WORKING THE SYSTEM

WORKING THE SYSTEM

A POLITICAL ETHNOGRAPHY
OF THE NEW ANGOLA

JON SCHUBERT

CORNELL UNIVERSITY PRESS
Ithaca and London

First published 2017 by Cornell University Press

Printed in the United States of America

Library of Congress Cataloging-in-Publication Data

Names: Schubert, Jon, 1982– author.
Title: Working the system : a political ethnography of the new Angola / Jon Schubert.
Description: Ithaca : Cornell University Press, 2017. | Includes bibliographical references and index.
Identifiers: LCCN 2017004031 (print) | LCCN 2017004739 (ebook) | ISBN 9781501713699 (cloth : alk. paper) | ISBN 9781501713705 (pbk. : alk. paper) | ISBN 9781501712333 (epub/mobi) | ISBN 9781501709692 (pdf)
Subjects: LCSH: Ethnology—Angola. | Politics and culture—Angola. | Angola—History—2002– | Power (Social sciences)—Angola. | Postwar reconstruction—Social aspects—Angola.
Classification: LCC DT1304 .S38 2017 (print) | LCC DT1304 (ebook) | DDC 967.304/2—dc23
LC record available at https://lccn.loc.gov/2017004031

Cornell University Press strives to use environmentally responsible suppliers and materials to the fullest extent possible in the publishing of its books. Such materials include vegetable-based, low-VOC inks and acid-free papers that are recycled, totally chlorine-free, or partly composed of nonwood fibers. For further information, visit our website at www.cornellpress.cornell.edu.

Maps and photo are by the author.

Pour Agathe

CONTENTS

Preface

Since the end of its civil war on 4 April 2002, Angola has often been cited as a paradigmatic case of "illiberal peacebuilding," of successful postwar transition to economic recovery and formal, political liberalization, closely managed and tightly controlled by a neo-authoritarian, dominant-party regime. This book offers an empirically and analytically innovative perspective that challenges the "Africa rising" narrative pervading mainstream media reports of postwar Angola, and complicates the clientelist account of Angolan politics that predominates academic literature. It does so by privileging an ethnographic approach rooted in urban life, encompassing social strata commonly studied separately. This book seeks, in doing this, to delocalize the anthropological gaze and capture the radical social and spatial mobility of everyday life in Luanda.

How political authority and legitimacy are sustained in societies marked by socioeconomic inequality and political exclusion is a long-standing preoccupation in the social sciences. By working through the emic notion of the "system" (*o sistema*), this book pays attention both to material practices and symbolic repertoires mobilized in the coproduction of hegemony. For Angolans the system is simultaneously a moral ordering device, a critique, and a *mode d'emploi* for their current political and socioeconomic environment. The system is characterized by multiple internal tensions: between the stasis and speed of urban life, between blockages and mobility, between the past and the future, between memory work and selective amnesia, between fear and hope, and between the affects and aspirations of power. Through detailed analysis of the practices through which people work the system, and of the political imaginaries and discursive repertoires that make the system work, this ethnography looks at the myriad processes through which relationships between "power" and "the people" are constantly remade, renegotiated, and dialogically constructed. The analytical value of this notion of the system is that it avoids reproducing a simplistic distinction between state and society. By revealing the multiple linkages between these two spheres, we can think beyond resistance and complicity, drawing out a more subtle account of hegemony, beyond the cultivation of consent by the dominant.

Examining the functioning of the system through the eyes of its users, the book therefore builds on anthropology's critique of dominance as something produced by a group of select individuals, and investigates instead what it means and how it feels to live in and be part of such a polity. Its chapters explore the interweaving strands that make up this mutually dependent relationship: history and the disjunctures between official and affective memories, ideas of racial and class identities, the idioms of kinship, and the practices and symbolisms of money making. However, instead of reifying notions of memory, tradition, identity, or corruption as analytical concepts, this work shows how social actors mobilize and modify these idioms in their everyday interactions with power. Both in practice and in imagination, this "New Angola" is constituted as essentially urban—upwardly mobile and aspirational—with rural areas left behind. Thus Luanda epitomizes both a lived reality and a political project that stands for the entire country, as well as a laboratory of the global, offering new insights into the politics of the everyday in dominant-party regimes in the twenty-first century.

ACKNOWLEDGMENTS

My gratitude goes first to my informants, who appear throughout this book, some anonymously and some named. Their willingness to share their stories and daily lives with me made this book possible and shaped my understanding of Angola. Their readiness to find time for me and my questions despite the hectic pace of life in Luanda and their multiple obligations and commitments, as well as their openness and generosity, still overwhelm me. You know who you are, and if the results of this book find their way back to Luanda in one form or another, still only a very small fraction of my debt to you will be repaid.

Anyone who knows Luanda also knows how impossible it is to get anything done without a functioning support network. I truly only got by with a little help from my friends. For their invaluable support during my fieldwork in Luanda, generous hospitality, unfailing help, and precious contacts in the administration; for *boleias*, broadband access, and little escapes; for lending me household items and novels, and sometimes even a car; for *funge* and wining and dining; for singing and dancing and inspiring conversations; and most of all, for their wonderful friendship and kindness, many thanks to Pedro Quinanga, Dee, Bea, Doby, Jerry, and Lauretta Geraldo, Hilla and *Cavaliere* Augusto Poma with Nico and Vittoria, Nuno Beja and family, Andrew Kempson and Kristina Nauer-Statham, Isidora Marcela, Nuno and Delphine Burnier Macedo, Branca Gonçalves, Adelina Rosa, Sónia Dias Serrão, Katiana da Silva, Hendrik Selle, Lioba Gansen, Rita Soares, Vineira Kongo, Bento de Jesus, Isilda Hurst, Pedro Chamangongo, Oliver Dalichau and Alfons Üllenberg, Helena Marinho, Machteld Catrysse and Job Beeckmans, Cristián Castro, Tânia Manso de Oliveira, José Tiago Catito, Helga Borges Silveira, Murielle Mignot, Julia and Allan Cain, Cristiano Makiese, Elad Strohmeyer, Rev. José António, Rev. Jerónimo Panda, Rev. Alberto Daniel, Rev. Gonçalves Augusto Damba, Rev. Pedro António Malungo and Dona Noémia, Amb. Giancarlo Fenini, Dr. Júlio Mendes, Dra. Ginga Neto, Dr. Cornélio Caley, Dra. Alexandra Aparício, Dr. Francisco Dias Costa, Dra. Irene Neto, Gen. Peregrino Wambu, and Dr. Manzambi Vuvu Fernando.

Several Angolan institutions and associations facilitated the fieldwork that forms the basis of this book, in terms of affiliation, sponsorship of the research visa, access to information, and general support: Ministério da Cultura, Arquivo Nacional de Angola, Museu de Antropologia, Fundação Agostinho Neto, Fundação 27 de Maio, and Development Workshop Angola.

The other essential precondition for doing research, especially in Luanda, is money. Despite the deteriorating funding climate, I was extremely fortunate to always obtain the next grant before the situation got really desperate. I am thus truly grateful to the following funding bodies which, with their generous and timely support, helped finance my research: the School of Social and Political Sciences, University of Edinburgh; Theodor Engelmann-Stiftung, Basel; Janggen-Pöhn-Stiftung, St. Gallen; Bolsa Rui Tavares, Lisbon; and Het Familie Heringa Vereneging, Utrecht. A postdoctoral fellowship of the German Research Foundation's Priority Programme SPP1448 at the University of Leipzig allowed me to make the necessary revisions and finalize the manuscript.

I thank Joost Fontein and Sara Rich Dorman at the Centre of African Studies, University of Edinburgh, for their concise, frank, open, and insightful feedback and critique, as well as their targeted encouragement. Their input at various stages of my thinking process was very inspiring, and their counsel on academic life was most welcome. Ramon Sarró and José-Maria Muñoz were the first reviewers of this book and have provided critical fresh input and much-appreciated support ever since.

At Cornell University Press, Jim Lance believed in this book from the beginning and has, with enthusiasm, grace, humor, and very hands-on advice, helped me move this book from the manuscript stage through the review and revision process to its final form. Marissa Moorman and Ricardo Soares de Oliveira were intellectual polestars from my earliest academic engagement with Angola and became fantastic supporters of this book. Their insightful comments helped me refine some of my arguments in the final stage of revisions.

During my postdoctoral fellowship in Leipzig, my project directors Ulf Engel and Elísio Macamo were tremendously generous in their support for this endeavor; Ulf Engel and Richard Rottenburg, as directors of the Priority Programme SPP1448 of the German Scientific Foundation (DFG), provided ideal material conditions for finalizing the manuscript. In Edinburgh, James Smith, Barbara Bompani, and Paul Nugent encouraged me very actively to join the Centre of African Studies. My gratitude also goes to Harry West, formerly of the Department of Anthropology at the School of Oriental and African Studies (SOAS), whose guidance was essential and who has continued to follow my progress with interest. In Switzerland, Patrick Harries, who sadly passed away before this book was published, and Tobias Hagmann were important early catalysts for discovering the joys and challenges of academic research and writing, while Henning Melber and Veit Arlt have been a constant source of support and valuable contacts. David Birmingham and Franz-Wilhelm Heimer, doyens of Angolan studies, opened many doors, for which I am very thankful. Special regards also to Natznet Tesfay at the Africa Desk at IHS for providing me with gainful employment and giving me ample and flexible time to focus on research.

Some elements of this book have been presented elsewhere and have also greatly benefitted from previous critical commentary. Parts of chapter 1 have appeared as Jon Schubert, "2002, Year Zero: History as Anti-Politics in the New Angola," *Journal of Southern African Studies* 41, no. 4, 835–52 (4 July 2015), and parts of chapter 5 as Jon Schubert, "'A Culture of Immediatism': Co-optation and Complicity in Post-War Angola," *Ethnos* (8 February 2016); both are reprinted by permission of Taylor & Francis Ltd. Many thanks to the publisher for giving their permission to reprint these passages here.

Over the past few years I have found that people working on, and passionate about, Angola are a small, tight-knit community. Many of those people have become good friends rather than just fellow Angolanists, and their feedback and ideas at various stages of this project have been invaluable sources of inspiration. During my year in Luanda, I was fortunate not to be entirely alone, and I am happy and grateful that I could count on the support of my brilliant and inspiring fellow researchers and *companheiros de luta* Claudia Gastrow and Aharon de Grassi. Our late-night discussions over improvised dinners in my dingy flat in B. O., or over Somalian street food and *cucas* in Mártires, are fond memories. Justin Pearce and Lara Pawson have been extremely loyal friends and unflagging supporters of this book since its very first stages, while Chloé Buire has given me enthusiastic comments ever since I put the first results out into the public. Didier Péclard and Ruy Llera Blanes have provided support and encouragement throughout. Sylvia Croese, António Tomás, Paulo Inglês, Abel Paxe, Gilson Lázaro, Cláudio Tomás, Jess Auerbach, Juliana Lima, Louise Redvers, Aslak Orre, Lisa Rimli, Anne Pitcher, Jeremy Ball, and Cláudio Silva have all been highly valued interlocutors on all things Angolan over the past ten years. Any limitations, mistakes, or misinterpretations in this work, however, are solely my own responsibility.

Although writing a book is ultimately a rather solitary experience, I am thankful to my wonderful friends for spirited discussions at various stages of my research and writing. For their steady support and intellectual companionship over many years, my warmest thanks go to Henri-Michel Yéré, Laurent

Cartier, Heid Jerstad, Jenny Lawy, Luke Heslop, Wim van Daele, Julie Soleil Archambault, Jason Sumich, and Tristam Barrett. Many other good friends also have provided moral and logistical support, feedback and comments, and happy dinners. In Edinburgh, many thanks go to Leila Sinclair-Bright, Gaia von Hatzfeld, and Ben Epstein. In Pristina, Vigan Jashari, Shpend Emini, Laurent Moser, Natasha Froejd, and Ludwig Román were invaluable sources of support. In Germany, I am especially grateful to Andrea Behrends, Judith Beyer and Felix Girke, Friederike Stahlmann, Maarten Bedert, Solange Guo Châtelard, Hadas Weiss, Katja Naumann and Geert Castryck, Forrest Kilimnik, Lena and Chris Dallywater, and Dmitri van den Bersselaar and Alba Valenciano for their friendship and support in matters both academic and practical.

My family in Switzerland and Belgium—and elsewhere—have provided constant moral and emotional support, as well as temporary homes to facilitate my constant moving during these years of academic wandering. My parents, especially, have encouraged me throughout my career with their love and their trust in my choices. Because it is thanks to my family history that I ended up in Angola in the first place, this book is in many ways also for my siblings, Ulrich, Paul, and Agnes, who share an Angolan childhood with me.

Above all, I thank my wife, Agathe Mora, to whom this book is dedicated. Without her love and support none of this would have been possible. Her constructive input has helped me overcome moments of doubt and aimlessness and has led me to sharpen my arguments in unforeseen ways. More important, life with her and our son, Emile, is a fantastically joyful and fulfilling journey that gives meaning and purpose to all these endeavors.

A NOTE ON LANGUAGE, NAMES, AND MONEY

Angolan Portuguese words, including words borrowed from Kimbundu, Umbundu, or Kikongo (e.g., *funge*, *kota*, *zungueira*, *kamba*) are italicized and translated at first mention and given in parentheses (see also in the glossary).

I have italicized common forms of addressing people, such as *Mamã*, *Papá*, *Senhor* (Mister), *Dona* (Madam), *Irmão* (Brother) and *Irmã* (Sister), if used as a generic term. However, for better legibility I have opted not to do so when used together with / as a name, as in Mamã Rosa, Irmão Pedro, or Dona Laurinda, for example.

The correct spelling, especially of place and personal names, is complicated in Angola by the fact that usually two or three spelling variants coexist—very often within a single document. Generally speaking, the Portuguese "c" and "q" were replaced with the Bantu (mainly Kimbundu, Umbundu, or Kikongo) "k"; the "ç," with "ss"; and the "g," with "j." However, even in official documents, one can find different versions in the heading and the body of a text, as for example in the spelling of the River Cuanza / Kwanza / Kuanza or of localities such as Quiçama / Kissama, Viquenge / Vikenji, Malange / Malanje, and the like. Because there is no official policy or unequivocal rule, I have tried to use the most common spelling of names and to be consistent throughout the book.

The spelling of people's names follows Portuguese-Angolan naming conventions: normally, people have one or two given names, followed by two family names, inheriting the mother's last name and the father's last name. As a fictive example, the daughter of José Francisco Lopes Bungo and Rosa Maria Panzo Rodrigues would be named Adelina Paula Rodrigues Bungo. Exceptions apply, though, especially when one of the double family names has to be preserved, if belonging to this specific family indicates a certain social status (e.g., Vieira Dias, Vieira Lopes). Furthermore, with sons the father's first name is also often passed on as a second given name. Family names thus change with every generation, hence the need to state the filiation (often two generations back) on official documents. In common usage, however, only one of the names is used when addressing a person, although which one is used varies according to situation and rapport (see chapter 4). In my case, I would be addressed as Senhor Jon (Mister Jon), Gabriel (my second given name), Benedito (my father's name), or just Schubert (as one would use a first name), or any combination of the above. Talking about someone, however, often requires reference to a combination of two names in most of the cases, to allow for a clear identification, especially if the given name is a common one (João, Maria, and so forth). That is, unless the person is so well-known that the first name alone suffices: when people in Angola talk about Isabel, for example, they usually take it to refer to Isabel dos Santos, the daughter of President José Eduardo dos Santos. Moreover, many public figures in Angola are commonly known by their noms de guerre, mostly from the time of the independence struggle. Here I follow the Angolan practice of writing the full name, with the nickname in quotation marks (e.g., Fernando da Piedade Dias dos Santos "Nandó," or Manuel Hélder Vieira Dias "Kope-lipa"), using only the aliases later. However, as I elaborate in the introduction, political matters are a sensitive topic in Angola. Therefore public figures are identified with their real names when they speak on the record or are quoted from the press. I have, however, anonymized most of my informants to allow them to speak their minds freely, and assigned them a single pseudonym to make them recognizable to the reader throughout the text.

"Taxi" always refers to *candongueiro/táxi*, and means the collective taxis, usually Hi-Ace minibuses, that ply more or less fixed routes. The Luandan *bairro* is only insufficiently translated as slum, shantytown, or township, or the more generic neighborhood. Historically, Luanda was divided between the *cidade*, the colonial cement city, and the *musseques*, the surrounding "indigenous," informal quarters built on sandy ground. Due to the gradual upgrading of certain of these areas into more permanent cement homes, and the pejorative associations with *musseque*, the more neutral *bairro* (literally: neighborhood) has come to largely replace *musseque* in popular usage, thereby eventually engendering a slippage of meaning through which *bairro* nowadays normally means a high-density neighborhood of lower socioeconomic standing that is not part of the planned cement city, even if certain *bairros* have permanent cement block homes, sometimes even boasting standards and dimensions more evocative of middle-class suburbs. By contrast, *musseque* now connotes poor, insalubrious shantytowns of more provisional homes, while the neighborhoods of the cement city are usually referred to by their names (e.g., Maculusso, Alvalade, Miramar).

The Party with capital P is—following my informants' usage—always the Popular Movement for the Liberation of Angola (MPLA, for the Portuguese Movimento Popular de Libertação de Angola). Both the MPLA and the National Union for the Total Independence of Angola (UNITA, for the Portuguese União Nacional para a Independência Total de Angola) come with a definite article in Portuguese (*o MPLA, a UNITA*). In English usage, however, only the MPLA is commonly used with the definite article; UNITA is usually written without it. For ease of reading, I have followed this convention.

Finally, when I translate "they" it is either the ominous *eles* (they) that my informants often used, or a passive-reflexive construction that obliterates clear authorship, like in *começou à criar-se a democracia* (democracy started to be created). All translations from Portuguese, as well as from French and German literature, are mine, and I am solely responsible for any errors.

Due to the high costs of living in Luanda, money is a very important element of this work. During the main fieldwork for the study that forms the basis of this book, the exchange rate on the streets was initially 95 kwanza to the dollar, just a little better than the official bank rate of 92 or 93 kwanza to the dollar, but it soon went up to around 100 kwanza to the dollar (bank rates 95 to 97:1), which is the rate I use throughout the book. Due to the oil price shock in late 2014, the kwanza depreciated over the course of 2015 and 2016, with street rates as high as 490 kwanza to the dollar at the time of going to print.

Examples of Prices at the Time of Research

A small bread roll: 30 kwanza (subsidized)
A kilogram of tomatoes: 500 kwanza
A liter of gasoline: 60 kwanza (subsidized)
A liter of gasoil: 40 kwanza (subsidized)
A taxi ride: 100 kwanza
A beer (330 ml): 75 kwanza
Minimum wage (equivalent to what a guard earns): 150 dollars/month
Salary of an *empregada* (domestic employee, cleaner) in a well-to-do
household: 350–400 dollars/month

FIGURE 1. Map of Angola

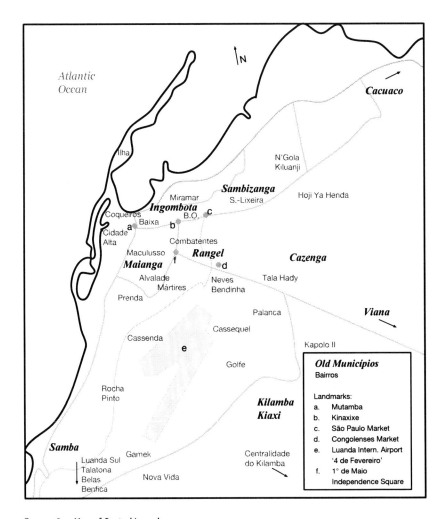

FIGURE 2. Map of Central Luanda

WORKING THE SYSTEM

Introduction

Working the System in Boomtown Africa

"Why do you want to study the relation of people with power?" Bela and Clarisse laughed out loud. "It's really bad, for every individual the relationship is *péssima* (very bad). You don't need a doctorate for that! It hasn't changed since the war, or if it has at all, it's changed for the worse," Bela said. *"Their* children can do anything they like, while we can't do anything at all." "I won't vote again in 2012," Clarisse asserted, but Bela berated her: "Don't you know that if you don't [vote] you help them? Don't you know that if you put in a blank vote it's counted for the M (*o Eme*)? It's evident. How else would they get 82 percent?"

We were walking toward the Neves Bendinha Hospital for Burn Injuries, near the Congolenses market, where a friend of Clarisse and Bela's was recovering from serious burns she had sustained from the explosion of a butane cooking gas bottle at home. The hospital was overcrowded and understaffed, and the only such specialized institution for this in Luanda, Angola's capital city of 6.4 million people. Clarisse and Bela were not the only people to be amused by my research objectives, or to find them hard to believe, and many of my informants echoed the sentiment that the relation between *o povo* (people) and *o poder* (power) was really, really bad. Nonetheless, it is a relation, and one that is dialogically constructed and constantly negotiated, subverted, and remade.

The Contours of the System

During my fieldwork in Luanda, many of my informants understood and casually referred to their society as *o sistema* (the system). Though not necessarily a direct subject of daily discussion, the system is a shared understanding of social realities that resonates in the background and is expressed through jokes, offhand remarks, or resigned sighs. Evoking a set of assumptions, the notion of the system carries specific implications, connotations, and meanings very characteristic of everyday life in contemporary Angola. To its inhabitants, the system works in totalizing ways, as there is a sense of inescapability. But the notion of a system also suggests a set of rules, or a set of interconnected mechanisms that make the system work. For people living in Luanda, life is characterized by great inequality and daily complications, and unwritten guidelines that delineate the parameters of the political—that is, the limits of what is publicly sayable and thinkable. As a citizen of that polity, you have to possess this arcane, yet for Angolans self-evident, knowledge to be able to safely navigate the politics of everyday life. Referring to the system is thus simultaneously evocative of those limits, of Angolan *jeito* (know-how, street-savvy) in navigating these, and a means of social commentary.

The system has, in the eyes of its inhabitants, multiple dimensions—the relational, the practical, and the symbolic that they must manage if they are to make sense of life. In essence, you need to know how the system works to make it function, and to function in it. And the way you work the system directly mediates and produces people's political subjectivities. For Angolans, the system is therefore a moral ordering device, a critique, and a user manual for the political and socioeconomic environment they inhabit.

So indeed, while the relation between people and power is, in the words of my informants, "bad," the system's analytic lens allows us to work through and analyze this relationality. In this book, I investigate the elements—both discursive and material—that make up this relation, by analyzing the social imaginaries, mundane practices, and everyday politics that daily recreate, remake, and renegotiate this system. Examining through the eyes of its users how the system works, I therefore build on anthropology's critique of dominance as produced by a group of select individuals and investigate instead how the dominated and the dominant jointly inhabit and recreate their lifeworlds.

Looking at the coproduction of hegemony through the system, then, avoids reproducing a simplistic distinction between state and society: by revealing the multiple linkages between these two spheres, we can think beyond resistance and collaboration, drawing out a more subtle account of hegemony, an account that is based on the idea of complicity and that goes beyond the cultivation of consent by the dominant. In this, Luanda serves as a "laboratory of the global" (Piot 2010: 18): thinking through the idea of the system we can explore how contemporary neo-authoritarian statecraft and an unbridled, turbo-capitalist economy affect the people living in and with regimes such as Angola's.

The opening dialogue sketches out three key elements of the system: relationality, inequality, and its inherent tensions. As Bela and Clarisse state, *"Their sons can do anything, while we can do nothing at all."* Like the ruling Movimento Popular para a Libertação de Angola (MPLA), the former anticolonial Popular Movement for the Liberation of Angola, which is often almost euphemistically circumscribed as "the party in power," or "the M," "they" are seldom mentioned by name and have an almost phantasmagorical quality, and yet everyone seems to know exactly who is meant by "them," which invests this power—*o poder*, a vague yet very concrete term of everyday usage that I render here as "power"—with menacing concreteness and a manifest capacity to disrupt citizens' lives.[1]

Since the end of its decades-long internal conflict in 2002, Angola has been internationally fêted as a miracle of postwar reconstruction and economic growth. Fuelled by oil production, a construction boom has transformed Luanda's cityscape. Until a drop in crude oil prices on the world market in late 2014, the country regularly posted record growth rates, attracting investors and economic migrants from across the African continent and the wider world.

However, this "Africa rising" narrative of the New Angola carries a flip side: under the leadership of the "Architect of Peace," President José Eduardo dos Santos, in power since 1979, the MPLA government is skillfully managing this reconstruction, tightly managing the spaces for the expression of dissent and restricting democratic freedoms.[2] Despite the centrality of oil-generated wealth both to regime maintenance and this infrastructure reconstruction, a significant majority of the urban and rural population remains excluded from economic growth and the benefits of peace. The promised trickle-down effect of liberal economics remains elusive, and Angola's oil industry is socially "thin" (Ferguson 2006, 198).

These internal tensions are characteristic of the system of contemporary Angola. Despite rapid economic growth and fabulous wealth for some people, most people struggle to make ends meet, living on less than two dollars per day.[3] The postwar oil-fuelled urban reconstruction boom goes hand in hand with large scale "urban regeneration"; that is, the violent expulsion of poor residents from informal inner-city neighborhoods. The hectic pace of daily life regularly grinds to a standstill, as rainfall or the passing of the presidential mo-torcade cause monstrous hour-long gridlocks during which nothing moves. Constant power and water cuts interrupt the functioning of public and private services (as well as people's domestic lives), and the horrendous costs of living make it necessary for people to embark on countless *esquemas* (schemes), *biscates* (small commerce), and *biznos* (businesses) to make ends meet.[4] Al-though the neoliberal mantras of efficiency, streamlining, and new public management are repeated to present to the outside world the image of a mod-ern, investor-friendly land of plenty, most Angolans experience the daily has-sles of a slow, cumbersome, inefficient state bureaucracy with an exceeding love for formalism, paperwork, and triplicate documents authenticated by white seals, fiscal stamps, and notary signatures. The New Angola is project-ing itself as the "country of the future"; but this promised future seems a long way off for its citizens. Although the unruly, often unresolved past keeps ir-rupting in the present, the "conquest of peace" in 2002 is held as the greatest good for all Angolans, and any criticism of the status quo is equated with a return to the *confusão* (confusion, mess) of war.

Faced with such contradictions, a recurring theme in people's lives is the "lack of system" (*não há sistema*, or "system down"), which is regularly given as the reason why, for example, in a public administration service documents cannot be processed.

This lack of system may be due to power shortages, computer failure, or one of the frequent administrative reshuffles, but it also stands by metonymy for the malfunctioning of society in general and the inequities of the "*Sistema dos Santos*."[5] Or, in the words of my informants, "For the Angolan, things are not good since the end of the war, *as coisas vão mal*. Maybe for Angolan A things are good, but for Angolan B and C, things aren't. And we here are Angolan C! Angolan A is the son of the ministers."

And yet the system evidently works: despite the seeming absence of a clas-sical social contract between citizens and political leaders, a relation between the rulers and the ruled exists through which political legitimacy and public authority are constantly renegotiated and remade. Despite stasis and block-ades, people experience social and physical mobility and find strategies to make the system work. And although political repression and a widespread feeling of the impossibility of talking politics exist, people do develop and formulate substantive political aspirations. Evidently, as I will show, how this system works, and for whom, is eminently positional—clearly, not everyone has the same capabilities and resources to navigate and work the system—but it has still prevented a fundamental reordering of social, economic, and political re-lations since the end of the war.

The system is thus constitutive of power relations in Angola. It is more than class relations, or power and economic inequality; it points to the reciprocity and consociality of those power relations, their sensuous, aspirational, complicit, and creative character. It shows how spheres often thought of as separate—people and power—are caught up in and thus use and reproduce the same discursive framework. This allows us to analyze both the material practices and the popular imaginaries that make up this common framework.

Empirically, this book is centered on Luanda because both in practice and in imagination this New Angola is constituted as essentially urban—upwardly mobile and aspirational—with rural areas left behind.[6] However, rather than an ethnography of a place and its people, this book is an investigation of the symbolic and material affects of power on social formations and relations in a specific social and historical context, or, an ethnography of emic understandings of the political in postwar Angola. In the New Angola, Luanda epitomizes both a lived reality and a political project that stands for the entire country, and offers new insights into the politics of the everyday in dominant-party regimes in the twenty-first century.

Indeed, since the end of the war, Angola has justly been cited as a paradigmatic case of "illiberal peacebuilding" (Soares de Oliveira 2011). We know about the "menu of manipulation" in "electoral authoritarian" contexts—that is, the restrictions of press freedom, the rigging of electoral processes, and the abuse of the privileges of incumbency, as well as the disappointed expectations of a "vibrant civil society" and donor assistance to democratization.[7] It is fair to say that Angola has had it all—but how does it feel to live in such a regime? How does living in an oil-rich, neo-authoritarian state shape the lifeworlds of its citizens?[8] And how do citizens participate in the political imaginaries that negotiate, subvert, and sustain political authority, legitimacy, and the relationship between power-holders and their populations? How do people situate themselves vis-à-vis this dominant power, and how are political subjectivities formed under these circumstances?

These questions are important because the subtext of much of the commentary on Angola tends to explain the "authoritarian dispensation" in Angola (and often, too, in similar sociopolitical contexts) through a combination of patronage, coercion, and an apathetic citizenry still too traumatized by the effects of the civil war to develop an independent political consciousness.[9] But these explanatory models can only give us partial, often unsatisfactory answers. While Angola might today not be an ideal-type liberal democracy, it is clearly not a totalitarian dictatorship where people live under constant state terror or in a state of siege similar to, for example, Guatemala (Green 1994), Northern

Ireland (Feldman 1991), or the Basque Country (Aretxaga 2000) in the 1980s and 1990s, where violence was routinized and fear had become a "way of life" (Green 1994). There has been and still is a recurring element of state violence and coercion to the maintenance of the regime. Nonetheless, although violent repression of suspected dissent has been on the rise since 2011, the threat of violence is largely still only latent, and rarely acted out in the everyday lives of the population. Rather, Angolans cite a "culture of fear" that impedes them from overly political engagement (Schubert 2010, 665–66).

Similarly, "patronage" might be a useful approach to understand high-level politics and the balancing of competing factions within the ruling party by the president and his close entourage (Roque 2011, 6; Corkin 2013, 126) but it fails to account for the political subjectivities of the majority of the population who are usually excluded from those material benefits. A scholarly focus on neoliberal "transitions" and their challenges that dovetails with the politics of *rayonnement* of the New Angola also overlooks "the persistence of historical memories, the symbolic and discursive continuities, and the institutional ruptures and restorations in those African countries that once embraced socialism and have now relinquished it in favor of neo-liberal reforms" (Pitcher and Askew 2006, 2). And although the trauma of the Angolan conflict may point to why the specter of a return to civil war that is regularly raised to call for stability and the maintenance of the status quo resonates with the electorate at large, such trauma cannot sufficiently account for the processes that produce political authority in a context where historic claims to legitimacy are reaching their limits.

In trying to come to grips with these ethnographic puzzles, my analytical approach to the system has probably most profoundly been colored by the notion of hegemony. Bierschenk and Olivier de Sardan criticize Africanist anthropology for aligning itself with the "ethereal realms" of dated European and thus by extension Eurocentric political philosophy rather than with its closest disciplinary (and empirically oriented) neighbors (Bierschenk and Olivier de Sardan 2014, 20). They decry anthropology's obsession with "the philosophical fashions of the moment," which "continues to shy away from empirical engagement but instead aims to produce an often second-hand philosophy" (54), and single out the concepts of Foucault and Gramsci for being "particularly resistant to operationalization for empirical research" (53).

I think their emphasis on empirical grounding and methodological rigor is a welcome counterweight to some of anthropology's loftier tendencies. Nonetheless, I am convinced that Gramsci's original question remains valid and can be a useful guiding heuristic framework in a context such as Angola. The problem of how a system of unequal political and economic dominance is reproduced by means other than brute coercion very much resonated with my attempts to grasp and make sense of the glaring contradictions of social life in Angola. Similarly, Foucault's notion of *assujettissement* (1978) opens up analytical perspectives that might help us understand the formation of subjectivities in a political society that is experienced by its citizens as totalizing as the system. The question why Angolans do not do more to contest the regime is one that baffles many observers of Angola. This exploration of the system intends to offer at least a partial answer to that question.[10]

By analyzing the different elements that coproduce hegemony in the system of contemporary Angola, I seek to understand how dominance and political legitimacy are negotiated in neo-authoritarian contexts, and to sketch the contours, characteristics, and limits of hegemonic dominance. This line of inquiry makes this research timely and important beyond the disciplines of anthropology and African studies because globally neo-authoritarianism is emerging as a norm rather than as an exception to the much-vaunted trend toward liberal democracy. The Angolan experience, far from being an exception, is "a magnified version of a dynamic occurring across many resource-rich states around the continent" (Soares de Oliveira 2015, 206). Because countries in the West increasingly depend on oil and oil-related investments, they are increasingly willing to overlook "democratic shortcomings," not just in Angola, but also in other oil-rich, neo-authoritarian countries around the globe—for example, Gabon, Equatorial Guinea, Chad, Kazakhstan, Azerbaijan—in exchange for economic benefits.[11] At the same time, these countries also bear strong parallels with prerevolution Arab countries: the political compromise that rested on certain imaginings of authority and legitimacy (socialism, anticolonialism) has come to its limits, and in its place a younger, educated, globally connected generation is emerging that is less easily satisfied with the crumbs from the master's table. Last, understanding hegemonic formations remains important also as a first step to countering hegemony, not only in neo-authoritarian contexts but also in Europe and the United States, where people are increasingly seduced to vote against their own best interests and dehumanizing discourses gain political traction again.[12] Building "Theory from the South" (Comaroff and Comaroff 2012), then, helps us gain new insights into the nature of political authority, the ways in which societies deal with inequality, and the possibilities of change.

On the Relational Nature of Hegemony

This ethnographic puzzle—how does a polity such as Angola work for its inhabitants—and the empirical questions that result from it—how does it feel to live with such a regime—translate into larger conceptual questions that guide my analysis: first, how can we understand the symbolic and material dimensions of dominance (i.e., what practices and discourses create, negotiate, subvert, and sustain power and political legitimacy in postwar Angola)? Second, what popular practices, such as gossip, rumor, humor, performance, and the "inventions of the everyday,"[13] produce the popular political imaginary, seen as a "set of emic interpretations of the political" (Friedman 2011, 7)? Finally, how does the relationality and reciprocity of these practices through which people make the system work affect the formation of their oftentimes ambiguous political subjectivities? These overarching questions evidently need to be translated into more operational analytical questions that point to the heart of larger current academic debates. Here, I chart out how these questions can be broken down to make the tensions in the system analytically fruitful and point out the lines along which the investigation in the chapters operates.

First, talking about the symbolic and material aspects of dominance directly echoes Gramsci's understanding of the negotiations of hegemony, where the dominated participate in their own subordination through rituals and practices that inculcate values of allegiance to the system, and naturalize the relations of power, thus making them invisible.[14] Gramsci directs our attention to the material and symbolic elements that remake a "lived hegemony," seeing both aspects as inextricably linked (Crehan 2002, 172–4, 200). However, this is not simply a case of the distribution of the means of production, or relations of ownership, as a more classical Marxist analysis would posit. As Gramsci develops, hegemony is also negotiated in the field of culture and through the institutions of civil society. Discourse actively shapes what is commonly seen as material reality, along the lines that a more poststructuralist, Foucauldian discourse analysis posits: "the production of social reality which includes the analysis of representations as social facts [is] inseparable from what is commonly thought of as 'material reality'" (Escobar 1996, 46). This resonates, for example, with Lisa Wedeen's suggestion to analyze the vocabulary and grammar of power—that is, to analyze "the meaning of symbols, rituals, and practices in a way that avoids a simple functionalist interpretation" to understand "how ordinary people live their lives under conditions of authoritarian rule"—in her case, in the context of Hafiz al-Assad's

Syria in the 1990s (Wedeen 1999, 25). Not a finished or uncontested ideology, then, but rather "a common material and meaningful framework for living through, talking about, and acting upon social orders characterized by domination" (Roseberry 1994, 361).

These are powerful impulses, ones which direct the analysis toward how dominant discourses are negotiated and circulated and how the dispersedness of power materially affects how people live their lives in the everyday. As we shall see in the following chapters, this intertwining of material and symbolic power—the feedback loop between discourses and lived reality—is a central element to how the system works.

Beyond that, a careful attention to the historicity and cultural embeddedness of these discourses is necessary to allow us to understand how and why they resonate with and affect people in a specific context. This includes, for example, taking Angola's socialist past seriously. The MPLA's recourse to its past as a Marxist-Leninist vanguard party may appear to the casual observer today as mere rhetorical posturing, a populist tactic by which the party speaks the language of "the people" even though its practices today epitomize Angola's transition to predatory capitalism charted by Hodges (2004) and Soares de Oliveira (2015) and thinly fictionalized by Pepetela in his *Predadores* (2005). However, socialist imaginaries of progress, modernity, solidarity, and unity did find resonance with "ordinary Angolans," and "the hopes that socialist values brought to women, workers or youth" still echo today (Pitcher and Askew 2006, 2).

Looking at the past in its affective dimensions also allows us to grasp a further aspect of the materiality of power in people's lives. For example, the "culture of fear" that Angolans often cite to explain the impossibility of talking politics openly is, according to them, rooted in events of the past that still affect people today. This points to the affective, sensuous character of the system. Pushing off from Foucault's idea of the "conduct of conduct," I take up an analytical concern with the bodily and emotional affects of power in people's lives. Piot's (2010) ethnography of post-Cold War political changes in Togo is a good example of how such an approach can be put to use. Looking at how rumors of the state's eyes and ears are circulated, he states that the "truth" of those rumors is beside the point: "People thought there were, and the state wanted people to think there were. As such, the belief alone served state interest" (37). Thus, he writes, "the chilling effect of this culture of paranoia on public discourse was near-total, so that people never would say anything in public that could be construed as 'political'" (37). This can help us understand how the system has indeed totalizing effects, shaping how and what can be said and done by different actors across the social spectrum—and that definitely includes the seemingly powerful as well, thereby complicating simple distinctions between the people and the state.

The second analytical focus of the book is on popular practices and the mobilization of specific repertoires in their context. In contemporary Angola, where people often say that it is dangerous to talk about politics, I found inspiration in James Scott's work that directs our attention to the "'micro' pushing and shoving" that is indicative of the daily negotiations of power relations (Scott 1990, 188). Investigating those micro-processes that make up the "unobtrusive realm of political struggle" in everyday life is thus one of the cornerstones of my analysis of the system in Angola. Two points are especially worth highlighting: first, Scott's notion of the "hidden transcripts" under conditions of political dominance is especially productive in the context of Angola, where the political is seldom openly addressed, as it requires us to investigate in everyday social actions the "noninnocent meanings using our cultural knowledge" (184). Second, as Gramsci does, Scott highlights the bond between domination and appropriation, in the sense that it is impossible to separate symbolic resistance against the symbolism and ideas of subordination from practical struggles over material exploitation (Scott 1990, 188). Taking this as a point of departure, I pay detailed attention to the mundane politics of the everyday. This includes taking into account the situational nature of culturally embedded repertoires, which allows us to analyze how, for example, the idioms of race, class, and family are polysemous and ambivalent, and utilized by the same actors to express seemingly contradictory positions of both accommodation and resistance.

This inherent contradiction points to a problem with Scott's focus on the micro-struggles, which is that it sees "political struggles" as essentially conflictual. Against this, I assert that it is rather a coproduction, where the seemingly powerful and powerless are jointly negotiating and producing, subverting and endorsing the system. Here, Achille Mbembe's notion of complicity (2001) is especially fruitful. In a way, this issue highlights the tension between Gramsci's understanding of hegemony as negotiated or fought over between the dominant and the subordinate, and Foucault's idea of the dispersedness of power. But as Tanya Murray Li (2007) writes, it is not a case of using one against the other: some practices of power are visible, and people resist or accommodate them actively; some forms of power are more diffuse, as are people's (embodied) actions in relation to them.

The joint production of the framework of the system leads us to the third conceptual anchor, which is the idea of relationality and reciprocity of power relations. Reciprocity is a central trope in Africanist scholarship and is often used as analytical shorthand to point to the "functionality" of vertical relations of patronage.[15] However, reality is much messier and more complex than this imagery of big men and clients conjures. Indeed, it is, for example, hard to find fault with Soares de Oliveira's analysis of "illiberal peacebuilding," especially his mapping of the MPLA's "development vision" (2011, 296–8). However, his analysis of this transition as "masterminded by the Angolan elite" and a ruling party that "firmly consolidated a party-state domination" (288) and his exposition of the cleverness and ruthlessness of Angolan rulers (2015) implicitly rest on an idea of hegemonic power as something imposed from above, which ultimately reinforces rather than deconstructs this imagery.

As Krohn-Hansen (2008) points out in his research on popular experiences of the dictatorship in the Dominican Republic, a hegemonic Western discourse on autocratic rulers, based on the idea that one man (it is usually a man) wields power, results in an obsession with personal rule.[16] President dos Santos is nothing if not a shrewd political operator, but "even in the most repressive regimes, political power is far more dispersed and transactional than is most often assumed" and "even a form of dictatorial rule may have a (surprisingly) broad backing among the population, or parts of the population" (Krohn-Hansen 2008, 8, 9). Thus "the analysis of authoritarian rule ought to be solidly rooted in examinations of everyday life" and should "view authoritarian states as sets of cultural processes" (Krohn-Hansen 2008, 5).[17] In the following chapters, I carefully unpack these cultural processes to see how links of familiarity, relationality, and ideals of consociality produce these transactional elements that at the same time reproduce and contest political legitimacy.

Looking at the coproduction of the system can then help us disaggregate the regime, complicate terms like corruption, and challenge the idea of hegemony as something imposed from above. Here, my analysis borrows from Navaro-Yashin's study of the coproduction of "the political" in "public life" in Turkey, which gives us tools to understand how social actors commonly connoted with either civil society or the state—bureaucrats, police agents, and so on—jointly produce the social environment they operate in. I follow her interest in "the public *participation* in and *perpetuation* of, rather than resistance to, state power" (Navaro-Yashin 2002, 129, emphasis hers), and her approach of studying "humor, rumor, imaginary stories, projections, and irrational fears as intangible sites for the making of the political in . . . public life" (16). However, this emphasis on the joint production of the political—possibly influenced by her research's context of liberal, secular, urban Turkey in the 1990s—to which I subscribe from a conceptual point of view, may overlook the real power inequalities, the violence of everyday life, and the more coercive aspects of domination that we see in a context like Angola.

We should not reproduce an artificial distinction between people and power, or between citizens and the state—to do so would run the risk of reifying those concepts—but some inequalities are very concrete. In the experience of my informants in Angola there is a difference between people and power, this simultaneously nebulous and yet very concrete and identifiable force that acts as a shaping and disrupting force in people's lives. These distinctions are clear in the eyes of my informants, who position themselves—at least in discourse and imaginary—as separate from *eles* (them), even if in practice that division may be less clear-cut.

Indeed, although the distinction between "us" and "them" is often reproduced and upheld in people's discourse, their practices under the current conditions complicate that separation and point both to the messier realities of life in contemporary Luanda and to the compromises they have to make to navigate their everyday lives. As Michael Herzfeld writes, maintaining these dichotomies at a conceptual level risks inhibiting analysis by concealing common ground and "obscur[ing] complex processes of creative co-optation in economic, political, and administrative practices" (2005, 3). What my focus on coproduction in the following chapters thus reveals is how the seemingly powerful and the dominated jointly produce—and are caught up in—a common framework that defines the parameters of the political in contemporary Angola.

This leads us to my final point, the formation of political subjectivities, which allows us to look at political culture in Africa without falling into the "deterministic trap." Indeed, one of the dangers of talking about "political culture" is the risk of (unwittingly) espousing a cultural determinist understanding of political dynamics. Scholars of politics in Africa have often explained the "incompatibility" of African societies with democracy by reifying culture as typically African "traditional rationalities" like patronage, elite rule, and authoritarianism. Such theorists of state failure or collapse often produce symptomologies that recognize neither for whom state failure works nor the creativity, production, and expansion state failure engenders (Jackson 2010, 61).

In many ways, I thus take up Patrick Chabal's challenge to "tackle African politics from a different angle," analyze "the stuff of politics . . . from within," and answer the question of "what politics means for people who are not political actors" (2009, xi). While a welcome corrective to the widespread Afro-pessimism of the late 1990s, Chabal's project (Chabal and Daloz 1999; Chabal and Daloz 2006; Chabal 2009) has been criticized for making sweeping, "excessively reductionist" generalizations about Africa (Young 2007, 156), lacking attention to empirical detail and variation (Hagmann 2009, 1284), and essentializing notions such as reciprocity (Dorman 2009), tradition, and modernity, ultimately leading to cultural primordialism (Bryceson 2000, 426; Meagher 2006, 590). These are justified, if sometimes harshly voiced critiques, but the investigation of the "stuff of politics" remains nonetheless a valid academic endeavor. To do so, however, Kaarsholm has suggested that "instead of adapting—as Chabal attempts—'modernity' and 'tradition' as analytical concepts with which to think in terms of an 'African modernity,' we would do better to look at how such notions have been mobilized during political struggles" (2012, 357). Instead of reducing political culture to a set of fixed attitudes—a sort of cultural determinism that emphasizes continuity and teleology—I understand it as a set of culturally meaningful repertoires from which social actors can freely choose. It is thus a culture that is constantly renegotiated and remade (Hagmann 2006, 606).

Similarly, one might justifiably criticize democracy as a Western concept and denounce any attempts to measure the progress of African democracies against normative, Eurocentric benchmarks of success. However, this critique has been overextended to the point that, again in a culturalist vein, some authors (as well as journalists and pundits) deny African political subjects their political aspirations. By this logic, because democracy is "not really African," and because "African political culture" privileges, for example, the "Big Man" mode of authority—or similar analytical shorthands like "neo-patrimonialism"—African citizens are almost portrayed as being happy to be governed by authoritarian rulers and as being complicit in their own subjugation. This is dangerous and false on a number of accounts. On the one hand, although it seems self-evident to set out to understand "African politics" on its own terms, authors such as Chabal and Daloz (1999) reproduce old stereotypes by noting how "different rational registers" of—what they see as—"the modern" (cell phones, polling) and "the most archaic" (witchcraft, "traditional" rationalities) seem to coexist in Africa (146). Such stereotyping makes it easy to negate the historical, transnational entanglements that have shaped African polities, often leading Western commentators to overlook the complicity of Western political and economic actors in perpetuating existing inequalities. On the other hand, a culturalist interpretation of African politics also discounts the pervasiveness of the "meta-narratives of democracy," and how these have "affected Africans' imaginations and the way they represent multi-party politics" (Ndjio 2008, 105).

Ndjio ultimately presents us with a bleak picture when he stresses the "ability of African autocrats to invent their own democracy," a "product of the

African genius" that "sustain[s] both the hegemonic and accumulative project of the dominant classes in sub-Saharan Africa" (2008, 120). While obviously true, this underplays the substantive aspirations of African citizens for their everyday lives. Especially in a context such as Angola's, accountability and transparency are not just abstract concepts, transposed or grafted from a different cultural context; they should also be seen as repertoires that can be deployed situationally. Although such terms might originate in the boardrooms of donor organizations, they are reappropriated locally for very real and concrete claims, to raise specific questions such as: "How can Angola have one of the fastest-growing economies of sub-Saharan Africa when the majority of people live on less than two dollars a day?" Or, "If the oil wealth belongs to all Angolans, how come the generals and ministers have everything while we do not even have clean water, electricity, schools, or hospitals?"

My analysis of the agentive, creative, subversive, and aspirational character of political subjectivities is thus close to Mahmood's take on the contested notion of agency.[18] According to her, we should see "agency not simply as a synonym for resistance to relations of domination, but as a capacity for action that specific relations of *subordination* create and enable" (Mahmood 2005, 18, emphasis hers). This allows her to focus on how "norms are not only consolidated and/or subverted, . . . but performed, inhabited, and experienced in a variety of ways" (22). This resonates with Holston (2008), who defines "citizenship as a relation of state and society" in which we neither conceptualize mobilization as resistance nor demobilization as co-optation (9), but instead "emphasize the *experiences* of citizens with the elements—such as property, illegality, courts, associations, and ideologies—that constitute the discursive and contextual constructions of relations called citizenship and that indicate not only particular attributes of belonging in society but also the political imagination that both produces and disrupts citizenship" (13, emphasis mine). As the chapters will show in greater detail, the experiential aspect of the system—the way people inhabit and perform its parameters—is key to understanding its functioning.

I thus ultimately posit that living in Angola today demands a mastery of the codes and practices of the system, to both work the system and make the system work. The practices and discourses of the system's inhabitants reveal how complex everyday life is, and how people position themselves within it. In a context where politics is seldom a subject for open discussion, people form ambivalent, complex political subjectivities: they inhabit and express sometimes openly oppositional ideas about the moral order of society and are at the same time well aware of their complicity in the system. Although the lack of system poses very real material and symbolic limits to their possibilities, they live, work, love, dream, and aspire in this polity, and through their daily lives constantly negotiate and reproduce the system.

I aim not to present a unified body of theory from such eclectic a selection of sources of inspiration. Rather, having staked out the wider parameters of my analysis, I aim to create in the chapters that follow a dialogue between my empirical data and the ideas and concepts sketched out here, and to examine in detail the different aspects of the system that make up people's relation with power in Angola. Ultimately, looking at the formation of political subjectivities through the lens of the system will allow us to gain a better understanding of what it means to be Angolan today.

These lines of inquiry raise the question why this research should just not be termed an anthropology of the state—justifiably so, because a growing body of work is interested in the workings of "the state" as a social system of symbols and meanings "at the margins of the state" (Das and Poole 2004). Such poststructuralist analyses of government as a "mode of structuring the field of action of individuals or groups" in a given sociohistorical context (Hibou 2004, 21) include the forms of knowledge, techniques, and other means employed, but also the entity to be governed, and how it is conceived by the governing agency, which ends it seeks, and the outcomes and consequences of its attempt to control, regulate, and direct human conduct (Dean 1999, 11). Such an approach enables us to take the idea of the state as seriously as its materiality and investigate how "state-related political imaginings . . . are not only products of the State, but they are also productive of the State" (Friedman 2011, 4–5, 8).

By contrast to this poststructuralist analysis, a strand of research seminally influenced by the work of the Laboratoire d'Etudes et de Recherche sur les Dynamiques Sociales et le Développement Local (Laboratory for the Study and Research on Social Dynamics and Local Development, or LASDEL) in Niger and Bénin is more interested in examining the interactions of people with "agents of the state" at the local level—looking at "street-level bureaucrats" (Blundo 2006), "everyday corruption" (Blundo and Olivier de Sardan 2006), or the everyday functioning of public service (Bierschenk and Olivier de Sardan 2014). The empirical rigor of their take on the state allows us to disaggregate the state and treat it as a bundle of practices and a system of social relations.

Much of the analysis in the following chapters engages these ideas more directly. However, I am wary of defining this book as an anthropology of the state. For one, I doubt the analytical usefulness of the term. In this, I follow Krohn-Hansen (2008, 7), who argues that by positing a "veiling separation of the state and society, analysts, politicians and citizens have provided the state with a misplaced concreteness [and] have fetishized it, turning complex historical processes into a person, a will, a spirit, or a thing" that masks the realities of political practice. Also, contrary to an anthropology of the state at its margins,[19] Luanda is very much at the heart of negotiations over the meaning of politics and Angolanness; mine is an anthropology of the affects of power in everyday life in the urban center of the New Angola, not at its periphery. Most important, I am too much influenced by my informants' perspective on this ubiquitous "power" to limit myself to a subset of social actors that could be termed "agents of the state" or, conversely, "citizens" or "the dominated." Because of the increased, intentional blurring between state, party, and government in Angola, and the "changing enmeshed relationships" between people and power,[20] I would be hard-pressed to offer clear-cut definitions or to empirically demarcate the state from civil society at large.

With regard to research on Angola more specifically, this book primarily adds to the growing, but still slim body of scholarship on postwar Angola, especially when it comes to in-depth ethnographic studies of contemporary social realities in the country. This is largely because, due to the war and general difficulties of access, there has been a hiatus in research in the 1990s. Research resumed after the end of the war in 2002, albeit still limited by the prohibitive costs of living in Angola, as well as by the difficulties of obtaining a long-term research visa and the general distrust (or lack of interest) of the authorities in independent research.[21]

For the time until the end of the war, Christine Messiant's work stands out as the most comprehensive and nuanced account of the political and economic transitions of Angola from a Marxist, single-party regime to the post-1991, multiparty but wartime democracy. Building on her doctoral thesis, published later as *1961. L'Angola colonial, histoire et société. Les prémisses du mouvement nationaliste* (2006), a rich and detailed historical sociology of the "social roots" of the MPLA, she analyzes the failures of the 1991 peace process and the 1992 elections (1994, 1995a) and details how the MPLA transformed itself from a socialist vanguard party to a predatory capitalist elite that has privatized state resources for personal gain (1999). However, her increasingly critical writing has impeded her from returning to Angola in the last years, and due to her untimely passing away in 2006, her latest work only just about captured the end of the war (2002, 2007). For the same period in the English-speaking world, Tony Hodges's book (2001; revised version 2004) has long been the reference work on Angola, detailing Angola's transformation "from Afro-Marxism to Petro-Diamond Capitalism," as the title of the 2001 version alludes to. Additionally, some accounts of the brutalities of the war were published by journalists or aid workers active in the country (Maier 1996; Moorhouse and Cheng 2005); other research on the second phase of the Angolan conflict often used Angola as an example of a "war economy" to contribute to the then prominent "greed v grievance" debate (Cilliers and Dietrich 2000; Cramer 2006; Greenhill and Major 2007).

Since the end of the civil war, new research has been carried out, with works focusing in the early years on the (im-)possibility of political transition and new elections in Angola (Miranda 2004; Ennes Ferreira 2005; Vines, Shaxson, and Rimli 2005; Amundsen and Abreu 2006), the peace process or lack thereof (Comerford 2005; Pearce 2005), or urban planning and poverty alleviation (Cain 2002; Croese 2010). Spurred on by Angola's economic growth and increasing geopolitical importance, scholars have also focused on the economy, formal politics, and high-level corruption (Kibble 2006; Soares de Oliveira 2007; Vallée 2008; Soares de Oliveira 2011; Sogge 2011; Ovadia 2013), the preparation and holding of elections (Roque 2009, 2013; Schubert 2010) or more specifically on China's engagement in Angola (Power and Alves 2012; Corkin 2013). Of these, Ricardo Soares de Oliveira's *Magnificent and Beggar Land* (2015) provides the most comprehensive account of Angola's postwar political economy, albeit with a declared focus on high-level, elite politics.

In terms of a more "popular" perspective, Marissa Moorman's history of music and nationalism in Luanda (2008) stands out, although her discussion of contemporary dynamics is limited to the postscript. Research by Heywood (2000), Heywood and Thornton (2007), Péclard (2015), and Pearce (2015a) also offers valuable new insights into processes of social formation during colonial times and the civil war. However, few ethnographic studies of postwar Angola have been undertaken.[22] Notable exceptions include Calvão's study of diamond traders in the Lundas (2013), Ferrão's research on "communities of suffering" under UNITA control during the war (2012), and Blanes's work on the Tokoist Church (2011, 2012). This is not to disregard the body of work from the 1960s, 1970s, and 1980s, or to dismiss the important contributions coming out of Angola, Portugal, and Brazil, but as I will engage in greater detail with existing Angolanist scholarship in the following chapters, I limit myself to this very summary overview here.

As a largely ethnographic exploration of the system, my research aims to offer a different, complementary perspective on power in Angola and how this constitutes a lived reality for "ordinary Angolans." My aim here is to direct the focus of the analysis away from the person of President dos Santos and his reshuffles of power behind the façade of official government positions, thereby going beyond "Kremlinology" modes of understanding Angolan politics.[23] My other intention is to take the discussion further from a somewhat dominant line of analysis concerned with oil (or diamond) extraction, economic growth, corruption, and patronage politics, by complicating these concepts from an emic perspective. Or, in the words of one of my informants:

> We think it's a good idea you spend time here, it's only like this that you will know Angola. If you are only in the Baixa [downtown] and the Cidade Alta [government quarter] this country is ranked first in economy [in Africa]. It's a disgrace. The enterprises we contracted are building disposable roads (*estradas descartáveis*), they have holes, they [the authorities] are not inspecting.

I thus intend to update and revisit the "social roots" of the MPLA's political legitimacy today. As a by-product of this analytical work, I also hope to provide a modest corrective to existing historiography, especially with regard to certain key events of Angolan history that serve as one of the structuring elements of my analysis.

On Methodology, Positionality, and Limitations

Doing research in a postconflict environment such as Angola's presents the researcher with the problem of how to address topics that are considered to be too sensitive to be talked about openly. Time and again, informants told me that it was dangerous or problematic to raise "political" questions, even if they were often happy to talk politics with me after this initial caution (see below on positionality). Indeed, the idea of a "culture of fear" is a recurrent topos in Angola, deployed by activists and opposition parties, government and ruling party figures and ordinary Angolans alike to explain the lack of citizen engagement or, conversely, to appeal for calm and order.

Early in my fieldwork, I had an audience with Dr. Caley, the vice-minister of culture, who warned me to talk politics only with "appropriate" persons because Angola was still a "young country" where politics was a sensitive issue. Another informant gave me similar advice on how to conduct my interviews: "You have to take all the political things out of it, otherwise you won't get anything. You have to explain people very carefully what you are doing otherwise they will distrust you. In fact, I first mistrusted you. Don't talk about the state."

Because of this "culture of fear" Angolans have long been afraid to talk politics or speak out against their government. This is usually explained by the experience of living in a surveillance state, with the allegedly omnipresent state security service monitoring every expression of dissent. Ruthless purges against an alleged opposition faction within the MPLA in 1977 (the notorious "coup attempt" of 27 May 1977), and the disastrous 1992 elections, which saw a return to conflict, are seen as deeply traumatic events that reinforced the message that it is better not to get mixed up in politics.

As a lapsed historian my initial interest for doing this research lay in popular memory narratives and the tensions between the official historiography and the hidden transcript of the liberation struggle, the 1977 coup attempt and the Angolan conflict. This proved a useful entry point for conversations and interviews, and a formal justification for my research that did not raise too many suspicions. I soon realized, however, that my interest in how power shapes social processes required a much broader, more holistic approach to the different elements that make up the political society—the system—in Luanda.

Doing an urban anthropology in a hectic, chaotic, and sprawling multimillion metropolis such as Luanda presents logistical and epistemological challenges. The notion of participant observation has to be complicated when people juggle multiple obligations—often accumulating several jobs, studies, and family commitments—and when people's daily routines include time-consuming commutes from one part of the city to another. Although I probably made the most "participant" observations in dealing with services of the public administration and my own daily movement through the city, these were complemented by observations of the stuff of everyday life: family lunches, motorized transport, petty commerce, police harassment, birthday and engagement parties, funerals, church services, and street-side chats.

The backbone of the study that forms the basis of this book, however, is formed by long conversations, often with regular interlocutors. My original plan was to seek out informants with a specific "historical capital," in extension of Ortner's idea of culture as a contested resource (1990, 59). Those were people who had personal knowledge of key events of Angolan history, as well as those who might be in a position to leverage that historical capital, be it through their standing in the community of the *bairro* (neighborhood), their formal position, or their personal links with power. Although this provided me with a good entry point, I soon came to understand that such a narrow focus and quasi-mechanistic understanding of the importance of history and of memory as merely the narratives was not overly productive to investigate the questions that really interested me. I had to expand my range of interviews and observations, building on my initial contacts to make sense of the realities of everyday life in Luanda.

I would assert that this is more than "snowballing"—*horribile dictu*—because it involves planning and method, even if it does include a good dose

of serendipity. Thus chance encounters in the street and referrals from ac-
quaintances and friends were vital in expanding my network of interviewees.
More important for an ethnographic study, I could not afford a car. Walking
in the physical environment of the city, and observations in and from the
ubiquitous collective taxis (*candongueiros*), the thousands of blue-and-white
Toyota HiAce minivans that ply the city's main transport routes, gave me a
richer understanding of the tapestry of life in Luanda.[24] Spontaneous interactions with fellow passengers in the collective taxis were especially fruitful
because they recreated "countless times a day in myriad ways . . . the interactions that encapsulate much of everyday life and economy in many versions of urban Africa" (Myers 2011, 22). This was especially true because
with such long-term fieldwork and under conditions where no one openly
wants to speak of politics, it is key to attuning oneself to the fleeting manifestation of the political, that which "blinks, momentarily shows itself, and
escapes" (Navaro-Yashin 2002, 15).

For all these points—initial and secondary contacts, chance encounters, and
physical and social movement in the city—my own position as a researcher
was key, which requires a brief biographical digression. I grew up in Luanda
from the age of two to ten (1984–92). My parents had been sent to Angola by
the Département Missionaire of Lausanne, Switzerland, at the request of its
Angolan partner church, the Evangelic Reformed Church of Angola (IERA),
a protestant church founded in 1922 by Archibald Patterson, an Anglican lay
missionary, and Ernst Niklaus, a Swiss pastor.[25] Impeded by the war from accessing the church's heartland in the northern province of Uíge, we stayed on
in Luanda, with my younger siblings adding to the family over time. My parents were working with the church in the rapidly growing informal *bairros* of
Luanda, improvised shantytowns of huts made of corrugated iron sheets
where internal refugees from the war made their new homes. Due to the in-
adequacy of the Angolan education system, however, we children followed
French school, together with children mainly from the expatriate diplomatic
and oil circuits, but also a few privileged Angolans. Thus I grew up in a strangely
in-between position, participating in and being familiar with both common
Angolan and privileged expat lifeworlds, but being part of neither. The flar-
ing up of conflict in Luanda in 1992 prompted an unplanned return to Switzerland, and I only returned to Angola in 2007 (then aged twenty-five) for my
master's research (Schubert 2010). There I carried out shorter research and
worked in collaboration with an Angolan NGO, processing the biographical
shock of return (and the impossibility thereof).

This put me in a unique position to carry out this research. First, I had an established basic network of contacts to fall back on, which was essential for the logistics of living in the city. This included less my few remaining (or returned) childhood friends, but more people of my parents' generation, as well as new contacts in NGOs, churches, and academia that I cultivated since 2007. Second, for this kind of research, linguistic competence was key. As I am fluent in Angolan Portuguese, I could share jokes and capture subtle nuances, when informants would, for example, switch speech repertoires to indicate a higher or lower social status. Third, because of the "in-between-ness" of my upbringing, I had access to informants across the social spectrum, from *mamãs* in the *bairro* to upper-middle-class youths and people in executive positions in the administration or the church hierarchies.[26] I thus spoke to street vendors; war veterans; police officers; administrative clerks; bishops and pastors of the Catholic, Reformed, and Methodist Churches; politicians and party members (opposition and ruling party); reporters; authors; scholars; activists; students; and shoeshine boys. This may sound like a random enumeration, but it was in fact an invaluable asset: as the following chapters show, it is highly representative of the multiple social links that exist in Luanda, and of the social and spatial mobility of its inhabitants.

Last, and perhaps most important, although I had this broad access and the necessary linguistic and contextual cultural knowledge for "thick" ethnographic encounters, I am visibly not Angolan—because of my physical appearance (e.g., blue eyes) and my name, I do not fit the general mold of the white Angolan. Thus I was evidently not part of the system or connected to any of the "big families" or to particular interests. This proved a huge advantage. Before starting fieldwork, I was concerned that people would only reluctantly speak about sensitive political issues; quite the contrary turned out to be true, and I was surprised at the openness and candor with which people spoke to me.

It is also true that many people seeing me for the first time had initial difficulties in placing me. Indeed very few "European" foreigners walk the streets or enter the *bairros*—except for those in a jeep with a big NGO logo on the side, or those wearing a priest collar—and passers-by or fellow passengers in the taxi would often assume I was Russian or Czech, possibly recalling the *cooperantes* (accredited co-operators) of the socialist era. Thus introducing myself through my biography helped people situate me and make sense of my presence. This is especially the case in a country where, depending on which social milieu one frequents, one of the first questions people often ask is not "Do you go to church?" but rather "Which church do you go to?" I am hardly an avid churchgoer in Europe, but it is in Angola part of the reality I grew up in and a primary social frame of reference for people. Referring to my father having been a pastor of the IERA placed me in a clear social context.[27] This positionality will become more evident in the subsequent chapters, as it informed my access to and take on specific situations.

Thus although I radiated out of a more or less defined place, the urban district of Sambizanga, and structured initial encounters around key events of Angolan history taking place there, this is not an ethnography of a specific locale. It is illusory to try and replicate a spatially bounded ethnography in an urban context like Luanda where people's lives are profoundly shaped by social and physical mobility (the two being of course connected). To decenter and delocalize the anthropological gaze, the text moves between different social strata and locales, not only imitating my own movements as a researcher across spatial and social divides but also attempting to connect seemingly disparate realities that are in fact intimately connected.[28] The analysis is thus a construction that is fundamentally shaped by the anthropologist's "voice and vision, which themselves become significant sites of connection between the . . . phenomena [she/he] engages" (Biehl and McKay, 2012: 1213, writing about Tsing, 2005). The text then offers glimpses of local realities to convey specific context, rhythms, and flavors, and to offer insights at a more abstract level.

This is not to say that it was all plain sailing, as the variety of sources and directions my fieldwork took made me regularly doubt the validity of my purpose. And experiencing the brutal disjunctions between different social realities of Luanda was at times hard to assume. For example, when I spent Sunday morning at a church service in a *bairro* where the congregation of perhaps a hundred people struggled to collect around 120 dollars among themselves for the weekly offers, and on the same afternoon had lunch with upwardly mobile young professionals in a luxury "beach hut" on Mussulo, the peninsula off Luanda. While we were feasting on grilled meat, a friend showed up, stepping off his gleaming white yacht with a magnum bottle of champagne that easily cost double the 120 dollars collected by the church congregation. I also experienced "periods of despondency, when I buried myself in the reading of novels, as a man might take to drink in a fit of tropical depression and boredom" (Malinowski 1922, 4). Nonetheless, I rekindled old friendships and made new ones, and despite phases of boredom and aimlessness, I always found something to see and do in Luanda, and inspiration came to me from unexpected places.

As a final note on methods and sources: because of my attention to the circulation and public life of stories, rumors, and political events, I have often resorted to news items and their reception during the writing of the book, to complement my firsthand ethnographic data. Most of these are referenced in the notes with URL and date accessed. Archival sources from the postindependence, pre-Internet period were more difficult to get by, for reasons of access, physical availability, and time constraints. For example, at the archives of *Jornal de Angola* (*JdA*), I was told that the holdings were under reorganization for an undefined period of time that lasted until the end of my fieldwork. While the municipal library at the provincial government of Luanda also holds *JdA* back issues, archival research such as the one I did there only serves as a minor complement to my ethnographic data; it is not the mainstay of my analysis.

Two further considerations regarding my own position and my relation to the social context of the research are necessary. One is to do with research ethics and the protection of informants. Despite my readiness to anonymize informants, some interviewees insisted on having their names written down and their photos taken (this was especially the case with "survivors" of the political purges of 1977). Accordingly, I have given aliases to most informants, and recorded others with their real names, especially those who through their public personas are known for their positions or those who wanted to be identified with their statements. Also, because of a widespread distrust of the recorded voice and the taking of photos—due to the perceived omnipresence of the state security service—I mostly jotted down notes, which I typed into full field notes in the evenings and, with a few rare exceptions, made no recorded interviews.

The second point is linked to the politics of writing an anthropology of power in the context of Angola. Even if we agree that anthropologists have a historical and theoretical duty to study unequal power relations (Bourgois 1990, 45), research and activism must be clearly separated (Hastrup and Elsass 1990, 301). Nonetheless, and especially because of my personal background and obligation to my informants, objective research and personal commitment are sometimes hard to disentangle, and "it is obvious that a study like this is at least partly inspired by an interest in scholarship as a form of political action" (Englund 2006, 24). This is not to engage in some form of "militant anthropology" (Scheper-Hughes 1995), but considering that "scientific objectivity" is a futile pursuit in all production of knowledge, it would be useless to try and mask my own sympathies in the text.

Although through this book, I aim to present as complete as possible a picture of life in Luanda and people's relation to power through the system, my analysis is of course limited, due equally to material constraints, analytical choices, and personal proclivities. Three main limitations come to mind: the first is that although religious life plays a central role in the lives of a large number of Angolans, I only touch on churches as social environment or organized religion. This is certainly to do with my own position and my desire to stake out my own field of research, separate from any possible focus on churches in Angola.[29] But it is also a result of the general thrust of my analysis: although biblical imagery was often invoked to make points about the moral order of society, most churches are decidedly apolitical and refrain from addressing political issues.[30]

The second is that although this book is about political culture, there may seem to be relatively little about popular culture as in music, film, and literature. This is not due to a lack of personal interest or potential for empirical research; the intertwining of popular music and political subjectivities in Angola, for example, has been charted by Moorman (2008).[31] Especially in the context of the 2011–2017 youth protests, my argument could have taken a very different spin if I had focused on the tensions between and political instrumentalization of kuduro and protest rap, Luanda's home-grown styles of "ghetto-music." Although listening to the latest rap tracks blaring from the loudspeakers of the taxis was an exhilarating and definitely political experience, I did not collect the data to formulate such an argument more authoritatively. Work by Tomás (2014) and Moorman (2014)—on the dulling of kuduro's political edge—and by Buire (2016)—on underground rap music and political contestation—shows the way forward.

Finally, based primarily on fieldwork carried out between October 2010 and October 2011, the work engages chiefly with ethnographic data collected during this period. Complementing this longer research by earlier research trips (2007, 2009), personal correspondence with informants, and continuous monitoring of media and social media, I engage with events until the 31 August 2012 general elections in chapter 6, and tackle subsequent developments only in the conclusion and the epilogue.

Structure of the Book

Considering the wide-ranging and often overlapping themes that this book seeks to investigate, as well as the physical and social mobility inherent to an ethnography of the system in an urban space as heterogeneous and complex as Luanda, breaking down the analysis into discrete chapters is no easy task. I was initially tempted to structure the book around key events of Angolan history to tease out the different elements that make up these social realities, but this idea ultimately proved unwieldy. I thus decided to draw together the themes of everyday life that make up a common sociopolitical field and to present in each chapter a specific facet of the relation of people to power. These themes follow each other logically, as building blocks of the argument, and can be divided into three pairs of chapters: a first pair (chapters 1 and 2) on history and the uses of memory discourses, a second (chapters 3 and 4) on social relations and the articulations of cleavages and connections, and a last one (chapters 5 and 6) on the practices of negotiation, accommodation, and resistance.

Following this overarching structure, in chapter 1, I investigate the master narrative that provides the foundation, or ideological underpinning of the system. At the same time, I provide an overview and critical reading of the existing historiography of Angola. Departing from scholarship on memory politics in postliberation regimes, I analyze the discursive strategies and performative acts deployed in these processes and explore the symbolic and material effects of this "technical" hegemonic discourse in Luanda. Because national reconciliation is limited to the reconstruction of infrastructures, the master narrative of the New Angola is also physically imposed on the urban cityscape; similarly, any substantive political dialogue about the war is precluded because it is a threat to the gains of peace, which are measured again in purely material terms of the built environment.

In chapter 2, I present the flip side of the politics of concrete and the processes of "spatial cleansing" discussed in chapter 1. I discuss the multiple ways in which memories are a central element to the renegotiation and dialogical construction of the relation of people with power in postwar Angola. In this chapter, then, I look at the affects of place in the historic neighborhood of Sambizanga: how does the material transformation of a specific place seep into people's memories? How do holes and gaps in the cityscape evoke feelings of loss, melancholia, nostalgia, and fear, and how do these feelings inform people's relationship with power? And how does such "memory work"—that is, the making of narratives through engaging with urban space—stabilize the unruliness and disruptive potential of past violence that cannot publicly be spoken of? Chapter 2 thus serves a dual purpose: it enables discussion of the multiple ways in which the hidden transcript of Angolan history is a central element to the renegotiation and dialogical construction of unequal social relations, and how political subjectivities within the system are shaped by central affects such as fear, melancholia, and "nostalgia for the future" promised at independence. At the same time, it allows me to ethnographically ground my thesis in Sambila (as the district is sometimes colloquially called by its residents) and to provide the reader with the physical, social, and historical context of my fieldwork.

One of the key issues of postindependence history is the question of racial and ethnic identities, raised in the 27 May 1977 coup attempt and acted out in the anti-northerner postelectoral violence of 1992–3. In chapter 3, I explore the interplay of race, ethnicity, class, and nationality in contemporary Angola—all unresolved issues that remain politically taboo and potent identitary discourses. Through the idioms of race and ethnicity, Angolans express ideas of social hierarchies and political legitimacy in the very unstable, contested notion of *angolanidade* (Angolanness). For reasons I expand on in the chapter, *angolanidade* is a slippery, ambivalent notion that, in contrast to other African countries where autochthony has become a central means of political mobilization, is a nonracial, "nontribal" concept that cannot (or only to a very limited degree) be deployed in formal politics. I contend that the reluctance of political actors to address the question of national identity has mainly to do with the political elite's unstable identity as a socially white or *mestiço* privileged class governing a socially black, African country, as well as the way in which the war was won.

However, the idiom of race is very much part of the popular political imaginary of the system: people in Luanda often perceive their ruling class as strangers and denounce them as a foreign elite disconnected from the realities of the people. Race, ethnicity, and citizenship are recast in terms of class within the Angolan political scene in statements such as, "They don't care about the country or us *because they're not really African*" (emphasis mine). And yet "Africanness" is not simply the oppositional discourse to the MPLA's hegemonic vision of multiracial *angolanidade*. Because race and class are intimately intertwined, people shift in and out of different categories situationally, so that even if they might denounce the ruling elite as foreign, they also endorse and reproduce a fundamentally urban, anti-indigenous project of "civilized" modernity.

Chapter 4 makes a parallel movement to add a further facet to the reproduction of hegemony by looking at practices of "situational kinship" in everyday interactions between citizens and agents of the state, and the ideas of power and hierarchy expressed in these practices. Because of Angolan social history, and the ambivalent social roots of today's urban elites explored in chapter 3, the instrumentalization of idioms of kinship for purposes of state power is less straightforward than it is in other African contexts we know from anthropological literature. The idioms of kinship and the "traditional" foundations of "correct" social interactions then assume a more subversive character. These practices and discourses thus reveal the tensions between what people see as the real functioning of society, and their perspectives on how society should work.

However, the idea of kinship as an oppositional discourse must be complicated again through the exploration of the everyday practice of mobilizing *cunhas* (personal connections) for one's own purposes. Exploring these *cunhas*—based on intimate knowledge of Luandan family networks—allows us to trace the multiple linkages between state and society, to combine in the analysis social strata commonly studied separately, and to challenge facile notions of nepotism and corruption. In chapter 4, I suggest interpreting the personalization of interactions in everyday practice as a much more fluid and reciprocal process of negotiations that coproduce the system and sustain, subvert, and redefine political legitimacy in postwar Angola.

In the last part of the book, I turn my attention even more closely to how those social relations are acted out in practice: in chapter 5, I turn to the intended or actual results of activating the *cunhas* discussed in chapter 4. I look at the desires produced by Angola's oil wealth and analyze the material and symbolic effects of the postwar economic boom on the lives of Luandans. I do so by exploring the vernacular imaginary of a "culture of immediatism" to show how the dynamics of economic growth and the commodification of politics are perceived and utilized by the population. Based on the stories of three key informants, this chapter thus ethnographically unpacks the aesthetics of power and the coproduction of hegemony to map the popular lifeworlds in a resource-rich, dominant-party regime such as the regime in Angola. As I show in the chapter, the fabulous overnight wealth of some people contrasts sharply with the lived reality of most Luandans; nonetheless, this wealth is very visible and "almost within reach" for most. This has had, according to many, a corrosive effect on class solidarity and the work ethic of Angolans, an effect that goes hand in hand with a commodification of politics, where displays of wealth and largesse, and of quick consumption (*maratonas*), trump programs and substance. Although many Luandans recognize and deplore their complicity in maintaining the system, immediatism also points to the limits of hegemonic domination, opening up a terrain of contestation of the regime.

In chapter 6, I analyze these contestations in greater detail to show what happens when the system frays. I show how antigovernment youth protests that started in 2011 utilize the discursive repertoires of dominant ideology to challenge the dominance of the regime. Empirically, I pursue the question of what happens when the ordinary course of social life in Luanda is disrupted by open defiance and more explicit resistance to the dominant social and power structures. Analytically, by disassembling the discursive and performative re-actions by various social actors to those events, I draw back together the different elements that define the parameters of the political in Angola, analyzed separately, and in greater detail, in chapters 1 to 5. Even the most oppositional of the manifold social actions taking place around these events, and even the most novel vectors of communication, resorted to existing, culturally significant repertoires to make sense of the situation and articulate their interests. Although this contributed to reproducing and reinforcing hegemony, by tapping into and manipulating these repertoires for oppositional purposes, these first protests did significantly impact on the dynamics of Angolan political culture, triggering strong reactions by a vast array of social actors and sketching out the possibility of change. This then allows me to make a more general point about the emergence of new political subjectivities under conditions of neo-authoritarianism.

In the conclusion, I draw these various elements together to reiterate and formulate the key argument of the book: working through the emic under-standing of contemporary Angolan society as a system that needs to be un-derstood, mastered, and managed to successfully navigate daily life, this study advocates a heuristic approach that encompasses both the symbolic and ma-terial effects of power in people's lives. I argue that we need to take into account the relational, sensuous, and reciprocal dimensions of power to understand the coproduction of the political in a neo-authoritarian political environment such as the one that exists in Angola. I argue that by paying de-tailed attention to the more subtle cultural processes and everyday politics of the ordinary in the system of contemporary Angola, we can begin to under-stand how a regime such as this one functions, and gain insights into the mul-tiple ways in which political authority is sustained in social contexts marked by rising inequality and less-than-perfect democratic mechanisms across the globe. This is followed by an epilogue that gives a brief summary of events between 2012 and 2017 and sketches out the potential for change within and through the system.

Throughout the analysis I have tried to stay true to the voice of my infor-mants in my translations, and to give space to their stories, which throw into sharp relief the dominant themes shaping people's relation to power and demonstrate people's strategies for managing their everyday lives in Luanda. Equally, I have aimed to convey the exhausting and exhilarating speed of life in Luanda, its rhythms, its flavors, and its textures. Now let us start with a closer look at this New Angola.

CHAPTER 1

2002, Year Zero
The Foundations of the New Angola

In 2011, Rádio Mais—*"a rádio da Nova Angola!"* (the Radio of the New Angola)—repeatedly played a short jingle that cut together snippets of Barack Obama's inauguration speech, Kofi Annan's farewell speech, and a previous State of the Nation speech by President José Eduardo dos Santos.[1] The message of this New Angola was clear: President dos Santos was on an equal footing with those renowned world leaders. Since the end of the war, there have been concerted efforts to rebrand dos Santos as the "Architect of Peace." He is hailed in public media as a "Great African Statesman" or compared to Nelson Mandela and Desmond Tutu.[2] A constant barrage of speeches and media reports extolling the virtues of "the executive," singing the praises of the president, and praising the successes of both in reconstructing the country hammers home the message that the MPLA is the party of peace and material reconstruction.

In this chapter, I examine the production of the Angolan postwar master narrative as the discursive underpinning of the system, and its effect on the sociopolitical and physical environment of Luanda. I contend that the Angolan narrative relies on, and has promoted, a very selective reading of the history of the Angolan conflict, a reading that involves shrouding the conflict's ideological or political root causes and silencing the more unsavory aspects of the ruling MPLA's part in the conflict.[3] Although the MPLA's past as an anticolonial liberation movement has been subject to patriotic rewriting, its position after independence, as both the legitimate government of Angola and, at the same time, a participant in the civil war, has proven much more problematic for straightforward political appropriation. Because of the MPLA's role in Angolan postindependence history, especially with regard to key events such as the 27 May 1977 coup attempt and the 1992 elections, even a tailored version of the past would stir up too many unwanted questions. The postwar master narrative thus selectively conceals the conflict's postindependence period. According to this reading of history, the end of the war in 2002 functions as Year Zero of the country's independence, which was delayed only by the conflict.

It is a teleological reading of history, one which starts with the heroic independence struggle of the MPLA, in which the movement prevailed over internal and external enemies. The Angolan conflict, in that perspective, was thus merely the continuation of this struggle to overcome the last obstacles keeping Angola from fulfilling its manifest destiny. All the promises of independence that were never fulfilled because of the civil war can now finally be honored. As all blame for the conflict is laid on UNITA's insurgency against the state, peace and the rightful predominance of the MPLA are the just rewards of this *luta continua*.[4] Finally, the New Angola is entering history and taking up its rightful place in the community of sovereign nations.[5] Through this hegemonic discourse of peace and national reconstruction and a selective silencing of postindependence history, the MPLA and President José Eduardo dos Santos have been recast as the sole guarantors of peace and stability.

Based on this image of the Architect of Peace, the second core element of the narrative is the reduction of the Angolan conflict to its material effects, in which the war has been resignified as a technical, material issue, as a largely actor-less calamity that befell the Angolan people as a whole. In this perspective, 1975–2002 was a time of "massive destruction of lives and infrastructures," but was not in any way linked to personal agency or political agendas, ideologies, or economic motivations. It was, rather, a *situação* (situation) beyond anyone's control.[6] The war is spoken of in terms of "material and human losses" and "large-scale destruction of infrastructures," often quantified in terms of monetary costs, or depicted as an obstacle to economic growth and progress that has held back the country for too long on its path to prosperity and subregional influence.

More important, if peace equals infrastructure reconstruction, there is no need for reconciliation (i.e., a political dialogue between former enemies, or any form of institutionalized dealing with the past). There is no need to revisit the past in this New Angola, a country of promising futures, manifest destiny, and unparalleled economic growth. Ideology, when it is hegemonic, is couched in the language of reason, commonsensical knowledge, and the greater good; any dissenting opinion, by contrast, is denounced as ideological, irrational, and antithetical to the will of "the people." And it is on this dominant discourse of peace, stability, and reconstruction that the MPLA today bases its claim to political legitimacy.

In the first section, I review the historiography of Angolan nationalism and of the civil war by juxtaposing the dominant narrative with how scholarly literature has addressed these periods. This more historical section of the chapter allows me to build my argument about why the MPLA's relationship to its past is so tenuous, and why memory politics in Angola focus on the liberation struggle rather than on the postindependence Angolan conflict. This also provides the reader with an overview of the Angolan conflict. Here, I specifically look at two key events of postindependence history, the 27 May 1977 coup attempt and the elections and postelectoral violence of 1992–93, which despite official silence continue to strongly impact debates, discourses, and practices.

Having thus laid the groundwork for my analysis, I examine in the second half of the chapter how, since the end of the war, the Angolan conflict has been resignified in dominant discourse. By unpacking the core elements of the master narrative, and the discursive strategies, tools, and performative acts employed, I look at how the MPLA is projecting a forward-oriented, materialist conception of national reconstruction to promote the idea of a New Angola, one that starts with a clean slate. Rather than ascribing intentionality to specific social actors (which would be hard to prove empirically), I aim to demonstrate how this dominant discourse structures the terms of the debates; that is, how it creates the conditions for what can be thought and said publicly. The circulation of these ideas then produces certain kinds of subjectivities and, in turn, shapes material reality.[7] To the extent that reconciliation has been equated with, and limited to, infrastructure reconstruction and a politics of concrete, so has the built environment become a key site of contestations over history and meaning. This is nowhere more evident than in Luanda. I thus argue that the destruction of historic neighborhoods and key mnemonic sites also works as the material manifestation of the MPLA's will to impose the ideology and vision of a New Angola on the cityscape.[8]

In this chapter, then, I read the transformations of the urban environment through the totalizing effects of the dominant postwar political discourse rather than retrace the history and development of urban planning per se.[9] Instead, I look at the physical transformation of the built environment as the material effect of the political project of the creation of a new country.

Although these large-scale infrastructure and building projects invoke the imperatives of (neoliberal) economics, safety, health, and urban planning, I argue that these processes of urban upgrading (*requalificação urbana*) are better understood as practices of "spatial cleansing" (Herzfeld 2006). Moreover, in this first chapter I very much focus on the public transcript of Angolan history. Numerous hidden transcripts and popular memories about national history circulate, of course, that more explicitly contest and subvert the master narrative. I address these in chapter 2.

Memory Politics in Southern Africa

Ever since Werbner diagnosed a "postcolonial memory crisis" in Southern Africa, it has been taken almost as a given that former liberation movements across the subregion instrumentalize and appropriate national history for their own means to assert their claims to national leadership and discredit political opponents (Werbner 1998).[10] Primorac, writing on Zimbabwe, describes the creation of a "master narrative" by which the state "seeks to govern the production of all other socially constructed meanings" (2007, 434). Because of the conflicts and discrepancies between state and popular readings of national history, memory then becomes a political space where ideas of nationhood, political legitimacy, and identity are contested (Werbner 1998, 95).

Over the past fifteen years, such processes of memory making have received sustained scholarly attention, especially in Zimbabwe, Namibia, and Mozambique, which share with Angola certain characteristics of postliberation dominant-party regimes. In Zimbabwe, the ruling ZANU (PF) has monopolized the history of the independence struggle "as means [sic] of reasserting its own legitimacy whilst also undermining the 'liberation credentials' of the opposition party the MDC" (Fontein 2009a, 15). This resignifying of history includes promoting a "patriotic history" in school and university teaching, a history that is, as Ranger explains, "narrower than the old nationalist historiography" and resents "disloyal" questions about nationalism (2004, 218). This patriotic history promotes a kind of "exclusive nationalism" to discredit any opposition challenges to its political primacy (Alexander and McGregor 2007) and helped reconfigure the political crises of the 2000s as "Third Chimurenga" to justify the fast-track land reform and position violence as the main form by social and political conflict was acted out (Kössler 2010, 41).

Namibia has followed similar paths of using national history for political means: the former liberation movement and ruling party, SWAPO, has promoted a narrow reading of the history of the liberation struggle, premised on its heroic role and sacrifices in freeing the country from the South African yoke (Becker 2011, 520). This one-sided history is embodied in the National Heroes' Acre (based on the Zimbabwean model and designed and built by a North Korean art workshop) and in a selective canonized set of materials and national holidays (Kössler 2007, 363–4). As both Kössler and Becker show, individual and collective contestations over this history are played out in a variety of arenas, including alternative sites of commemoration and community memorial practices, with varying success.

In Mozambique, history remains a main site of political contestation, with the former civil war opponents, the ruling Frelimo (Mozambican Liberation Front, Frente de Libertação de Moçambique) and main opposition party Renamo (Mozambican National Resistance, *Resistência Nacional Moçambicana*) both openly trading accusations about the civil war in parliament and "us[ing] memories as weapons to settle accounts with former wartime foes" (Igreja 2008, 539).[11] For example, both the root cause of the civil war and the creation of the newer, second-largest opposition party, MDM, can be traced back to Frelimo's killing of Uria Simango after the assassination of Eduardo Mondlane. The resurgence of armed conflict in Mozambique since 2013 is arguably also made intelligible through the history of the civil war, with Renamo justifying their return to arms with the fact that Frelimo "violated the Rome Accords" (the 1992 Rome General Peace Accords), an argument that finds surprising resonance even outside of Renamo's traditional central heartlands.[12]

The Public Transcript of Angolan History

Similar observations can be made if we look at how the history of Angolan nationalism and the independence struggle (1950s to 1975) has been reworked in official discourse for political aims. The social roots of Angolan nationalism have been explored elsewhere in great detail, and I will therefore limit myself to the most salient points here.[13]

In her analysis of the sources of the MPLA's history, Christine Messiant (1998) explains how and why the MPLA has rewritten its history, and why national history is still the object of strong polemic. Her central argument is that the MPLA never was, despite later efforts to portray itself as such, the first or only expression of Angolan nationalism, and has only a tenuous claim on having won independence for Angola. In Mozambique, Frelimo was, at the moment of independence, the sole recognized representative of the Mozambican people; in Angola, the three nationalist movements, the FNLA (National Front for the Liberation of Angola, *Frente Nacional de Libertação de Angola*), the

MPLA, and UNITA, had already rivalled and fought each other before independence—rivalries that the Portuguese colonial power skillfully nurtured to
play off the groups against each other.[14] The Alvor Agreement of 15 January 1975, which stipulated the gradual withdrawal of Portugal and a power-
sharing transition government composed of the three movements, soon fell
apart. Negotiations failed, and "elections were foregone for military engagement between the three parties, each emboldened by Cold War resources and
rhetoric" (Moorman 2008, 169).

Armed confrontations escalated from June 1975, with the three movements
trying to extend their territorial control and thereby strengthen their claims to
representing a majority of the Angolan people in view of the planned elections (Pearce 2015a), and the MPLA holding on to the capital. The FNLA and
UNITA marched on Luanda, but the MPLA, with Cuban help, prevailed in its
control of the capital, defeating the FNLA on 10 November 1975 in the Battle
of Kifangondo, and pushing back the South African Army that was moving
on to Luanda from the South in support of UNITA at Sumbe. Reflecting these
realities, there were then two separate declarations of independence on 11 November 1975, one by the MPLA in Luanda and one by UNITA in Huambo,
both claiming sovereignty on behalf of the Angolan people.[15]

Witnessing the intervention of the South African apartheid regime in support of UNITA, initial calls by the international community for ceasefire and
compliance with the Alvor Agreement fell silent, and a wave of solidarity swept
the continent, leading to the eventual recognition of the MPLA as the sole
legitimate government of Angola by a majority of states (Marcum 1987).
UNITA was routed, retreating to the far southeast of the country, from where
it slowly rebuilt (Pearce 2015a).

Because three movements with genuine, if divergent, bases of popular support fought the Portuguese, the history of Angolan nationalism was from the
start the object of fierce politicization and rewriting. Two contested "untruths"
have been maintained until today: the claim that the MPLA was founded in
1956 and already existed inside Angola before the foundation of the Union of
the People of Northern Angola (UPNA, FNLA's precursor) in 1957;[16] and the
appropriation of the attack on São Paulo prison, on 4 February 1961, as the
"the beginning of the armed struggle under the leadership of the MPLA."[17]
This canonized version of pre-independence history—materialized, for example, in Luanda's 4 de Fevereiro International Airport—also demonized the
other armed movements and eclipsed the role of internal dissidents such as
the Revolta Activa and Revolta do Leste factions.

This went beyond a simple war of words: older MPLA members told me
how they were tasked with planting human hearts at FNLA's Luanda head-

quarters to support the rumor that those "northerners" were cannibals, and sway the urban population. At the Pica-Pau school in the neighborhood of Rangel, the MPLA killed over four hundred UNITA members who were supposed to integrate into the national army under the Alvor Agreement.[18] Organizers of the 4 February 1961 uprising, who "claimed that [the attack] was an independent force, with a different nationalist consciousness," were "executed, to erase all this knowledge."[19] This last point, not commonly substantiated in the literature, was made by one of the sons of Virgílio Sotto Mayor, one of the instigators of the attack on São Paulo prison, who was executed after independence, allegedly on the orders of an MPLA leader with previous links to the colonial International and State Defense Police (Polícia Internacional e de Defesa do Estado, PIDE).[20]

So far, so "patriotic history," when we look at how the history of Angolan nationalism and the liberation struggle has been monopolized. This was true in the 1980s, when the Marxist government made concerted efforts to impose an official reading of history through schools and mass-based organizations (Amundsen and Abreu 2006, 6; Pearce 2015b, 108). And it remained so throughout the first civil war (1975–91), when the MPLA portrayed UNITA as apartheid stooges, puppets (*fantoches*) and lackeys of Western imperialism.

In present-day, post-2002, Angola, such impositions of patriotic history are still manifest in commemorations of earlier decades: pre-1975, pre-independence, and pre-civil war. A good example is the debate around a new law of national holidays in 2010–11. The draft bill, presented by the MPLA parliamentary group in December 2010, downgraded 15 March, the date of the FNLA's northern rebellion, which marks the start of Portugal's colonial war in Angola, from a national holiday to a "day of celebration," to remember the "expansion of the armed national liberation struggle," enshrining 4 February, the date of the attack on São Paulo prison, allegedly authored by the MPLA, as the beginning of the armed struggle.[21] The Baixa de Cassange massacre, on 4 January, would no longer be commemorated.[22] Opposition protests against this monopolization of history remained ineffective due to the MPLA's large parliamentary majority, and the law was voted into effect.

However, if we turn to how the history of the postindependence Angolan conflict from 1975–2002 is represented today, the situation is much less straightforward, and the MPLA is at pains to construct a coherent narrative. Until 2002 the MPLA was still fighting the enemy, UNITA. It could therefore project a Manichaean reading of the conflict, based on this previous rewriting of history, that followed a dominant MPLA narrative, justified by the MPLA defending the nation against *fantoches* in the first civil war, and against "bandits" in

1990s. Since the end of the war, however, the conflict has been largely silenced in public discourse and is only dug out sporadically to conveniently remind the public of UNITA's responsibility for the war's devastations.

To understand why this is so, we must look at the MPLA's role during the conflict, which is much less clear-cut than a linear, revisionist patriotic history would have it. Two events of postindependence history are central in the view of many Angolans: the 27 May 1977 coup attempt, and the 1992 elections and their aftermath. It is not my aim to establish the definitive historical truth about these events; rather, I seek to reflect on the representation of these events in scholarly and public discourse, and the meaning ascribed to these events later,[23] and build my argument about the need to silence this period of national history rather than stabilize it in patriotic history. A slightly more detailed account of these events is therefore necessary to set the backdrop for this argument, and for this book as a whole.

27 May 1977

In 1975 and 1976, just after independence, when the government was setting out to build a new, socialist nation, there was much debate within the MPLA about which path should be followed and which ideology promoted to create loyalty and mobilize the population to transform the country. Lively discussions were led in youth and women committees, trade unions, and Maoist debate groups, the so-called Amílcar Cabral Committees, in the neighborhoods (Birmingham 1978, 554).

Nito Alves, a former guerrilla commander, became the major proponent of this "people's power" (*poder popular*), as this more participatory, bottom-up political project became known. Proponents of people's power such as Alves especially criticized the privileges of the new party elite, who concluded oil deals with the United States—the imperialist enemy—and had access to *nomenklatura* shops, while the majority of the population did not benefit from the gains of independence (Birmingham 2002, 152).

More important, Alves denounced the predominance of whites and mulattoes in the party's leadership positions, identifying, sometimes openly, sometimes only by allusion, skin color with class situation (Mabeko-Tali 2001b, 209), a question I return to in chapter 3. In a statement later repeated by Alves's supporters and detractors alike, Alves said that Angola would only truly be free when whites swept the streets alongside the blacks.[24] Alves's criticism of the "presidentialist" wing of the MPLA around Angola's first president, Agostinho Neto, as well as his growing appeal among the population, made him a threat to the party leadership (Fauvet 1977, 92–4). In October 1976, the

MPLA's Central Committee condemned this "factionalism" (*fraccionalismo*), and the Directorate of Intelligence and Security of Angola (DISA, from the Portuguese, Direcção de Informação e Segurança de Angola, i.e. the security apparatus) intensified its raids of suspected factionalists in the informal neighborhoods (*musseques*). On 20 May 1977, Alves and José (Zé) Van-Dúnem were condemned as the ringleaders of factionalism and expelled from the MPLA's Central Committee (Birmingham 1978, 555; Moorman 2008, 173).

What exactly happened next is disputed among Angolans and scholars alike. According to the official reading, Alves and Zé Van-Dúnem planned a coup to overthrow the government and kill President Neto, backed by the masses from the *musseques*. In the early morning of the 27 May 1977, groups of *nitistas*—as the putschists were subsequently labeled—seized the central São Paulo prison and the National Radio. President Neto's first statement still left open the possibility of reconciliation (Mabeko-Tali 2001b, 183); however, when it transpired that the putschists had rounded up and killed several high-ranking civilian and military MPLA leaders, Neto made his now infamous statement, announcing, "We will not lose much time with judgments . . . we will be as brief as possible" (184). Cuban forces were called in to support the government, and the uprising was quickly quelled, its leaders captured after a prolonged manhunt in the "hot" neighborhoods of Sambizanga and Rangel.

The ensuing rectification (*rectificação*), an internal purge of the party, led to a crackdown on supposed dissidents all over the country. Hundreds of people linked closely or distantly to the coup, or simply suspected of such links, were executed (Mabeko-Tali 2001b, 184). While the government later admitted to about two hundred deaths, advocacy groups claim that between 12,000 and 82,000 people were killed or disappeared in the aftermath of the events (Comerford 2005, 91).

Whatever happened during and after 27 May 1977, my aim here is not to uncover the historical truth—a challenging endeavor that can only be undertaken by acknowledging the multiplicity and subjectivity of perspectives, as Lara Pawson (2014) does so well. Rather, I want to highlight why the "27 de Maio," as the event and subsequent purges are commonly referred to in Angola, is still such a key event for contemporary sociopolitical relations in Angola. A recurring theme in Angola is the notion of a culture of fear that, according to informants, kept and still keeps Angolans from openly speaking about political matters (see chapter 2). According to them, the 27 de Maio was the turning point that installed this culture. After the euphoria of independence, the purges within the MPLA and the prosecution of factionalists (*fraccionistas*) and dissenters by the state security apparatus (the Stasi- and KGB-trained DISA) installed a climate of arbitrary state violence and deep distrust. Before independence, the PIDE (the secret police of the Salazar regime) had installed a system of snitches and spies that pitted family members against each other; to the shock of many, this system was reproduced in the newly independent country.

Much of the persistent trauma of the 27 de Maio is because this was primarily an internal purge of the MPLA, with arbitrary arrests and summary executions, the use of torture, and bodies that were not returned to their families for burial. It is commonly said that all families in Angola were affected somehow by the purges.

As the MPLA continued in power, and as key perpetrators of the purges remained in key positions—including, allegedly, President dos Santos himself—it was for a very long time impossible to talk openly about the events (Kassembe 1995, 152). The imposed silence about this emotionally highly charged event reinforced its determining status for Angolan political culture. For older generations, it triggered an almost automatic warning not to talk about politics (see chapter 2).

However, complete silencing is not strategically desirable either; it is an "open secret" that serves a purpose: the rumors and half-truths about this taboo event (Mendes, Silva, and Cabecinhas 2011), more than criticizing and undermining the authority of the regime, have actually contributed to reinforcing the dominance of the MPLA. Through this opacity, the 27 de Maio functions as a sigil, symbolizing the capacity of the MPLA to make people disappear. Indeed, when the authorities arrested fifteen "youth activists" in June 2015 for allegedly "plotting a coup," President dos Santos responded to popular calls for their release with a none too subtle allusion to the *vinte e sete* (27 [May]), saying: "We cannot allow that the Angolan people be submitted again to a dramatic situation like the 27 May 1977 because of a coup."[25]

Let me briefly return to the established historiography of the Angolan conflict and its subsequent reinterpretations. While the MPLA was fighting internal enemies in the 27 de Maio, the young country was also beleaguered by "external enemies": the FNLA, supported by Zaire (and the United States), was militarily defeated soon after independence; UNITA, with South African backing, regrouped in the far southeast of the country. Due to Cold War funding and military assistance for both sides, the conflict evolved from a small-scale bush war into a conventional land war, opposing two increasingly heavily armed forces. Throughout the first civil war (1975–91), and following the logic of internal and external enemies, the MPLA proceeded to portray the UNITA as apartheid stooges, *fantoches*, and lackeys of Western imperialism (Messiant

1998, 161). Such processes of identifying internal and external enemies are typically part of the state-building that young states undergo: "Far from being pathological, the identification and prosecution of treason are constant, essential, and 'normal' parts of the processes by which attempts are made to reproduce social and political order" (Thiranagama and Kelly 2010, 2).

Under socialist, single-party rule and during the civil war, talk about the "enemies of the nation" was an integral part of the MPLA's discourse. However, as I elaborate below, and in greater detail in chapter 6, the rhetoric of traitors and the branding of the opposition as "stooges of foreign powers" is a continuing underlying theme of the postwar political discourse.

Influenced by the Cold War context, most of the research of and on this period of the 1980s—with a few notable exceptions, such as Birmingham (1993)—also depicted UNITA as either a South African-funded tribalist and racist movement that had little political legitimacy,[26] or as champions of democracy and freedom fighters struggling against a godless communist regime.[27] And as Pawson (2014) illuminates, there was especially among the British Left a great reluctance to assess the events of 1977 critically, so that the official reading of a "counter-revolutionary" coup attempt also became enshrined in subsequent scholarship.

The 1992 Elections

Much as it does the coup attempt of 1977, controversy surrounds the aftermath of the 1992 elections. Facing a military stalemate and the drying out of external Cold War support in the late 1980s, the MPLA converted to multiparty democracy and agreed to negotiations with UNITA.[28] The Bicesse Accords of 1991, under the auspices of the United States, the USSR, and Portugal, foresaw the disarmament of the warring parties, the creation of a new, united Angolan army, and the holding of the country's first democratic elections (Messiant 1994, 158).

Polls were held on 29 and 30 September 1992. In the parliamentary elections, MPLA gained 129 of 220 seats in the national assembly, against 70 for UNITA. In the presidential election, 49.7 percent of the vote went to dos Santos and 40 percent to Savimbi, making a second round of voting necessary (Roque 2009, 139).

While the elections were quickly proclaimed "free and fair" by international observers, UNITA cried fraud. Savimbi withdrew to Huambo, and both sides raised the stakes by verbally attacking their opponent. Before the second round of presidential elections could take place, however, conflict broke out in Luanda. Because of the large number of armed troops it had in the city, UNITA was blamed for this return to fighting—but the MPLA had already issued small arms to the population "for self-defense" (see chapter 2).

Throughout the period immediately before and after the first round of elections, *Jornal de Angola* depicted UNITA as warmongers and ran stories of violence and killings in the provinces. Unsurprisingly, the local population in Luanda was intimidated by bands of swaggering UNITA soldiers circulating between the party headquarters in Bairro Operário and Savimbi's residence in Miramar. *Jornal de Angola*'s headlines from the period depict a growing threat coming ever closer to Luanda and include, for example, "UNITA accused to prepare military operation in Bié";[29] "UNITA injures and kills police agent in Kwanza-Sul";[30] and "UNITA beats up children for wearing MPLA shirts"[31] at Luanda's São Paulo market. A cartoon published in *Jornal de Angola* after the first round of elections depicts a UNITA supporter threatening a voter with violence if he does not vote for the right candidate, and photos of UNITA's armed troops allegedly at the ready in the interior upheld the specter of a return to war.[32] Looking back, Leandro, who was a child at that time, remembers:[33]

> In 1992, the government armed the population of Luanda and said they should defend themselves against the terrorists because the army were in the other seventeen provinces. Luanda had no experience of fighting, and all of a sudden the UNITA troops were in town. I was only seven or eight, but I remember it was a struggle to go to school—the schooling system was in shambles, anyway, back then—and even to buy bread. Most people wouldn't go out of their houses, only some grown-ups went out to buy food for everyone. The problem was the false communication. The UNITA was fighting for a just cause, we recognize that now, but back then the media told us that they did eat people.[34] "They eat people? What? *Xê!* I won't vote for these guys . . ." So it was better to arm ourselves.

In such a tense situation only one spark was needed. It came when UNITA were alleged to have attacked the provincial police command from their downtown lodgings in the Hotel Turismo on the night of Sunday, 10 October 1992.[35] MPLA raids on Savimbi's residence and on the Barrio Operário headquarters followed, while the security forces, aided by the armed population, started to root out suspected opposition supporters. In the "Halloween massacres" of 30 October–1 November 1992, numerous Ovimbundu and Bakongo, supposedly natural allies of UNITA, were murdered in the capital; several high-ranking UNITA members were killed when trying to escape the city. While UNITA intensified its fighting in the countryside, extending its control over large parts of the territory and occupying major cities, the military and the police in Luanda continued to kill civilians of Bakongo origin, culminating in the "Bloody Friday" of 22 January 1993 (Mabeko-Tali 1995). No undisputed figures exist, but in the "period of political purges, revenge killings and ethnic cleansing from both sides" that followed, as many as three hundred thousand people are said to have lost their lives (Roque 2009, 139). Already, then, people interpreted the killings as an echo of the events of the 27 de Maio, saying "Blood is again flowing down the streets from the Kinaxixe."[36]

After the elections derailed and the conflict flared up again, international opinion shifted against UNITA. Although some scholars rightly have pointed out the failures of the international community in overseeing the transition to elections (Messiant 1995, 2004), the blame was largely put on UNITA: Savimbi was perceived as a "greedy spoiler" and an authoritarian madman with a "messianic sense of destiny," unwilling to share power (Greenhill and Major 2007, 16). Clearly his personality certainly did not help the search for a negotiated solution, but this perspective also neatly dovetailed with (or fed into) a scholarly trend to interpret conflicts, especially in Africa, as "resource based" and driven by greed rather than by grievance (Collier and Hoeffler 2000; Malaquias 2007). In this light, UNITA's fight was seen as "an increasingly pointless and personal bush war of sheer destruction," driven by the desire to loot Angola's diamond riches in the East (Brittain 2002, 128). The international community labeled UNITA a terrorist group and subjected it to ever-increasing sanctions (Hodges 2004, 16). Although civil society initiatives lobbied for a negotiated peace, the MPLA, dominating a Government of National Unity and Reconciliation born from the 1994 Lusaka Accords and now internationally recognized as Angola's legitimate government, successfully depicted Savimbi as the last obstacle to peace and pushed for a military victory and "total annihilation" of the enemy (Miranda 2004, 23; Malaquias 2007). The killing of Savimbi, on 22 February 2002, finally proved to be the "one-bullet solution" to the conflict; six weeks later, on 4 April 2002, the exhausted military commanders of UNITA signed the Luena Memorandum of Understanding, which ended the war.

This depiction of UNITA as rebels without a cause, which became widely accepted in the 1990s, has several problems. As authors such as Beck (2009, 2013), Pearce (2015a), and Ferrão (2012) have demonstrated, UNITA always also pursued a political, state-building project that created strong links of sociality and imagined and implemented (or enforced, if we follow Beck) alternative models of Angolan society in the territories it controlled. But, as with the conflict in Eastern DRC ten years later, "simple narratives" predominated (Autesserre 2012). These narratives were necessary—not least for foreign journalists and international organizations—to frame the conflict and conceive of possible solutions, and justified the government's pursuit of a purely military solution. True, UNITA had not complied with the disarmament requirements in the interior. Nonetheless, placing the responsibility for the Angolan conflict wholly on UNITA obscures the fact that the MPLA leadership was willing to share neither power nor state revenues, and that the failure of negotiated solutions to the war must be imputed to them in at least equal measure. Furthermore, the 1992–93 killings in Luanda, which have left such a deep imprint on the urban population, cannot simply be explained by Savimbi's megalomaniac personality or UNITA's "loss aversion," as has often been the case (Greenhill and Major 2007). However, this reading of the conflict prevailed throughout the last phases of the war.

Until the end of the conflict in 2002, we can still observe a rewriting of history following a dominant MPLA narrative, justified by the MPLA defending the nation against "UNITA rebels." But the picture changes when we turn to how the period of the Angolan conflict (1975–2002) has been resignified since the end of the war to create the New Angola. Here I think we need to nuance Pearce's reading of postwar memory politics in Angola (2015b). I agree that periodically reminding UNITA of its role in destructive civil war whenever an opposition demonstration is announced serves a political purpose. However, much like the problematic place of victims of the Matabeleland massacres in the 1980s in Zimbabwe's national history (Fontein 2010), the events of Angola's postindependence history—such as the *vinte e sete* or the postelectoral violence of 1992–3—undermine the dominant narrative of the MPLA as the representative of all Angolan people, and thus resist being stabilized in a dominant, patriotic history narrative. This helps explain why the postindependence period is so notably absent in postwar memory-making processes.

Constructing the New Angola

In the following section I turn to the construction of a hegemonic "peace and reconstruction" discourse and a selective silencing of postindependence history. I discuss how the MPLA and President José Eduardo dos Santos have been recast as the guarantors of peace and stability, and how this impinges on the ways in which "national reconciliation" has been reframed. I do so by unpacking the core elements of this master narrative—the discursive strategies, newspeak, and performative acts—and explore how this antihistorical stance is echoed in the physical transformation of the city.

> In the last ten years, the Architect of Peace has been working to rebuild Angola and guarantee more social justice and less poverty to his people. Under his leadership, Angola has recovered and built infrastructures like roads and railways and power plants, and has transformed itself into one of the countries that grows most on the entire planet.[37]

The designation of the president as the Architect of Peace—a designation bestowed on him by "his grateful people" for his "key role in the peace process and the reconstruction of the country," according to party propaganda and state-run media—epitomizes this process of resignifying war as an issue of infrastructures.[38] Whenever the president inaugurates a new road bridge, railway section, or hydroelectric power station, people are reminded of the "gains of peace" (*os ganhos da paz*), in opposition to the destruction and confusion brought about by the war.

Because the war has been equated with the "senseless" destruction of infrastructures, large-scale reconstruction projects have since been one of the government's top priorities, thereby depoliticizing the question of national reconciliation as national reconstruction. In the same way that the "destructions of the war" are quantified in billions of dollars in speeches allusive to the anniversary of peace, or of national independence, the MPLA has pursued a politics of concrete by which peace is conceived in GDP growth figures, numbers of roads rebuilt, kilometers of rails laid, and numbers of classrooms reconstructed. Posters exhort the population to "Build the Future Together" (*juntos construimos o futuro*), or to stand "Together for Growth" (*juntos para o crescimento*). Even before the official period of electoral campaigning in 2012, oversized MPLA posters claimed "MPLA—More Democracy, More Development." In a similar shift of signifiers, the former "government" has been rebranded as the "executive" in public and state media discourse. Through this depiction, President dos Santos stands above the fray of party politics and is, as the head of the executive, merely implementing the national reconstruction program that clearly represents the will of most, if not all, Angolans. Stability and tranquility, which are always contrasted with the *confusão* of war, are praised as the most fundamental gains of peace and the necessary precondition for reconstruction and economic growth. So while the fundamentally "high modernist" project of the Marxist MPLA of the 1980s—including the creation of a New Man (*homem novo*)—has metamorphosed into its neoliberal, market capitalist offshoot, its five- and fifteen-year master plans of state-led progress and development, which could be threatened by "enemies of stability and progress," remain strikingly similar.[39]

It is well known that development processes of technocratization and "rendering technical" depoliticize issues that are, at their core, deeply political (Ferguson 1994; Mosse and Lewis 2005; Murray Li 2007). However, paradoxically, similar processes of rendering technical are, in Angola, not just a by-product of national reconstruction; they are at the very heart of the postwar political project of resignifying the Angolan conflict. Because this dark period has been framed as a *situação* beyond anyone's responsibility, and because people have been constantly reminded of the *confusão* and material damages it brought about, the war has been emptied of any political agency or meaning. And because the war has been reduced to its material dimension, peace and reconciliation have equally been conceived as technical solutions.

Stability and the gains of peace are thus the cornerstones of the master narrative of the New Angola, providing the discursive foundation of the system. In this logic, anyone who criticizes the government is an enemy of this newfound stability, desiring to jeopardize the gains of peace, and is thus, ultimately, an enemy of the Angolan people. This subtext equates UNITA, now the major opposition party, with damages caused by the war. If the government talks about stability as opposed to *confusão*, the message is clear for Angolans: if you support an opposition demonstration, vote for the opposition, or even question the government's performance, you will bring back the past as a material reality, those thirty years of war, as new infrastructures will remain uncompleted or be destroyed. In that sense, a road that the government rebuilt just before the elections might not withstand the next rains, but if they (UNITA) come back it will never be finished. Most of the time, those allegations are only implicit, and the question of responsibility, motives, and political agency in the Angolan conflict is shirked, though these accusations are conveniently trotted out whenever UNITA questions the government.

If peace equals reconstruction—a common goal shared by all Angolans, according to the master narrative—any other form of reconciliation (such as dialoguing with former enemies) is not merely absent; it is unnecessary, counterproductive even. And because the MPLA's historical legitimacy as the sole representative of the Angolan people is tenuous at best, the reconstruction of the country becomes the sole basis of its claims to political legitimacy.

The totalizing effects of this discourse are revealed in the way actors across the social spectrum have bought into and reproduce it. For example, I attended a conference on national reconciliation, organized by the Episcopal Conference of Angola and São Tomé (CEAST), at which, ironically—or rather, typically—the question of reconciliation was almost never directly addressed. Only one Angolan presenter, Justino Pinto de Andrade of the unrepresented opposition party, Bloco Democrático, actually talked about questions of reconciliation: "Is reconciliation merely the physical reconstruction of the country?" he asked. "I don't think so. Acts of political intolerance, aggressions against those who have a different opinion still happen."[40]

Most other presenters, however, were content to talk about the need for "social justice" (i.e., a more equitable distribution of wealth).[41] During group discussions, only a few expressed the need for more open debate; most emphasized peace and tranquility and the need for better services. When I asked the participants directly about reconciliation, they said, "We have social problems, we should forget and reconcile," or, "Each one should work in his own corner, in the parishes, families, villages, neighborhoods. The church can work more in this community area, and talk about domestic violence, for example." Here, too, it appeared that a large part of the public had bought into this master narrative, which tends to equate reconciliation with a technical problem that can be fixed by government programs (wealth distribution, access to services) and to voluntarily retreat into the sphere of the personal and the parochial.

For peace to be reimagined as the New Angola's Year Zero, a thirty-year hiatus in Angolan history has been both the precondition and the consequence of this master narrative. Of course parallel attempts by the MPLA still exist to promote a coherent, unified historical narrative that would include the period of the conflict, through the convening of MPLA-sponsored history conferences, or a commission working on defining which of Angola's national heroes should be included in the school history curriculum. But the messiness of the war has so far proven surprisingly resistant to straightforward appropriation.

The celebrations, on 11 November 2010, of thirty-five years of independence were thus more about the "conquest of peace" and the *ganhos da paz*—and so the logical culmination of the independence struggle—than about remembering publicly what had happened during those thirty-five years. After a host of parades and official speeches, the theme tune, a slick new kuduro production, blasted out slogans like "Leaving this mess behind" and buzzwords like "unity," "democracy," and "development." Two years later, opposition politicians said that Angolans had nothing to celebrate for the thirty-seven years of independence, which were only a formal gain, but that they enjoyed no "qualitative gains" seeing that the country was still colonized by the same boss (*chefe*) who had been in power for thirty-three years.[42] State-controlled media, however, immediately lambasted opposition parties for questioning the gains of independence, saying that *dipanda* (the Kimbundu word for independence) was an achievement of all Angolans, and that criticizing the government was unpatriotic.

Two years later again, the secretary-general of UNITA, Vitorino Nhany, expressed the idea that Angola needed a "second independence." As he said, "We are lacking total independence, based on freedom—which does not exist—social justice, the respect of human rights and equal opportunities."[43] This demonstrates how oppositional social actors also tap into and subvert—but at the same time reproduce and reinforce—the dominant discourse, that the gains of peace can be equated with the fulfillment of the promises of independence (see chapter 6).

Overwriting the Urban Palimpsest

If we follow to its end the logic of 2002 as the Year Zero of Angolan independence and the beginning of the materialist master narrative of reconstruction, the cityscape of Luanda must also be wiped clean of the chaos and the messiness of those thirty years of war. Since the end of the Angolan conflict, Luanda has experienced a remarkable construction boom. Gigantic, ambitious urban redevelopment programs have been deployed. Prestige projects—such as the controversial "new centrality" of Kilamba, a Chinese-built model city of 82,000 apartments forty kilometers south of the old city center, or the redesigned Marginal, the avenue lining the Bay of Luanda—have been planned and undertaken, and sometimes even completed on time with great pomp. New, gleaming high-rise buildings, built to create offices, hotels, and apartments, have transformed the city's skyline. Informal, unplanned settlements that had appeared during the civil war due to the massive influx of refugees from the interior have been cleared, and their residents resettled to new model "social housing" schemes in Luanda's periphery—officially for reasons of health, safety, and urban planning.

Despite being condemned by international human rights organizations, forced evictions of poor residents from informal inner-city *bairros* in Luanda continue, and slum-dwellers are evicted to make way for new, profitable property developments (Human Rights Watch 2007, 2011; Croese 2010). People have been relocated to peri-urban zones, in many cases without adequate compensation, where they live in social houses and tents. More crucially, these new settlements have been established between twenty and forty kilometers outside the city center, in new neighborhoods like Zango I–V and

Panguila, offering very limited access to employment, informal business, or schooling.[44]

Although these schemes follow economic and urban planning imperatives, I contend that this politics of concrete should also be read as the material manifestation of the postwar master narrative and the MPLA's project of creating a new country. Similarly, the New Angola not only is a discourse but also concomitantly shapes its reality, in that it establishes the country as an emerging global power, and Luanda as a global capital or an "African Dubai," where a very specific imaginary of global modernity inscribes social cleavages in the cityscape.[45]

This urban remodeling of Luanda is thus not simply a neoliberal project driven by economic imperatives. In postconflict environments, history is incomplete and liminal, and the "remainders of the past"—objects or places, for example—produce anxiety (Bryant 2013). As I discuss in chapter 2, that is very much true for Angola. Urban upgrading therefore appears as a fundamentally ideological project that is about creating certainty. It reworks older—colonial and socialist—ideas of modernity,[46] efficiency, and civility to construct a new future and obliterate the remnants of the chaotic past and the *confusão* of war.[47]

During the civil war, socialist (and post-socialist, wartime) Luanda represented, much as did socialist Havana, a "mnemonic device, reminding people of their past, and confer[ring] a morality on their past struggles, thus giving meaning to their . . . struggles" (Gropas 2007, 531). Since the end of the civil war, however, it appears that this revolutionary reading of the cityscape is no longer desirable for the regime because it does not conform to the vision of the New Angola.

After independence, many colonial street names were changed to reflect the MPLA's Marxist, pan-Africanist, internationalist position. Street names such as Avenida Lenine, Rua Kwame Nkrumah, Avenida Ho Chi Minh, and Rua Gamal Abdel Nasser embody the spirit of these times. The martyrs of the anticolonial struggle were also glorified—as witnessed by the countless streets named after this or that comandante of the guerrilla war—as were mythical figures of Angolan history, upheld as early resisters to colonial invasion, such as Rainha Ginga or the kings Mandume and Katyavala. Even the names of the victims of the 27 de Maio—Comandante Eurico, Garcia Neto, Comandante Bula—were inscribed onto the street grid of Bairro Operário. Street names thus served as a reminder of those martyrs as well as of the MPLA's vigilance against internal enemies.

Street naming is "a set of performative practices which authorities seek to monopolize by devising 'official' toponymic systems backed up by the force of the law" (Rose-Redwood 2008, 877). Refusing to adopt official names and instead using informal names can be seen as challenging authority and undermining the order of the master narrative.[48] Responses to street names can also be interpreted as struggles over memory and meaning. Street names become repositories of memory because "through particular events or regular use, specific places become focal points for memories to cluster around" (Field 2007, 24). The grid of streets and place names becomes a palimpsest on which successive histories of place are sedimented but where traces of the original inscriptions of place still can be found. Colonial street names are often privileged in daily use over the names of Marxist postindependence heroes. Informal place names like Bagdad or Pau da Cobra (Stick of the Snake) are local reminders of significant events or evocative locales—Bagdad emphasizes the dire living conditions, "like in a war zone"; Pau da Cobra alludes to "a huge tumult, a rumor in the eighties, when people said that a man had transformed himself into a snake." If "place is a product of political work upon the land" (Navaro-Yashin 2012, 41), eradicating inconvenient names from the public space—or razing and rebuilding entire parts of city, as I detail further on—can be read as the physical imposition of the master narrative on the cityscape. Because of the potentially subversive character of informal practices in places charged with historical significance, locales have to be erased, traces blurred, names removed. The fewer traces remain of disappeared people and of the focal places of conflict in the city, the less the master narrative is subverted and the better can the nation be reconstructed.

In the monumentalization of national history, too, there is a notable difference between the treatment of pre-independence history—the glorious liberation struggle won by the MPLA for the Angolan people—and postindependence history, where the ambiguities and messiness of civil war resist straightforward appropriation. Although a few socialist-realist monuments to the liberation struggle exist—the statue of President Neto on Independence Square and a monument to the heroines of the struggle, to name the two most visible—any intentional or politically coherent memorialization of the civil war, or even of the conquest of peace, is conspicuously absent from the Luandan cityscape.[49]

We can observe a tentative reconnection with the MPLA's pre-independence history, as exemplified in the reappropriation (and distortion) of first president Agostinho Neto's quotes in speeches and on party posters, or—perhaps most visibly—in the completion in August 2012 of the Agostinho Neto Mausoleum, a concrete "rocket" of Soviet design, the construction of which started in the 1980s, its hulk looming over the Bay of Chicala, uncompleted for over twenty years for structural and financial reasons. Now finally completed with North Korean support, it has been rebranded as the Cultural Center Agostinho Neto and was used as the stage of President dos Santos's swearing-in ceremony in September 2012, thereby repressing more unsavory associations with an embalmed "eternal leader of the revolution," which run counter to the vision of a modern, efficient New Angola.

This remodeling of the cityscape is, however, not just about erasing inconvenient place names or practicing a selective memorialization through monuments (which in itself is a common trait of Southern African postliberation regimes). It also includes removing from the city the people and memories that do not conform to this vision of the New Angola. In 2011, in a masterstroke that can be seen as the momentary culmination of this process of spatial cleansing, the president promulgated an administrative reform of Luanda province. By redrawing the province boundaries, the undesirable locality of Panguila to the north of the city, populated originally mainly by forcibly resettled urban poor, was zoned out to neighboring Bengo province, while the largely undeveloped areas of Quiçama and Ícolo e Bengo to the east and south of the city were incorporated into Luanda province as new municipalities to make space for special economic zones, a planned new international airport, and prime residential areas.

More important, the seven old inner-city municipalities were merged into a new municipality of Luanda. Historic municipalities associated with nationalism and anticolonial resistance, such as Sambizanga and Rangel, ceased to exist as municipalities and were downgraded to urban districts. The municipalities of Samba and Viana, a "reminder of the unruly Southern expansion of the city in the 1980s and 1990s" were replaced by names with more positive associations, such as Belas (Angola's first shopping mall) and Quiçama, the national park south of the Kwanza River (Buire 2012, 22). Buire interprets this as a marketing strategy designed to attract foreign investors and rebrand Luanda as an "emerging world city" (22). Following Nigel Thrift, however, we could interpret the razing of *bairros* and the construction of a shiny new cityscape as part of the "microbiopolitics" of producing specific, politically desirable effects, docile bodies of good, modern citizens (Thrift 2004, 67). Urban upgrading and rezoning is thus also about imposing the master narrative of the New Angola on the palimpsest of names and memories that Luanda's urban geography represents for its inhabitants, and about excising the unwanted associations and (poor) people that stand in the way of this grand project.

Nowhere is this better to be seen than in the former municipality, now district, of Sambizanga (see chapter 2). Sambizanga includes the Bairro Operário, the "cradle of Angolan nationalism" and the birthplace of Agostinho Neto. It is also home of the soccer club Associação Progresso Sambizanga, where the coup leaders of the 27 de Maio 1977 held their first meetings; and in the street names of São Paulo the martyrs of the coup are commemorated. Sambizanga was the site of the heaviest confrontations between the armed population and UNITA in the aftermath of the 1992 elections. It is also officially the birthplace of President José Eduardo dos Santos.

But as most Luandans today will tell you, *"Bom*, it is his 'birthplace' *entre aspas"* (in inverted commas), referring to dos Santos's dubious credentials from the liberation struggle and persistent rumors about his "foreign" origins in São Tomé (see chapter 3). Not only is the Barrio Operário directly linked to those grisly events of Angola's conflicted history, its physical presence—the impossibility of finding dos Santos's birth house while Neto's childhood home stands visible—also questions the president's identity as Angolan nationalist "of the first hour," and thus his political legitimacy. Instead of preserving this heritage—even in a politicized form tailored to the MPLA's revolutionary past—the neighborhood will thus be razed as part of the urban requalification drive.

The clearing, in September 2010, of the Roque Santeiro market in Sambizanga—allegedly Africa's largest open-air market, servicing up to a million people per day—further exemplifies the materialization of the political imperatives of the New Angola. The Roque, as it was colloquially known, had sprung up in the 1980s, a time of controlled socialist economy, wartime supply failures, and *candonga* (the parallel market system established during wartime and socialism), and was named after a popular Brazilian telenovela. It was relatively centrally located in Sambizanga and could conveniently be reached by taxi.[50]

When President dos Santos launched the works to "rehabilitate" the Roque, he was quoted by official news agency Angop as saying this was "a new chapter in the history of the municipality of Sambizanga, and Luanda in general."[51] Comments on online forums were scathing, deploring that the "architect of corruption and discord" was again creating hardships for ordinary Angolans.[52]

Although the market was officially cleared to remedy the criminality, traffic chaos, and insalubrity it engendered, informants remarked that the area was a prime location, close to the city center, commanding sweeping views over the Bay of Luanda, and had great potential for a lucrative property development project to line the pockets of the usual suspects.[53] And while a model market with space, fresh air, and sanitary installations was created to replace it, it was built in Panguila, thirty kilometers from the city center. Few people could afford the time or money to travel there, and vendors consequently complained about a lack of customers.

But the Roque was also a mythical place (see chapter 2), where the creativity and resourcefulness of ordinary Angolans escaped the purview of state control, and people could make money, sometimes on a substantial scale.[54] Such an uncontrolled, anarchic place runs counter to the image of the planned, modern, orderly African Dubai that the master plan for Luanda's urban regeneration foresees. The symbolic violence of reducing a popular hub of bustling activity to a desolate rubble field further underscores the state's power and determination to shape the physical and social environment.

An Amnesiac Master Narrative

Because of its questionable role as a liberation movement and warring party in the Angolan conflict, the MPLA has a very ambivalent relation to national history. Thus its ways of instrumentalizing this history for political purposes—such as nation-building or constructing and reasserting legitimacy—are perhaps less straightforward than in neighboring countries. In the master narrative deployed, pre-independence history is prehistory, tailored to fit the image of the MPLA as the winner of the liberation struggle and the natural representative of the Angolan people as a whole.[55] During the civil war, while the government was fighting against UNITA it could project a black-and-white patriotic history into the postindependence period to support its claim of being Angola's legitimate government, defending the country against external enemies.

Since the end of the war, now that these enemies have become a political party, the MPLA's assertion of dominance and its pretensions to political legitimacy have followed a different track: a discursive strategy is employed that obfuscates the past and creates an almost thirty-year hiatus in Angolan history in official discourse. By resignifying this period as a *situação* beyond anyone's control or responsibility, and by constantly reminding people of the destruction and *confusão* it engendered, the war has largely been emptied of any political agency or meaning in public discourse. The MPLA, having conquered the peace for the Angolan people, leads the nation on the path of stability and unparalleled economic growth—without any discussion about how this peace was won or how the civil war came about.

After peace was achieved in 2002, the period of ambiguity and destruction of the civil war was firmly consigned to the dustbin of history. Thus the MPLA government has set out to finally fulfill the promises of independence and construct a new, better future for the country. Indeed, at the same time that the conflict has been reinterpreted almost as a natural catastrophe—casually obliterating the years of fierce civil war that divided the country and affected large parts of the population—the MPLA has embarked on an ambitious national reconstruction program to rebuild the infrastructure destroyed by the war. In this politics of concrete, peace becomes the material, physical, tangible antidote to the conflict, and anyone questioning the government becomes an enemy of stability and an agent of *confusão*, threatening to drag the country back into war and destruction. In such a reading, to support UNITA or criticize the executive would go against the common interests of the nation because it would physically bring back the past and the destruction of the war.

Like the conflict, which was framed as a problem of destroyed infrastructure, the end of the war end was also reduced to a merely technical question of implementing a previous ceasefire agreement, depoliticizing the question of reconciliation.[56] The end of the conflict is thus seen as the culmination of the independence struggle and the start of a new history as an independent country finally at peace. The reconstruction of infrastructure is then the most visible embodiment of this start into a brighter future.

If peace equates with infrastructure reconstruction, there is also no need for any substantial reconciliation, such as any institutionalized form of dealing with the past. To the extent that reconciliation has been equated with infrastructure reconstruction, the built environment could become the site of contestations over history and meaning, with countermemories expressed through nostalgia, loss, or mental affliction. The imposition of a hegemonic reading of history, then, is nowhere more evident than in Luanda. Although programs of urban requalification ostensibly follow economic, safety, health, and efficiency imperatives, I argue that the destruction of historic *bairros* and key sites of memory is the material embodiment of the will to impose this vision of the New Angola on the cityscape.

This discourse of peace, stability, and reconstruction provides the ideological foundation of the MPLA's claims to political legitimacy, and is how its development vision is communicated. But it also opens up a terrain on which hegemony can be renegotiated or even contested (see chapters 5 and 6; see also Gastrow 2016). However, the imposition of this narrative that underpins the system is remarkably effective, in the sense that few people demand to talk openly about the Angolan conflict. Most, if they dare, only do so by telling small, individual stories in private, stories that do not openly contest the official grand reading of history. However, neither erasing the history of the civil war from public debate nor destroying the physical reminders of the civil war in Luanda's cityscape can erase the individual histories of the civil war. These individual histories become more important exactly because of this silencing and because of people's individual emotional attachment to them. How these individual histories are embodied, lived out, and expressed to create a relation to power and renegotiate the historical foundations of the system is the focus of the next chapter.

CHAPTER 2

Sambizanga

The Affects of Place and Memory

The special place that Sambizanga holds in Luanda and the popular imaginary of Angolans is intimately linked with the importance of its places and constituent *bairros* in the national history of Angola.[1] This area of the city was the theater of key events of recent Angolan history that ran like a red thread through my entire fieldwork: Bairro Operário is famed as the cradle of Angolan nationalism and the birthplace of many early nationalists.[2] Further north, the grounds of the Associação Progresso Sambizanga (APS, the Progresso soccer club) were one of the epicenters of the 1977 coup attempt, while the UNITA headquarters, on the border zone between the neighborhoods of the Bairro Operário and São Paulo, were the setting of some of the most violent confrontations after the 1992 elections. In the 1990s, its Roque Santeiro market, which had started in the mid-1980s as an illegal but tolerated *praça* (open-air market) for *candonga* (black, parallel market), established itself as Africa's largest open-air market catering to, so the legend goes, up to one million people per day. By 2011, the Roque had been razed, and the government harbored ambitious urban requalification plans for the area.

In this chapter, I explore how the most contested episodes of Luanda's postindependence history are tangled up with the built environment, and how residents of one of Luanda's historic districts, Sambizanga, tie their personal biographies to that space. In opting for such an interpretation I have been influenced by my informants' recurring interpretations of their situation in light of past events, events that are in many cases fundamentally intertwined with the physical environment.

As the material presented here reveals, Sambizanga is a very real place where people live and die, and trade, shop, walk, love, try to make a living, and raise their families. At the same time, the spatial layout of the neighborhood acts as a structuring device, which allows me to link specific places to my informants' stories. When informants switch from the present to the past and back again, it is the *bairro* that holds those stories together. In the minds of Angolans, the purges of 1977 are linked to the killings of 1992, the same way the forced market clearances of today echo the disruptive capacity of state power manifested in the *rusgas* (conscription raids) of the 1980s, during which open-bed army trucks would prowl the streets and pick up teenage boys and young men to send them to the front. And these events are tied to specific places—streets in the Bairro Operário, Savimbi's former residence in the adjacent neighborhood of Miramar, São Paulo prison, the Progresso soccer grounds, the Roque Santeiro market—that elicit affects of melancholia, fear, nostalgia, and hope. Place ties together those very disparate and unsettling memories of key events, which are then stabilized in narratives or through "discursive somatization" (Oushakine 2006). Informants' stories serve as an anchor for the self, and as a moral compass by which to assess the present. How people position themselves within the system is shaped by affects such as fear and spatial melancholia, and nostalgia for the modernity promised at independence.

A great deal of scholarship has focused on the built environment and on the potency and efficacy of infrastructures—the material effects (or even agency) of physical structures.[3] This was, partly, in reaction to earlier, more semiotically oriented scholarship, which approached the city as a palimpsest waiting to be read.[4] Focussing on the materiality of structures and on what these structures do, has, however, sometimes resulted in downplaying issues of meaning. Through my exploration of Sambizanga and of the vernacular practices of tying places and memories together, I take up again the issue of meaning, but not to set up a simple opposition between meaning and materiality. On the contrary, what my informants' digressions through their neighborhood show is that *memory works in material ways.*[5]

I thus look at the multiple ways in which "the materiality of the environment seeps into, and provokes, memories" (Legg 2007, 458) and how these memories are inhabited and acted out by my informants. Through this, I aim to capture some of the messiness and disruptive capacity of these irruptions of the past in the present, and people's entanglement with this specific place and history. My ethnographic material charts the different forms that memory takes and points exactly to the relationality between places, things, and everyday embodied, sensuous engagement with objects and spaces, and the conscious retelling and narrative making that serves to stabilize the unruliness and disruptive potential of past violence that cannot publicly be spoken of.

The chapter thus serves a dual purpose: first, it allows me to discuss the multiple ways in which biographical memories are a central repertoire in the renegotiation and dialogical construction of the relation of people with power, and to discuss how these memories are mediated through and mutually constitutive of the urban environment. This allows me to show how political subjectivities within the system are shaped by central affects such as fear and melancholia, and "nostalgia for the future" promised at independence.[6] Second, it enables me to ethnographically ground my work in Sambila (as the district is sometimes colloquially called by its residents) and to provide the reader with the physical and historical context to my research.

I analyze the workings of place and subjectivities largely through the stories of *bairro* residents (as well as through my own eyes) to convey the rhythms, textures, and affects evoked by Sambizanga's places and history. By constructing the ethnographic narrative as a journey through the *bairro* through which certain events of the past—the 1977 coup attempt, the 1992 elections, and the 2010 market clearance—are retold and anchored in the physical environment, I have taken some authorial liberties: although the journey I describe is based largely on the stories of regular, key informants, it is clearly a montage. To denote it as such, as well as because these are typical stories and recurring observations, I have used the ethnographic present, in contrast to the rest of the book. Under the circumstances of everyday life and fieldwork in Luanda, one meeting per day must already be counted as a great success; in reality, the encounters I present were distributed over the duration of the fieldwork. By constructing the ethnography as my journey and impressions, this makes the chapter the most openly subjective and selective of the book. Equally, by structuring the chapter around a few selected places and ordering it along those key events, I impose a linearity on my informants' stories that these stories did not always have.[7] Although people do retell their stories using the historical course of events as ordering structure themselves, their narratives often jump between periods, drawing parallels between the past and the present. As Sarró, Blanes, and Viegas note, in Luanda "many interviewees make themselves the link [between past and present events], as if the events of 1993 provided a model through which to think what is happening today" (2008, 100).

My informants' stories may serve as a complement or modest corrective to existing scholarship about those key events; however, my aim is not to provide an oral history of Sambizanga; rather, it is to look at how my informants' "mythico-histories" (Malkki 1995) construct their subjectivities in and through the place and history of Sambizanga. The stories set in this "affective space" (Navaro-Yashin 2012) and the references to the above events that frequently were made in conversation serve as a core structuring element of the chapter. I largely renounce contrasting the statements of my informants with the existing historiography of the period. This is partially because I have reviewed the historiography in chapter 1. More crucially, it is because my interest is in understanding the affect and meaning of those stories and how these stories shape social relations within the system, not in debunking the myths of Angolan history.[8]

Through the *Bairro* of Revolutionaries

> Sambizanga is the neighborhood of revolutionaries [*bairro dos revolucionários*]. In reality it isn't, it's a seven-headed beast [*bicho de sete cabeças*; i.e., something difficult to grasp], but you can go around at ease [*à vontade*]. You see here on my ID? The municipality of residence is marked. For some time, I changed it to another neighborhood so I wouldn't be hassled all the time.
>
> Teixeira, Campo do Progresso, 13 January 2011

Until the administrative reform of September 2011, the city of Luanda was structured into nine municipalities, from the city center to the periphery: Ingombota, Maianga, Rangel, Samba, and Sambizanga (central); Cazenga and Kilamba Kiaxi (intermediate); and Cacuaco and Viana (peri-urban).[9] These municipalities (now urban districts of the central Luanda municipality) are divided into *comunas* (communes), in the case of Sambizanga into three: Operário, Sambizanga (where the seat of the municipal administration is), and N'Gola Kiluanji. The communes, in turn, are divided into *bairros* (neighborhoods). In the case of Operário, these are Bairro Operário (the B. O.), São Paulo, and Valódia.[10] There is some confusion over the naming of these neighborhoods because their administrative division does not always correspond to what residents see as their limits, and colloquial names coexist with the official ones. Furthermore, residents' perceptions of the limits of these zones, as well as the character of the neighborhoods, have shifted over time.

For my exploration of the affective spaces of the Luandan imagination-scape, the municipality of Sambizanga acts more as a symbol than as an administrative division. Hence its furthest *bairros* of N'Gola Kiluanji, toward the Cuca brewery, are less the focus of my investigation, while parts of Miramar, merely a stone's throw away from the Bairro Operário but technically in the district of Ingombota, or the São Paulo prison in Rangel—one of the starting

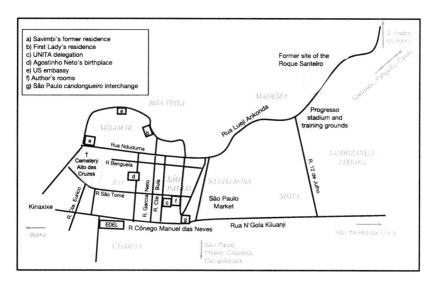

a) Savimbi's former residence
b) First Lady's residence
c) UNITA delegation
d) Agostinho Neto's birthplace
e) US embassy
f) Author's rooms
g) São Paulo *candongueiro* interchange

Former site of the
Roque Santeiro

BOA VISTA

MADEIRA

Rua Lueji Ankonda

Progresso
stadium and
training grounds

MIRAMAR

Rua Nduduma

*SAMBIZANGA-
LIXEIRA*

Cemetery
Alto das
Cruzes

R Benguela

B.O.

R São Tomé

*SÃO
PAULO*

SANTO ROSA

R. 12 de Julho

MOTA

Kinaxixe

R Garcia Neto

R. Cte. Bula

São Paulo
Market

Baixa

EDEL

R Cônego Manuel das Neves

Rua N'Gola Kiluanji

Hoji Ya-Henda, Cuca

KALÓPIA

São Paulo
Prison, Ciandela,
Congolenses

FIGURE 3.   Landmarks, streets, and *bairros* of Sambizanga

points of the independence struggle as well as a place of detention for many
factionists arrested after 27 May 1977—are inextricably tied to the same space
(see figure 3).

Among Sambizanga's neighborhoods, the Bairro Operário, or B. O. as it is
often called, occupies a special place in the history and popular imaginary of
Luanda as the cradle of nationalism. According to Isilda Hurst, an Angolan
anthropologist, architect, and artist:

> The Bairro Operário was founded in 1948, for the workers of the port
> of Luanda. But the people living there were actually of the scribe class
> [literate, lower functionaries in the colonial administration]. And all these
> people were living next to each other. So twenty years later, you had a
> perfectly formed generation ready to make the revolution. This was fool-
> ishness [*asneira*] on the part of Salazar, and not the only stupid decision
> he made.[11]

Indeed, this proximity of younger, educated, upwardly mobile Luandans
served as an incubator for the development of a nationalist consciousness
and a modern, urban Angolan identity (Moorman 2008). I return to the question of Angolanness and popular discourses about the president's alleged
birth in Sambizanga in chapter 3, but as it is the oldest built-up area of the
district, and closest to the city center, it is an apt starting point for my journey through the stories of Sambizanga. In order to guide the reader, I also

start chronologically, with stories surrounding the 27 May 1977 coup attempt before moving on to subsequent events.

In this part of the district, the dirt roads follow the ordered grid pattern of the old Bairro Operário, when the colonial administration founded it as a "native" neighborhood. Some of the old wooden houses of the first B. O. remain, as does the childhood home of Angola's first president, Agostinho Neto. The older houses are interspersed with a few newer, self-built, two-story houses made of concrete, but there is no sewage, and only a few main thoroughfares further north are tarred. As I mentioned in chapter 1, several streets in Bairro Operário are named after the martyrs of the 27 May 1977 coup attempt, MPLA leaders killed by the "putschists."

I have sketched out in chapter 1 the controversies surrounding the history of the 27 May 1977 coup attempt; many of my encounters with *mais velhos* (elders) of the neighborhood and survivors of the purges revolved around recollections of this event.

One such influential figure in the Bairro Operário is Senhor Adriano. I first met Adriano when the municipal administration called a neighborhood meeting to set up a veterans' association, to have an "organized" civil society interlocutor it could deal with regarding issues of pension payments, and other grievances.[12] The participants almost unanimously nominated Adriano to be their representative in the consultative committee. Although he seemed somewhat reluctant to assume more formal responsibilities, he also enjoyed the respect that the veterans showed him and often told me how he was known as General Zanga Mbonga in the neighborhood: "Even though I left the military early, in the *bairro* I'm a general!" On the several occasions I strolled through the dusty streets of the neighborhood with him, people would shout "General" or "Zanga," a clear sign of his popularity.

Now he is standing in front of his house in Rua Benguela, drinking beers with a few young men from his street whom he has engaged to cement the pavement in front of his house. EDEL, Luanda's public electricity distribution company, ripped the concrete open for some repair works but somehow neglected to close the hole afterward. Luckily, it seems Adriano has had no difficulties in mobilizing half a dozen youths for the task in return for two crates of ice-cold Cuca beers. Holding court in front of his house, and waving the slim white cigarette he has usually stuck in a gap between his front teeth to orchestrate the work, he sends one of the youths to also get me some beer. We start chatting about the history of the neighborhood, and he proudly recalls his days as a youngster in the late days of the independence struggle.

When I enquire about the significance of the street names in the *bairro*, however, his mood darkens:

> Bula, Cristiano dos Santos, Garcia Neto, these were martyrs, gunned down by the putschists. Then their corpses were driven away and put into a Volkswagen and set on fire. Garcia Neto, he was never a military man, he wasn't even a violent individual. He went to visit [Comandante] Eurico, who was ill, and lived in this street in Cruzeiro [behind the cemetery]. Then came the kids from the neighborhood commission [*commissão de bairro*] and killed them, in his home. That's why the street is today named after him; it's where he lived. And the other streets also, we knew them. . . . I also knew Escorpião. He was a kid [*miúdo*] of twenty-three years, and he was already the commander of the operations of the military police. This shows that he was capable, that they trusted him with responsibility. I worked with him in the military police. And he was driving my car, because he had a Citroën, and he did not know how to change the tire, because of the hydraulic suspension, so he was driving in my Mini Austin. It was my luck that no one saw him in my car on that day, otherwise I would have been caught, too. So what was it that they wanted? They were just kids from the Bairro Operário.
>
> The problem was that they killed and burned these individuals. This was then the justification to be hard [on them]; they were shot without judgment. Many cadres of the MPLA were lost; they were either imprisoned or shot. In fact, it is a great sadness for me. Many of my friends who went with me on a day-to-day basis—more than twenty—were killed. And they were no soldiers either. I don't understand it.[13]

Adriano clearly still struggles to make sense of what had happened in 1977, and is using specific landmarks in the neighborhood to make his "memories intelligible to others" (Birth 2006, 193). By "locating what [he] was observing, rooting it with a specific date, a significant event" (Navaro-Yashin 2009, 10), he is tying the personal loss of his friends to a larger narrative and trying to explain to me how the high hopes of independence were shattered shortly afterwards in the coup attempt. Whenever we met, he would return to this topic and tell me that he did not understand what this mess was all about.

Being a *mestiço*, Adriano insists that the coup attempt was never about race and that the putschists' demands were unclear and confused (see chapter 3, on race). Adriano mourns the loss of his friends, the "martyrs," but he admits he escaped the persecution more by chance—many of those who were arrested and killed after the coup attempt were also in his circle of friends. This sense of confusion and the arbitrary nature of the arrests were also the predominant themes surrounding the *vinte e sete* when I later spoke to survivors of the purges. Most of them had been part of the military units that had participated in the uprising but had had little notion of the politics behind it and had just been following orders. Many of the nonmilitary prisoners were simply deemed guilty by association, for being relatives of alleged putschists, or "class enemies," members of the educated bourgeoisie.

Adriano is less equivocal about the events following the 1992 elections and his role in them. I had heard from many informants that the MPLA had distributed arms to the population. Adriano now confirms this. He tells me how he participated in the neighborhood committees that armed the residents of Sambizanga. According to him, although the final decision to arm the population was taken by the political leaders, the initiative had come out of the local party cells because the population felt threatened by the presence of UNITA in the neighborhood.

> There was the General Secretariat of UNITA there [in the B.O.; see figure 3], and the residence of Savimbi in Miramar, with a number of soldiers higher than in an army barracks [*quartel*]. We no longer had soldiers; it was the population who felt the threat. So we who had done military service [*nós que tinhamos feito a tropa*], we decided to make a popular mobilization. We knew some soldiers, so we got the weapons and distributed them. We knew the *bairro* so well—five individuals here on this corner, they got weapons and stayed all in their homes. Because the army were all demobilized and the police without much strength— they were even caught by the UNITA—the bulk of us were civilians. We went into attack to defend the government. It was "to kill in order to not die" [*matar para não morrer*]. All of them [UNITA troops] were well-armed and had radio units; we only had light weapons, but we were many more. We didn't have radio [communication]; we had to go on foot or by bicycle. Each one was responsible for his own block. We asked the assault cars of the police for help. The police were afraid, but they saw us and said, "Damn [*Porra*], you are well-organized!" and we said, "If we keep waiting for you, we will all die!" The families stayed further inside the *bairro*, in the sand [toward the Bairro Operário, with the dirt roads]—they could not advance until there, they would have had to sweep away [*varrer*, in the sense of kill] many more people. We didn't want to start the attack without being able to end it once and for all. We had to expel them from Luanda.

They never thought that there were so many armed people here. In '75 and in '92 this was the great strength of the MPLA. Even someone who is really annoyed with the MPLA will defend it against others—"I'll first resolve it with you, then I will deal with our own affairs." Back then, 80 percent of the population of Luanda were MPLA; today only 60 percent, maybe, because of all the people who came from the interior.[14]

Although Adriano emphasizes the bottom-up character of the arming of the population, the systematic distribution of weapons belies the official version, which still speaks of a "spontaneous uprising" of the masses. On the eve of independence in 1975, the city was beleaguered by the FNLA, and white militias committed acts of violence in the *bairros* to stave off independence. But the MPLA armed the local population, organizing them into the ODP (Popular Defense Organization) to secure its hold on the capital. Similarly, in 1992, "the MPLA used the same tactic . . . to ensure its survival" (Maier 1996, 95).

Adriano's position is also indicative of the mixed loyalties many long-time supporters of the MPLA have: many of them might not agree with the path the country is on, but if forced to do so would still protect "their" government against "outsiders" before turning against the MPLA.[15]

What is less present in Adriano's story, because he stresses the self-defense aspect of his actions, is how, shortly after the postelectoral violence, the citizen militias targeted not UNITA's delegation in Sambizanga, but anyone suspected of being an opposition supporter, which was more often than not equated with being a "northerner." In a dimly lit corner of the bakery-café (*pastelaria*) Vuzelens, I meet another *mais velho*, Chinguito. Although he insists that he is not afraid of discussing sensitive topics, we sit removed from other customers, and he lowers his voice, sometimes looking over his shoulder, when he tells his story. In 1992, he was working for the National Radio. When fighting broke out, he and his shift colleagues had to stay at the station for seventy-two hours to keep the broadcasts going because their other colleagues could not come into the station.

> C: I stayed without contact with my family for a few days, for lack of a phone and lack of time. Back then I lived on the eighth floor of the Prédio do Livro [the Book Building, a landmark building in the shape of an open book, standing on the border between the Sambizanga neighborhoods of São Paulo and Santa Rosa]. There were some big skirmishes; people were dying as if they were dogs or pigs.

After forty-eight hours, the collection lorries of Elisal [the public rubbish removal and cleaning company] came and picked up the bodies and buried them in common graves. The people were armed. The arms had been handed over by the coordinators of the residents' commission [*commissão de moradores*]. My wife told them I was not there and said, "No, no, I don't want this!" but they told her, "Just put a bullet in the chamber and shoot like this." The kids made a game of this. At night, they would shoot whoever moved. They gave out a password: "Who are you?" "*Eme*" ["M" = MPLA]. But if you hesitated just for a second and said, "Huh?" they would kill their own father. At the entrance to the *bairro* they would give out the password: "Who are you?" "Enjoy your meal" [*Bom apetite*]. If you didn't know the right word, you would die like a dirty pig [*um porco enxovalhado*]. On Bloody Friday [22 January 1993] every individual who used the Congo cloth [*pano do Congo*] of the Zaireans [*zairenses*] or the *langas* was killed in the streets.[16] If you did not know and used this type of cloth you would be dead, mostly in the area of the former Roque Santeiro market. They were considered Zaireans or Congolese; they were killed as if they were not Angolan.

JS: But why were they targeted?

C: There was already a party, the PDP-ANA of Mfulumpinga Lando, who had a great adherence. The PDP-ANA were mainly returnees from Zaire [*regressados*], so they were killed to reduce the motor force of the party. It was either the color of the skin or the type of clothing. Then also the accent.[17] They are darker and use a type of [skin] product that is different from what the population of Luanda uses. But the worst killing took place in '92 at the Roque Santeiro market. After that, it began to spread [*descair*] into the *bairros*, Cazenga, Sambizanga, Rocha Pinto, and Mártires de Kifangondo. Only in Palanca did they [the Bakongo] manage to create a block because they were the majority there. There were many unnecessary deaths. But to sum it up, things are rolling and we'll hope that things will get better. Let's hope that [*Oxalá*] we will have free and fair elections. We will continue. As Agostinho Neto said, "The struggle continues; victory—sooner or later—will be certain" [*a luta continua, a vitória—cedo ou tarde—vai ser certa*].[18]

The singling out of northerners, purportedly as opposition supporters, happened after UNITA had made substantial gains in the northern (Bakongo) provinces of Uíge and Zaire but it also tapped into popular imaginaries of the Bakongo as foreigners stereotyped as "introducing the worst aspects of 'African tradition' ('witchcraft,' tribalism, corruption, etc.)" to Angola, in contrast to the MPLA's socialist, urban modernism (Sarró, Blanes, and Viegas 2008, 99).[19] Like the accusations of factionalism in 1977, denunciations of being "of the UNITA" or a northerner were then often used to settle old scores, for economic jealousy of the successful northerner traders or for personal benefit, to appropriate someone's possessions. The ethnic profiling of the victims belies the official narrative of a postracial Angolan identity, where ethnoregional identifications are minimized (see chapter 3).[20] It also throws into stark relief the disjunctions between the MPLA's claim to speak for "the people" [o povo]—a universalizing category that includes all people "from Cabinda to the Cunene"—and its practice of differentiating both between the people of the MPLA and the people of UNITA, as well as between the Angolan povo and the populações in the provinces (the local "populations" that are in practice, by virtue of their "indigeneity," less than full citizens).[21] Distinguishing between the people and the non-people is a dehumanizing device that then makes it possible that some should "die like . . . dirty pig[s]."

The affects of the 27 May 1977 coup attempt and the postelectoral violence of 1992–3 are not simply "old men's nostalgia"—memories affecting a handful of traumatized survivors stuck in the past. On the contrary, they are "emblematic memories" that tell "the collective truth of a society." Through these emblematic memories, people recall not only what happened to them but also what happened to their kin, neighbors, and fellow citizens (Stern 2004, 68). The memories are tied to specific places or, as Michel de Certeau writes, "There is no place that is not haunted by many different spirits hidden there in silence, spirits one can 'invoke' or not" (1988, 108). These spirits of place then also serve as references and meaning-making devices for younger residents of the district, and of the city in general.

Compare, for example, Adriano's and Chinguito's accounts with Alberto's notions of the bairro. Alberto is in his midtwenties and lives in the Campismo area further up in N'Gola Kiluanji commune, where he is trying to make ends meet and offer perspectives to the local youth as a neighborhood activist. We first met at a civil society conference earlier in my fieldwork, but he has only agreed to meet me now that I have obtained my research visa (see chapter 4), as he was afraid that someone might otherwise question his talking to me. When we meet for a Saturday stroll through the neighborhood, I ask Alberto if it is true that the MPLA simply dropped off weapons here for the civilian population in 1992, after the elections. He replies:

Of course it is true; that's what they did. Do you think it is a coincidence that Salupeto Pena [the head of the UNITA negotiation team in 1991–2 and Savimbi's nephew] was killed here? This is a *bairro* that shed a lot of blood, so it also has to pay for it a lot. Maybe it is cursed.[22]

The notion of Sambizanga as a special place in the city, subjected to cyclic episodes of violence and bloodshed, is very pervasive. By metonymy, it is the *bairro* itself that is cursed, that "has shed a lot of blood." Oushakine, drawing on Feldman (1994), speaks of "discursive somatization"—that is, "loss and trauma . . . expressed through the signifier of the individual or collective body" (2006, 298). I return to the idea of somatization and embodied habits in greater detail below, but it is notable how even people of a younger generation, born later, who might only know of these past events discursively, draw on contemporary experiences—of arbitrary police controls, of blocked aspirations, or of popular culture (see chapter 6)—that loads these past events with affect.[23] Thus for Alberto, too, specific places in the *bairro* are intimately linked to certain events. Chinguito and Adriano mentioned UNITA's headquarters in Rua Comandante Bula and Savimbi's residence.

With Alberto, we now cross Rua Nduduma into the adjacent neighborhood of Miramar. What a contrast from the dirt roads and low, ramshackle houses of the Bairro Operário, literally across the street: airy, modernist colonial villas and newer houses today host expatriates, embassy residences, and some of Luanda's more established rich and famous. In 1992, Savimbi's residence was here. It is now a swanky reception complex for the state diamond mining company, ENDIAMA (from the Portuguese, Empresa Nacional de Diamantes).[24] Along the road, the first lady's residence has displaced an entire block of smaller houses. The house overlooks the bay—and, to the right, what is left of the slum and rubbish dump of Boa Vista (Good View).[25] I look down, taking in the view, but Alberto advises me not to linger there: "If we stay here, someone is bound to come and ask us who we are and what we are doing here." As we return to the Bairro Operário, he tells me, meaningfully, "There's a lot of tension in the *bairro*; many people 'working' here today." I do not understand his suggestion, and have to ask him, thinking he might be alluding to pickpockets. Stepping closer, he whispers, "For the secret service, of course. Haven't you noticed them?"

I return to the pervasive suspicion of the ubiquitous *bufos* (snitches for the state security service) later in the chapter; the point I want to highlight here is that specific places in the *bairro* are intimately linked to certain events, which in turn are refracted in people's stories to construct their subjectivities. These are not just academic questions; as I often observed during heated discussions about the "correct" interpretations of these events, they are intimately linked to people's position within the system. Adriano and Chinguito mentioned the house of the UNITA delegation, which was then "almost like army barracks" and was completely burned down by the neighborhood defense militias in 1992. Chinguito's reference to the Book Building, one of the few tall apartment blocks in the neighborhood, from which "kids would shoot their own father," reminds of the destructiveness and arbitrariness of the violence.

Savimbi's residence's transformation into a leisure complex for ENDIAMA speaks eloquently of the current reconfigurations of history in the cityscape (see chapter 1). The residence's status as a mythical place in the stories of the neighborhood, however, echoes more than just the violence that was unleashed against the UNITA delegation in 1992. It also echoes the stature Savimbi has acquired in the people's minds: in 1992, the MPLA—with the help of state media—successfully portrayed Savimbi as a bloodthirsty warlord, and international opinion shifted against the "greedy spoiler" of the various peace accords in the 1990s; today, a younger generation remembers Savimbi in a more favorable light. Leandro, for example, remembers the time after the 1992 elections as a time of profound insecurity and destabilization, but his assessment of Savimbi has become more positive over time, especially when compared with the current socioeconomic situation:

> In 1992, the government armed the population of Luanda, and said they should defend themselves against the terrorists because our troops were in the other seventeen provinces; Luanda had no experience of fighting, and all of a sudden the UNITA units were in town. I was only seven or eight, but I remember it was a struggle to go to school—the schooling system was in shambles anyway back then—and even to buy bread. Most people wouldn't go out of their houses; only some grown-ups went out to buy food for everyone. The problem was the false communication. UNITA were fighting for a just cause, we recognize that now, but back then the media told us that they did eat people. "They eat people? What? Oh no, I won't vote for these guys . . ." So of course it was better to arm. But the UNITA were better educated. They were educated like hell [pr'o caraças]! They fought for a just cause, but there was no open communication. What their leader was saying did not reach the population. This created a rage with Savimbi, so he took up the war again. The population thought he was an assassin. Today the population is seeing that what he predicted is happening. It's the foreigners who are in charge.[26] Savimbi said, "First, second, third, fourth, and fifth the Angolan!"[27]

Even among younger residents of the neighborhood, the events of 1992 remain an important reference. As in the case of the expectations and hopes of independence that were shattered in 1977, regret for the broken promise of elections and peace shines through in Leandro's statement.

Visible Absences: The Roque

The other key site of the affective landscape of Sambizanga that comes out of these stories is the former market Roque Santeiro, which Chinguito mentioned as the place where many "Zairean" traders were killed during the Bloody Friday of 1993. More than just a place of bloodshed, however, the Roque Santeiro acquired mythical status as "Africa's largest open-air market," where many of Luanda's inhabitants found a means of income or supplies for their families. As the Angolan author Pepetela writes in his secret agent parody, *Jaime Bunda, Agente Secreto*:

> Hence the famous saying, that others later copied, if it can't be found on the Roque it's because it has not been invented yet. Here was the true Angolan stock exchange, where the real exchange rate of money and the price of products were established. And from where the goods were distributed to other markets and the street vendors of the city.[28]

The Roque Santeiro also speaks to popular creativity and the evocative power of place names: like many of the informal, open-air markets of Luanda that sprung up during the 1980s, the Roque was named after the immensely popular Brazilian telenovela Roque Santeiro, which was aired in Angola in the 1980s; the main market in the neighboring district of Cazenga (now formalized and still existing) is Asa Branca, after the town in which the telenovela was set; while the former market in the heart of the Bairro Operário, Beato Salú, is named after the token *maluco* (crazy man) of the series. This crazy man was—as *malucos* are in Luanda today—immediately recognizable by his tattered clothes and tousled mane, as well as his distinctive trousers with one long and one short leg. The market was named after him because it was the home of tailors, where you could get a dress made for two crates of beer during the time of the *candonga*, when the kwanza exchange rate was rising daily.[29] Another open-air market was Calaboca ("Shut up!"), evoking the illegal origins of these markets in the 1980s.

Today, after the government's crackdown on street commerce as part of its urban requalification program, most informal markets have been cleared—ostensibly for reasons of safety and hygiene—and transferred to formal structures. Now, the women sell their vegetables, clothes, and cheap Chinese plastic goods in the streets of the cement city from plastic basins they carry on their heads, or along the lanes of the *bairro*, in small heaps arranged on plastic sheets on the earth, facing constant police harassment.

To get to the place of the former Roque, I walk past my house toward the São Paulo market and taxi interchange. In the *bairro* of São Paulo, which marks the border between the communes of Operário and Sambizanga, roads are mostly tarred, and the houses present a mix of colonial *vivendas* (detached houses) in faded pastel colors and with patchy tiled roofs, some terraced houses, and a few apartment blocks. At the curbside of Rua dos Quicombos, near the former Cinema São Paulo, the taxis are waiting to fill up, and the *cobradores* (fare collectors) are shouting out the destinations: "Cuca–Hoji Ya-Henda–Cuca lá'm cima!," "Roque–da Barra da Barra!," "Roque–DIMUCA!" (See figure 4.)[30]

There is a hectic bustle of *engraxadores* (shoeshine boys), *roboteiros* (porters, carrying loads on wheelbarrows made of wooden planks and a car wheel), and *zungueiras* (female street vendors). I manage to buy a *gasosa* (fizzy drink) just before the police break up the anarchic street commerce again. Armed with heavy batons and cable whips, they lash out at the women, upending the plastic basins precariously perched on rolled up cardboard, throwing their wares in the dirt and stepping on them for good measure. Most of the women flee, but those who get hit wail and try to protect their heads and their belongings. These police actions seem like such an arbitrary battle against the tide, as the entire main road is lined with street vendors—stalls at the regular, covered São Paulo market are few and expensive—and as soon as the police agents turn their backs, the *mamãs* will put up their goods again.

All of a sudden there is a commotion across the street—a thief! I see people crowding together at the entrance of a shop, a few hands and arms flashing, and someone trying to escape. The supposed thief is caught and brought back, and then things happen very fast. First, the crowd all strike him with their open hands; then the thief tears loose, and a wild chase ensues. Two or three men pursue the thief, and one of them throws a plastic stool at his head. The thief dashes across the street, now bleeding heavily from a head wound, but he is soon caught again. Everybody stares and yells in excitement. A man next to me comments, "The thief [*gatuno*] gets what he deserves. He tried to steal the generator. The police are useless; often they get a little money from the thief to look away." I feel slightly sickened at the sight of the blood, but then a policeman intervenes to take the thief into custody. Still, the shop owner slaps him in the face one more time. This time, the policeman tells him to stop and leads the robber away. I am glad the police

Central Luanda candongueiro routes

FIGURE 4.   Main collective taxi routes and interchanges of central Luanda

came, because I suspect this thief escaped a worse fate—thieves are still routinely necklaced in the *bairro*.[31]

In the meantime, my taxi is almost full, and I get in. Rua dos Quicombos has not yet been remade in the frenzy of pre-electoral public works that will start later in the year. As it is the rainy season, the brackish brown water stands knee-deep in the many holes and gullies in the road, but the driver knows the topography of the street like the back of his hand and skillfully steers us from one elevation to the other. A hip-hop track by MC K blasts from the speakers mounted below my seat, rattling my teeth and providing a mordant commentary on the conditions outside. We pass the Prédio do Livro (Chinguito's Book Building) and reach Rua Lueji Ankonda safely, but now we are stuck in dense traffic.

The *bairro* to the right of Rua Nduduma, aptly named Sambizanga-Lixeira (waste dump) is submerged in water from the rains, and residents have to balance from one stepping stone to the next to avoid muddied shins. However, in contrast to the commune of Operário, there is no running water at all here, and people have to buy water from cistern trucks. Electricity is provided by anarchic extensions from the main line or generators. Here, the informal *bairros* begin, with no tarred roads or planned street layout and mainly self-built houses of cement blocks, iron sheets, and wood. Although some are older and larger and more solidly built, many are still small and improvised, with annexes added over the years.

The taxi avoids the deepest potholes in the road, and after negotiating a "fine" with a traffic officer we finally reach the Roque police station, where I get off. I overlook the space of the former Roque Santeiro: what was once a thriving market, providing income for a substantial part of the urban population, is now a desolate rubble field dotted with rubbish deposits, improvised football fields, and heaps of red earth.

This is not to indulge in nostalgia or to romanticize the hardships of life in the *bairro*; the Roque did indeed bring its fair share of *confusão* and criminality with it.[32] However, the loss of livelihoods and meaning was palpable whenever I spoke to former traders. Arrived at the police station, I wait for Irmão Batista, a young member of the Roque parish of IERA, who will take me into the *bairro* below the former markets to meet with some *mamãs* who used to sell on the Roque.[33]

The road that goes off the former Roque and leads down toward the church is reduced to deep furrows of black mud, plowed up by the cars that, skidding and rocking, make their way through the *bairro*. The typical stench of soapy wastewater, human feces, and open charcoal fires that lingers in the streets is slightly nauseating; yet for me, like the fumes at fuel pumps, strongly evocative of childhood memories. We enter the church, a surprisingly large and high brick building with a solid zinc roof. It still lacks some finishing touches—due to a lack of funds—but is nonetheless a marked improvement on the improvised lean-tos of corrugated sheet iron of the 1980s. The pastor and the leader of the women's group greet me warmly, and we settle down on the rough wooden benches to start the group discussion:

> We thank you for this chance to share our experiences, and [to tell you] which are the difficulties. This *bairro* was famous for the market, not only with Angolans, but also with foreigners who worked here. The market started in '86–'87, when Roque Santeiro was showing on TV.

First, there were other small markets [*pracinhas*], and here, next to the [police] squad, there were some wooden houses, occupied by Cape-Verdeans.[34] Afterward, these houses were occupied by the FAPLA. The first women started to sell here from plastic tubs, not yet from stalls. From '86 to '88 it grew into a huge market, a market that is today destroyed. This is a destruction that affects all Angolans; we very much deplore this destruction. With the wars, Luanda accrued [*afluar*] much and turned into the center of the country. But there are no conditions of employment for all Angolans here, so any kind of business helped many people. It also paid for the school fees of the children. The [earnings from the] Roque formed many Angolan cadres. Luanda is now experiencing very difficult moments.

The area of the Roque was a meeting point for everyone. The place where the government put the new market is a good space, and secure, but it's very far out, and it is only open from 8 to 14h. Here, buyers came from all over the city; there, the streets are in no condition, and you lose 2–3 hours on the way [and spend 800–1,000 kwanza on taxis for one way]. Now it's calmed down a bit, but for days and days there was a lot of noise in the taxis; people were commenting on it a lot! Also, those who rented out the storage spaces here lost [their income] and some persons fell ill. I know a lady who is at home and does not speak. She was storing great tons of merchandise here and who became very afflicted. We all suffered. There [in Panguila], the people are surrounded by bush grass [*capim*]; there is no good space. Others have now too much merchandise and don't know what to do with it. The government gave some warehouses [*armazéns*] there, for 250 dollars a month, but they are very small; they don't yield sufficient return.[35]

Mamã Adelina is one of many who lost their livelihoods when the Roque was cleared. And, as she explains, this affected not only the sellers (physically and mentally) but also the whole ecosystem of subsidiary services that had grown up around the Roque. People who owned houses or plots of land along the Roque would rent out storage space; Norberto de Castro, who made a fortune by renting out parking lots and used his money to build his eponymous football academy in Viana, was now struggling to make ends meet and keep the school afloat. Although the *mamãs* admit that Panguila is more modern and cleaner than the Roque, moving the market out of town, away from customers, made life more difficult for everyone:

In '76 I worked for the government. I was a guerrilla and was in combat before, and my husband was also a soldier. In '77 we came to Luanda and worked in the military until 1996. Then the government paid very little, so I started selling on the Roque to pay for the house and the schooling. In 2001, my husband died of an illness. I continued on the Roque, but the money is not enough. Now I sell bread on the street. If I sell the whole box, I manage to eat supper; if not, I don't. I have one son who is studying, but now the professor said, "Give me 6,000" [kwanzas]. And he has seven teachers! 7 × 6,000, it's only with God's help that I'll manage. And the *Segurança* [State security service, colloquial for the former DISA, now SINSE], where my husband worked, is not helping anything.[36]

Mamã Luisa is referring to the widespread corruption in the public education system. Numerous times I have heard how, because of insufficient numbers of study places, members of the admissions boards and examiners demand extra "fees" (or sexual favors) from students to pass or admit them. Furthermore, although the government had claimed that removing the Roque would reduce disorder and criminality, the trade had spilled into the streets, and many youngsters who were working on the market as errand boys or *roboteiros* now had lost their income, turning to drink, thieving, violent assault, or other mischief:[37]

Our government has the system of only looking one way, toward the growth and development of the country, but is not looking at the people. Of 100 percent of Angolans, 95 percent are unemployed. How can we achieve to see true peace? They said that the removal of the Roque would reduce banditry, but now there is this in every corner [of the city]. They also wanted to reduce the rubbish, but it's not really that what is happening. It actually even raised the levels of criminality.[38]

I explore further this disconnect between "the government" and "the people" in chapters 3 and 4; for now, I merely draw attention to the metonymic quality of the Roque, whose "signification relies on [people's] ability to condense the whole in a remnant [and] one's willingness to unpack the fragment to trace missing links" (Oushakine 2006, 306). The stories and the sadness of the *mamãs* reveal the interconnectedness of a specific place with a better time, and the criticism voiced around the transformation of that space, as well as the different qualities of space and the attributes attached to it—proximity versus distance, order versus disorder, and so on—stands for the larger transformations of society since the end of the war.

The Affects of Place and Memory

> After this incident [the 27 May 1977 coup attempt] we
> lived in a state of terror. Society closed up more, and
> more than 60,000 died. If this had not happened, things
> possibly would be different today. It is a fact of Angolan
> history that those persons who think are the ones who
> die first. Like Salupetu Pena [the UNITA delegation
> leader] in 1992. Now we've walked through the *bairro*,
> and you've seen life here. We don't have much to cele-
> brate for our thirty-five years of independence.
>
> Alberto, Bairro Campismo, 27 November 2010

What to make of this digression through Sambizanga, beyond simply a first
impression of life in the *bairro*? Borrowing from Richardson's "kaleidoscopic"
ethnography of Odessa (2008), I argue that the interviews and observations
reproduced in my montage refract a history tied to a sense of place to render
visible specific political and emotional geographies (21).

The dominant sentiments evoked in the accounts above—fear, melancholia, and a strong feeling of exclusion from the grand narrative of postwar reconstruction and progress—are widespread not only among individuals who
witnessed particular events themselves but also among a younger generation
of Angolans who, like Alberto, have firsthand recollections neither of the independence struggle nor of the 27 May 1977 coup attempt nor, in some cases
even, of the elections of 1992. Throughout my fieldwork, these events and the
affects they induce served as interconnected points of reference to make a
larger point about the moral order of Angolan society and about my informants' place within that moral order. In many of my interviews and observations, the retelling of national history through individual biographies and
family histories appears as a central *Kulturtechnik* with a strong didactic element: the "correct" (in the view of my informants) interpretation of history
in relation to the dominant narrative. Indeed, many of my informants seemed
almost obsessed with history, interweaving their own biographies with
national history, retelling certain events in great detail, and combining narratives of redemption, destiny, and individual and national suffering.[39] Explanations of current events are then rooted in the past. Within those narratives,
certain key events have taken on the status of myth: because the "facts" are so
little discussed, they are reproduced in individual histories, which are tagged
onto and interweaved with the grand narrative of national history, and interpreted in moral terms.[40]

Although these personal narratives have often a considerable emotional
weight for individuals, I argue that because of the politicized, contested na-

ture of national history (see chapter 1), the insertion of personal recollections within what constitutes the socially acceptable version of the past is a means of stabilizing the messiness of the affects of the past, and serves to produce citizen subjectivities and assert individual agency. As in the case of the 27 de Maio, the 1992 elections, or the civil war in general, people's personal stories sometimes jar with the grand history. Angolan citizens tend to suspect the state and its explanations because "the national myth of the war of independence . . . failed to eliminate the vernacular memories of the atrocities committed" (Silverstein 2002, 651). To the extent that official history contracts and reduces, the realms of the personal, clandestine, and subversive expand,[41] and in retelling those illicit personal memories, people express not only alternative versions of history but also alternative political visions of what Angola is or could be.

As individuals project themselves as "subjects of a collectively held history," they simultaneously reaffirm, question, construct, and reconfigure national identity and their position within it (Sturken 1997, 13). Informants' stories fit within a culturally meaningful framework of discursive strategies, where they illustrate and emotionalize a national narrative and "nationalize" personal pasts (White 1999, 505). The personal narrative is tied to the national narrative and reinterpreted in function of the needs of the present. Thus socially circulated narratives of memory weave together individual and social memory to create a local social world (Cole 2001). This is especially true for memories of violence, which often undergo a process of sacralization by which the inexplicable is converted into the meaningful to bring the past to a close (Schramm 2011, 7).

Yet, as the ethnography shows, these memories are stabilized and transposed into narratives for a purpose, to anchor them, and make them intelligible to people themselves, and to a listener. Because I was an outsider to the social setting of Luanda and not connected (at least visibly) to the system, telling me the stories was also a way out of the "impasse," where there is no public space to voice these stories (West 2003, 356–7).

However, very often the experiences of past violence, state surveillance, or social inequalities remain "sedimented in the body" and transmitted in a number of ways.[42] As shown by Alfredo's nervousness in Miramar or in Chinguito's way of narrating his story, pervasive suspicion of the ubiquitous state security service is a dominant state of mind in Angola, which is expressed in bodily habits and specific modes of ingrained behavior, such as talking and reading between the lines.

People often refer to the shorthand of the "culture of fear" that, according to them, informs the way Angolans act and think in relation to power in everyday life. Popular knowledge about the state security service follows typical discursive patterns, when referring to its advanced technological capacities for monitoring cell phones—"even when they're turned off!"—or e-mails, for example. At the same time, it is always also an embodied knowledge, tied to specific spaces that are more dangerous than others, and shaping bodily habits in very specific ways. Informants in public places such as restaurants and *pastelarias* would instinctively lower their voice when broaching certain political subjects, or would point out that any of the other patrons could well be an eavesdropping snitch. Some informants preferred to retreat to a private place—my place was usually more private than their house, where family members, friends, or other visitors could be present—or, when they could, switch to another language: "I don't want your neighbors to overhear us. There are too many people of SINFO here."

The experience of *bufaria* (snitching) has also taught Angolans to talk and read between the lines very skillfully, and researchers must attune themselves to picking up the coded messages to make sense of conversations which, transcribed, might sound mundane. In the elegant words of novelist Viet Thanh Nguyen in *The Sympathizer*, "The unseen is almost always underlined with the unsaid."[43]

In that sense, the public discourse of stability and tranquility—as opposed to the *confusão* of war I describe in chapter 1—is a thinly veiled reminder not only of the destruction wreaked by the war but also of the MPLA's capacities for violence and for making people disappear. Whether the ubiquity of the security service is real or not is secondary in that respect—people think snitches are everywhere, and the state wants them to think it is so; thus the belief in snitching serves the interests of power.[44]

As Linda Green writes, under such circumstances for researchers, too, "self-censorship becomes second nature" (Green 1994, 231). And while I cannot speak for others, I certainly know that as a researcher in Angola I developed a deep-seated distrust of authorities and instinctively adopted certain veiled, coded speech repertoires when addressing politically sensitive issues. I have also always viewed policemen with initial suspicion (even if individual conversations were often very positive), a somatic flight reflex I had to actively unlearn after leaving Angola.

With regard to the transmission of such knowledge, the events of 1977 and 1992–3 serve again as the main points of reference. For example, several informants explained how a popular song of the 1980s taught them as children, "Hey, little boy, don't talk politics" (*xê, menino, não fala politica*).[45] The song portrays an old lady, Velha Chica, selling peanuts in the streets. She reprimands the children who ask her why Angola is in such a bad state. At the end of the song, she expresses her desire to see the country at peace, leaving it open to interpretation whether she talks about the independence struggle or the 27 de Maio and the civil war. In later recordings, after his fêted return to Angola, Waldemar Bastos added a verse in which Velha Chica says she can now die in peace, "as I have seen Angola become independent," thereby anchoring his song (and Velha Chica's fear) firmly in the pre-independence past. My respondents, however, growing up in the 1980s and 1990s, all interpreted the song as a "lesson they learned" as children and as a discourse that their parents reproduced.[46] "We were always told, 'You can't demonstrate, you can't complain, otherwise you'll go to the mass grave [*vala comum*]!' "—a clear reference to the killings following the 27 de Maio.[47]

More than just cultural transmission through song, people would say, Angolans "are breastfed" this fear from early childhood: "The problem of the Angolan is fear. The Angolan, already in his mother's belly, is fed this fear." The discursive somatization of this fear "locates and circumscribes traumatic experience; it provides a 'somatic interface,' a bodily vehicle able to convey and mediate 'people's sensory inscription' of pain" (Oushakine 2006, 298).

The examples above show that this is not limited to the very real experience of violence and torture of the people imprisoned after the 27 de Maio. Time and again, people would explain to me how they "have felt the political game in the skin and the flesh [*na pele e na carne*]," referring sometimes to events as recent as the 2008 elections. To express why it was not possible to talk about the war, people talked of scars or "wounds that are still open" under a skin that has only healed superficially: "It might be too hurtful and reopen the wounds if you talk about it now." Or, in the words of Gégé, Chinguito's blind, toothless octogenarian uncle—a proper *ancião* (old-timer) of the Bairro Operário—the people who fled from the provinces had felt the war "*in the flesh*. But here in Luanda, the most drastic thing happened in 1992. After the elections, there was here a very drastic situation, very drastic indeed. There were many dead in here."[48]

With the survivors of the purges that followed the 27 de Maio, the inscription of this history in the flesh takes on a more literal dimension. At meetings with the survivors' association, the Fundação 27 de Maio, many told me horrific stories of beatings, torture, summary executions, forced labor, and starvation in the concentration camps of the interior. Some even showed me the marks on their skin.[49] But the transposition of lived experience into stabilized narratives served, in the case of the Fundação, a political purpose that included the demand for recognition, reparation, and the identification and reburial of the dead.[50] More tellingly for the embodied nature of these memories, though, and contrary to most other informants, who preferred anonymity, the survivors made very clear their desire to have their names recorded, their stories written down, and their photos taken. At a public symposium about the *vinte e sete* at the National History Museum on 27 May 2011, survivors were asked to raise their hands. Standing up and raising their hands, these men's presence seemed to be an act of defiance against a regime that had made people and places disappear and had for so long oppressed any open talk about the events, to "tell the world" what happened (West 2003, 357). In this act of presence, and of public remembering, "memory reaffirms and validates suffering" (Becker, Beyene, and Ken 2000, 340).

We Could Have Had a Wonderful Independence!

As the walk through the *bairro* demonstrates, specific places and events call forth certain bodily affects, which are then reinscribed onto the physical space in a number of ways (Schramm 2011, 5). On the one hand, informants recall events tied to individual places, especially when they are in those spaces— which provokes the affect linked to both the events and the places. The materiality of the environment, as well as disruptive changes to it, seeps into and provokes memories (Legg 2007, 458). On the other hand, these places are also socially created by those memories. They are "produced historically through spatial relations" and at the same time a "phenomenological experience," rooted in the senses and the body (Richardson 2008, 20).

This is especially the case with the "spatial and material melancholia" I often felt expressed through my informants' stories (Navaro-Yashin 2009, 1). For example, when another informant, Teixeira, finally came to my place to discuss the 27 de Maio, he insisted that he had had little to do with it, and that the two years he had spent in the prison camp in Moxico had mainly taught him never to get mixed up in politics. As a former player of the Progresso soccer club, the epicenter of the coup attempt, he, like many other players, had been deemed guilty by association. The dominant theme of our conversation, however, was the sense of melancholia over the promises of independence that had been frustrated due to the conflicts and the *confusão*. This was prompted by his comments on my flat: "Nice house you have here, my man (*meu*)! This area used to be a prime residential area in my youth, with shops and all. Now look at these anarchic constructions—it's all going down, *meu*."

For the better part of my fieldwork I had rented a small bedroom-living room (*quarto-sala*) at the back of the upper floor of an old colonial villa in São Paulo, just around the corner from the UNITA secretariat. In colonial times, one family would have lived in the house, with the domestic employees living in the subsidiary building in the courtyard (*anexo*); today it is home to five families in the house and the several rooms built along the walls of the yard (*quintal*), which also doubles as a lunch canteen.[51] The front of the house is occupied by a small grocery store, which stands in direct competition to the half-dozen *mamãs* selling vegetables from plastic tubs next to gas station and the two small corner shops (*cantinas*) in the same street, held by Malian and Guinean petty shopkeepers. This flat that I was renting, half-furnished for 600 dollars a month, included a tiny, dark kitchen and a toilet, but initially no running water. Water from the grid only came early in the morning, but pressure was never sufficient to get it to the first floor, and I had to install a tank and a pump at great expense. However, as I only found out during the installation, the drainpipes were not functioning either, as they had all silted up during years of neglect.[52]

I had chosen this place for the sociality and therefore the safety it offered; for Teixeira, however, the state of my apartment was indicative of the general *confusão* that had befallen the country after independence: "This was an unnecessary fight. We delayed our whole process a lot because of all that fighting, because in all those years that we were at war, we should've been reconstructing our country. *We could have had a wonderful independence!*" He echoed a sentiment I heard several times, that the Portuguese left too early: the colonizers had built good houses and were building up a processing industry, with factories that produced car tires, matches, biscuits, and cooking oil in Cazenga and Sambizanga. Due to the conflict, however, these started deteriorating after independence. Several informants told me how during the anarchic privatizations of the 1990s, some politicians had lined their pockets by transforming these former factories into warehouses for import-export companies. Instead of producing its own food and consumer goods, the country was now "hostage" to two Lebanese companies, which in joint-venture with the then vice-president, Nandó, controlled the market for domestic food consumption. If the Portuguese had left ten years later, and without the conflict that flared up in the hasty transition to independence, so the reasoning went, Angolans would have learned how to care for and maintain the city's physical infrastructure.

This rose-tinted nostalgia of colonial expectations of modernity[53] glosses over the fundamental inequalities of the colonial system (see chapter 3), and yet the melancholia that Teixeira expresses is echoed by many. As Bissell argues, nostalgia is one form of memory work particularly linked to the order of the physical environment, in a context where there is "a quite contested interplay of diverse social memory practices" (2005, 226). For younger informants, too, the time of colonialism is recalled as a time of modernity and of an ordered built environment. Likewise, the period of socialism, albeit a time of wartime hardship and material scarcity, is now remembered as a bygone era of solidarity, social equality, and lost ideals that have today been swept away by the economic inequalities produced by the national reconstruction drive (see chapters 1 and 5). Today, Angolans, quite like "the masses in Tanzania, Congo-PR, Ethiopia and Mozambique may now be longing for a socialism that never existed, or its 'nonrealized potential' " (Pitcher and Askew 2006, 9).

This sentiment of regret is, however, not only about the lost opportunities of modernity and the current state of the city, but about the unnecessary conflict and the calamities that befell the country after independence as a consequence of the *confusão*. Events like the 27 de Maio purges and the 1992–3 killings in Luanda have left physical traces and "visible absences" both in the city and in people's lives. Adriano's sentiments of loss were evoked by the streets of the Bairro Operário, named after his friends and martyrs of the *vinte e sete*, and by his recollection of the killings that had taken place there. Similarly, for many the predominant feeling surrounding the 27 de Maio was one of loss—not just the loss of lives, of friends, and relatives, but also the loss of innocence of the newly independent country. After the initial euphoria, the crackdown shattered the dream of independence for many, and stands at the root of all the promises of independence—progress, modernity, peace, better standards of living—that were subsequently broken. Not just among survivors of the coup but also among younger residents of Sambizanga, there was a strong sentiment of lost or missed opportunities. The sense of melancholia becomes even more palpable at the site of the former Roque Santeiro: where before a thriving market provided income and supplies to a substantial part of the urban population, a dusty field of red earth was now the only visible trace left.

Nostalgia about the better times of colonialism, early independence, and socialism can thus indeed be seen as a "social practice that mobilizes various signs of the past (colonial and otherwise) in the context of contemporary struggles" (Bissell 2005, 218). And as in Bissell's work in Stone Town, Zanzibar, these feelings express certain countermemories by local residents when faced with the government's ambitious redevelopment plans for Sambizanga, which are ultimately "reifying urban history and severing the built fabric of the city from the social context that produced it" (228).

Visible Absences and Memory Work

In the lived experiences of many residents of Luanda, Sambizanga appears as one of the key nodes of the city, a place of symbolic importance and profound disruptions where the dynamics of power relations in postindependence Angola are condensed. Visible absences—holes in the cityscape, gaps in the master narrative—provoke affects of loss, fear, and melancholia, which people plug by memory work to find and assert their space within the system. Key sites of the urban imagination-scape, such as the (former) Roque Santeiro, São Paulo prison, or the Bairro Operário as the cradle of nationalism, are potent symbols of these relations and serve as nodal points for practices of making and reinscribing history. In that sense, the urban landscapes of Sambizanga as zones of violence and marginality are "palimpsests in which buildings, street layouts and monumental structures are interpreted and reinterpreted as changing expressions of relations of power" (Hall 2006, 189). At and through these mnemonic sites, personal recollections are entangled with the larger national history.

However, Sambizanga is anything but simply a passive signifier, even though it might be symbolic in some contexts—it is a real place where people live and die, trade, shop, shit, walk, love, try to make a living, and raise their families. At the same time, the spatial layout of the neighborhood acts as a structuring device, linking specific places to the stories of its residents. When people's stories switch from the present to the past and back again, it is the *bairro* that holds the stories together. And the events recalled in these personal stories are tied to specific places, which bring forth sentiments of melancholia, fear, nostalgia, and hope.

A place's affective charge then deeply influences how people live in it. These everyday embodied, sensuous engagements with place and space go beyond the subjective experience, as the transformations of the cityscape and the events located in specific places manifest the disruptive or shaping effects of power. And the affect of iconic places goes beyond the experience of *bairro* residents alone—Angolans who live in other parts of the city perceive Sambizanga as a special area, a zone of danger and of liminality.

The relationship between official discourses and countermemories as a contested terrain often implies that the two are mutually exclusive; in fact, they overlap each other in many ways (Schramm 2011, 5). As the experiences above tease out, many of the residents of Sambizanga, traditionally one of the strong popular bases of the MPLA, are ambivalent about their relation to power. Although some of them voice strong criticisms through their memory work, they often display an almost proprietary sense of attachment to the MPLA's ideals and promises at independence. Stories that locate their tellers in national history, and the events of national history in personal and family histories, are "utterly contemporary and experientially salient" in the present (Malkki 1995, 105): they serve as a frame of reference, an anchor for the self, and a moral compass by which to assess the present.

The emotions produced by the interaction between self and specific spaces of Sambizanga (Labanyi 2010, 223) are but one of the facets that produce and negotiate relations in the system. In the following chapters, I analyze in greater detail the other facets that make up this relationality and that produce citizen subjectivities in Luanda.

CHAPTER 3

Angolanidade
Mediating Urbanity through Race and Class

Dona Mariana, Dona Gabriela, and I were having coffee at Dona Mariana's flat, on the fourteenth floor of one of the Portuguese modernist high-rise buildings overlooking the Bay of Luanda. Our conversation halted as the two sexagenarian ladies were distracted by the exciting news on the television: Leila Lopes, Miss Angola 2011, had just been elected Miss Universe the night before (on 12 September 2011).

Dona Gabriela and Dona Mariana were both thrilled because Leila Lopes was, according to them, a creole (*crioula*): "Honestly, racism here was introduced by the Portuguese, but there is no one more racist than the blacks! I am so happy that this *crioula* has been chosen—it shows well that the mixture of races makes the most beautiful women," they rejoiced, chuckling. "This will shut up all those *matumbos* [backward yokels] who are always writing in the forums that the whites and mulattoes have to be kicked out—I will write this immediately on my Facebook and on Club K!"

My surprise came not from the fact that Dona Mariana used Facebook, as she had told me how active she was, commenting on internet forums like Club-K—"But I don't use my real name, there are too many men of the state security service on Facebook, controlling who says bad things about the president"—but rather from her and Dona Gabriela's classification of Leila Lopes as *crioula*. Indeed, most headlines and comments on official Angolan news websites, which proudly hailed Leila Lopes as the "first *negra* (black woman) to be elected Miss Universe," and at a first glance, to the totalizing white gaze, the new beauty queen might indeed appear to be black. However, while some forum entries praised her "typical Ovimbundu beauty," several other commenters, both online and in the streets, were venomous, saying that she had stolen the title and should go back to Cape Verde or São Tomé.[1]

Leila Lopes's case, and how her identity was deployed by various social actors, exemplifies the interplay of race, ethnicity, class, and nationality in Angola—all unresolved issues that remain political taboos and potent identitary discourses. In this chapter, I explore this interplay, and how through the idioms of race and ethnicity Angolans express ideas of social hierarchies and political legitimacy in the very unstable, contested notion of *angolanidade* (Angolanness). For reasons I expand on below, *angolanidade* is a slippery, ambivalent notion. In contrast to other African countries where autochthony has become a main means of political mobilization, *angolanidade* is a nonracial, nontribal concept that cannot (or only to a very limited degree) be mobilized openly in formal politics. I contend that the general reluctance to address openly the question of national identity has mainly to do with the political elite's own unstable identity as a socially white or *mestiço* privileged class governing a socially black, African country, but also with the way the peace was won.

However, the idiom of race is part of the system's popular political imaginary: Luandans often perceive their ruling class as strangers, denouncing them as a foreign elite disconnected from the realities of the people. Race, ethnicity, and citizenship are recast in terms of class within the Angolan political scene, in statements such as, "They don't care about the country or us because *they're not really African*" (emphasis mine).

There is obviously something to that sentiment: although the MPLA still constantly invokes "the people" (*o povo*) in political rhetoric harking back to socialist times, those very people feel left out of any progress and development. And yet, Africanness is not simply the oppositional discourse to the MPLA's hegemonic vision of multiracial *angolanidade*. Because race and class are intimately intertwined, people shift in and out of different categories situationally—even if they might denounce the ruling elite as foreign, they also endorse and reproduce a fundamentally urban, anti-indigenous project of civilized modernity.

Analytically, in this chapter I build on existing scholarship on race, ethnicity, and nationalism in Africa to take up Susan Hangen's postulate and "interrogate the meanings of claims to primordial identities, rather than just deconstructing them, by asking why people make such claims at particular historical moments, and why these claims work" (2005, 52). Empirically, I investigate the place of *angolanidade* and nationalism in contemporary Angolan politics, which is often overlooked for being such a strong political taboo. Here, I propose to take on a more emic perspective on the role of Angolan nationalism than do Pearce (2012a) and Péclard (2012), to see how representations of self and racialized other are inhabited, embodied, and lived out. Also, taking an explicitly political approach to build on Moorman's (2008) cultural history of *angolanidade* in the 1950s–1970s, my analysis challenges Krug's (2011) analysis of *angolanidade* as an essentially oppositional discourse.

First, though, to situate the issues of race and class historically and in the context of the Angolan conflict, I briefly review the literature on the formation of nationalist elites in Angola. Based on observations and interviews with people in administrative or party functions, I then look at how *angolanidade* is used in contemporary official discourse and ask why, contrary to what might be expected from both Angolan social history and broader continental dynamics, identity discourses are not mobilized openly in party politics or for populist strategies. However, identity discourses are very much part of vernacular political repertoires: I then analyze the popular perspective on Angolanness and its uses, investigating why and how the imaginaries of racial and ethnic identities are mobilized.[2] In a final step, I complicate the idea of *angolanidade* as an oppositional discourse by looking at how my informants made use of the language of race and class to position themselves in a dominant political project of urban modernity. Here, by highlighting the aspirational qualities of idioms of race, I aim to push the existing analytic of autochthony one step further. My analysis of the aspirations and boundary work inherent to the language of race also reveals some of the larger fault lines in Angolan society, especially the urban–rural cleavage and Luanda's special position in Angola.

Highly charged terms such as "ethnicity," "race," and "class" call for conceptual clarification. Since the 1990s, researchers in anthropology and cultural studies have been increasingly interested in race and ethnicity as cultural constructions. In such a perspective, individual and group identities are never singular but multiply constructed; never unified but fragmented and fractured; and constantly changing and transforming (Malkki 1995; Hall 1996; Trouillot 2001). Equally, it has become somewhat of a truism that national and group identities are also invented (Hobsbawm and Ranger 1983) or imagined (Anderson 1983). However, as subsequent scholarship has critically pointed out, constructions of ethnicity, race, and national identity do not take place in a cultural vacuum, simply fabricated by unscrupulous elites for their own political ends. These constructions (and, quite often, their subsequent political instrumentalization) are successful because they latch onto a historical, cultural context, lending them an emotional resonance (Geschiere and Jackson 2006, 3), which is why I insist on the historical contingency of these imaginaries.

More important, once we agree that identities are always multiple and constructed, the more interesting analytical question then becomes how people represent themselves, in what context, and for what purpose?[3] What are the objectives and consequences of transposing certain political claims (more or less consciously) into the realm of racial identities? By looking at the everyday politics of representation (that is, by looking at how people inhabit and embody these representations of self and other), we can transcend analytical categories and come to understand these lived social identities as the tangible materialization of discourse in the Foucauldian sense: as a dispersed power that defines what is sayable, thinkable, and doable in public. If certain things—such as the perpetuation in power by one party and one president—cannot be questioned openly, the positioning of political subjects must shift to a different terrain, in the case of Angola, to the terrain of *angolanidade*.

In that sense, terms such as black, white, *mestiço*, and *mulato* (mulatto) which recur throughout the chapter, should be understood not as essentialist categories but as "emic constructions" or cultural representations by my informants, a "strategic toolbox" to make claims on the state of the society they live in.[4] Finally, with regard to *angolanidade* itself, I deliberately eschew a clear-cut definition. Moorman (2008) traces back to Luanda's *musseques* in the 1950s the formation of a pluralistic, urban, African, cosmopolitan, and cultural *angolanidade* that stood in opposition to the homogenizing, imperial *portugalidade* of the colonial regime. But today, "the Angolan state and elites are trying to capture in a hegemonic way the notion of *angolanidade*, and to impose a common colonial and postcolonial history," which we have seen in greater detail in chapter 1 (Sarró, Blanes, and Viegas 2008, 86). Without defining this political *angolanidade* more closely, the authors state that "the very different and sometimes very inventive significations that the notion of 'Angola' can take on . . . prove contradictory to the will of the Angolan state to control 'Angolanity'" (87). Quite so: in my analysis, I show that because of competing ideas about what it means to really be Angolan, the notion of *angolanidade* is unstable and depoliticized and has more to do with representations of social (and regional) inequalities and class privileges than it does with any primordial or politicized identities.

Historical Elite Formations in Angola

A widespread backronym joke in Angola says that MPLA stands for *"Mulatos e Pulas Libertaram Angola"* (Mulattoes and *Pulas*—a derogatory term for white Portuguese—Liberated Angola). After the 1977 Congress, the party's name was amended to MPLA-PT (Partido do Trabalho, or Worker's Party), or, in the words of the joke: *"Mulatos e Pulas Libertaram Angola—Pretos Também"* (Blacks, Too). As with all jokes and gossip, this one has a kernel of truth in it, which is intimately linked to the history of elite formation in Angola, the racial politics of the colonial regime, and the genesis of the MPLA as an organized movement. As the social history of the Angolan liberation movements has been scrutinized in great depth elsewhere,[5] I limit myself to a very brief overview to give the backdrop to the contemporary dynamics that stand at the center of my analysis.

At least since the landing of the Portuguese explorer Diogo Cão at the mouth of the Congo River in 1483, and the conversion of the King of Kongo, Afonso I, to Christianity in 1491, there has been a history of cross-cultural exchange and intermarriage in the territory that is today Angola. This led to the rise of a coastal, merchant elite that has subsequently been identified as creole (Birmingham 2006, 7–8; Thornton 2002, 85–6).[6] Portuguese, but also Dutch and Spanish, traders and soldiers intermarried with local women, resulting in the growth of an "Afro-Lusitanian" population and the "Africanization of Portuguese settlers and their culture, thus illustrating that creolization was not a process that only touched African culture and peoples" (Heywood 2002, 91). By the eighteenth century, a creole culture had grown in Luanda and Benguela, but also along the slave trading forts in the interior. These were large African families with Portuguese names, and who were Christian. They dominated social, economic, and political life in the coastal cities until the late nineteenth century, where they developed a proto-nationalism resembling the Brazilian model (Moorman 2008, 32).[7] This explains why until today Angolans like Leila Lopes can appear phenotypically black but be socially identified as *mestiço* or creole— often by the "right" family name, like dos Santos, Van-Dúnem, or Vieira Dias.[8]

Only after the Portuguese republic was established in 1910 did new white settlers arrive in greater numbers and start to displace the creole elites from their previously privileged social positions in the administration and in commerce. These new settlers were often "forced by circumstance to marry black and give preferment to their own mestiço children" (Birmingham 1988, 95). Racial competition further increased after World War II, when the Salazar regime tried to reverse the dynamics of decolonization by forcibly Portugalizing Angola. A mass of Portuguese settlers—many of whom were poor illiterate peasants or former convicts—now started crowding out the black population, not only from administrative posts but also from petty trade and menial jobs (Clarence-Smith 1985, 14).

To justify its continued domination over its "overseas provinces" when the United Nations started pushing for decolonization, the Salazar regime propagated the myth of Lusotropicalism. Based on the theories of racial miscegenation originally developed by the Brazilian sociologist Gilberto Freyre in the 1930s, the regime glorified the "five centuries of Portuguese presence" in Africa, a supposed harmony of races under the civilizing banner of the Portuguese genius.[9] The colonial administration established a system of classification that legally and in daily practice divided the population, ostensibly according to their degree of "civilizedness."[10]

The status of *assimilado*, introduced in the nineteenth century as part of Portugal's civilizing mission, theoretically allowed black Angolans to legally be equal to Portuguese citizens if they could prove that they had assimilated "an almost pure, unmitigated Portuguese culture" (Bender 1978, 28). In practice, though, only one percent of the black population achieved the status of *assimilado*, and the higher echelons of administrative positions were barred to them. Moreover, the system distinguished between metropolis-born Portuguese and Angolan-born whites as Portuguese first-class and Portuguese second-class or Euro-Africans (Tavares Pimenta 2012, 181–82). In the increasing socioeconomic competition between the *degredados* (the former convicts sent to Angola "by decree") and the *assimilados*, the only difference that gave the whites an edge over the educated blacks was their skin color, as the notion that African people were inherently inferior predominated in European, social-Darwinist thinking (Bender 1978, 205; Cabrita Mateus and Mateus 2011, 26–27). Despite the myth of Lusotropicalist racial harmony, colonial rule was thus marked by "the same omnipresent white domination which had marked all other European colonization in Africa" (Bender 1978, 207).[11]

Due to these racialized social stratifications of late colonial society, the early nationalists in 1950s Luanda, who eventually formed the MPLA, largely comprised those urban elites that had benefitted from a higher education under colonialism but had found their aspirations blocked due to their status as second-class citizens under the Salazar regime.[12] They included not only old creole elites from the trading families of Luanda (and Benguela) but also new elites, both the parvenu *mestiço* children of the new settlers and a few *assimilados*, accultured black Angolans (Clarence-Smith 1980, 116; Birmingham 1988, 95; Mabeko-Tali 2001b, 50; Messiant 2006). From its inception, the MPLA was thus riven by internal tensions between these old creole and new assimilated elites.

As Messiant writes, the "mental assimilation" among these early nationalists was strong, especially among the "old *assimilados*," as was their awareness of being the elite of the Angolan population. To broaden their appeal, they needed to break with this elitism and culturally and ideologically approach the *indigenas* (Messiant 2006, 396). This entailed the "re-Africanisation" of these elites, a celebration of Angolanness in literature[13]—chiefly influenced by Brazilian creolization and *négritude*, but also influenced by the US civil rights movement (396)—and in music, influenced by Cuba, Brazil, and Kinshasa, which led to the formation of "a distinctly Angolan culture that was neither purely African nor predominantly European" in Luanda's *musseques* (Moorman 2008, 40). By positioning this cosmopolitan *angolanidade* in opposition to the imperial, Lusotropicalist *portugalidade*, this was a cultural project as political work, an assertion of national identity, a sort of counterhegemony on the cultural front in Gramscian parlance.

We can see in the 1950s the formation of a distinct Angolan identity first through cultural expression, then gradually through political action, and eventually through armed resistance. After the independence struggle began in 1961, the movement, now largely in exile, had to extend its support base to the countryside and mobilize the peasantry for a guerrilla war against the colonial army. A second internal tension thus existed: the inherent disconnect between the MPLA's intellectual leadership in exile and its fighting social base inside the country. In the case of the leadership, most of its early members were sophisticated urbanites who had benefitted from higher education and social advancement during colonialism—and were thus the "designated heirs of the colonizer" (Fanon 2004, 146). The fighting social basis, in contrast, mostly comprised rural blacks with little formal education, whose only claim to postindependence leadership was their reputation of being good combatants (Mabeko-Tali 2001b, 252). Outside the realm of organized nationalism, the nationalist aspirations developed in the distinctly modern urban culture of Luanda were "fundamentally distinct from the social and cultural world of the guerrilla struggle" (Moorman 2008, 108). Ultimately, the question was who the real liberators of Angola were, and who would govern the future independent country (Mabeko-Tali 2001b, 274). More specifically, the question was whether a group of urban, predominantly creole, mulatto, and white intellectuals could produce a political community and national project that included, credibly spoke to, and represented those mostly black peasants that they were claiming were their fellow citizens and for whose liberation they were ostensibly fighting.

This problem was partially resolved when Agostinho Neto, a black intellectual from Bengo province, who had studied medicine in Lisbon, replaced the *mestiço* intellectual Viriato da Cruz at the helm of the organization in 1964. Being led by the *mestiço* da Cruz, the MPLA could hardly have claimed to represent all Angolans and gain the much-needed recognition and support of the Organization of African Unity. The black African Neto was a much more credible leader in this regard (Mabeko-Tali 2001b). But although the MPLA's rural fighting basis was largely based on and eventually connoted with the Mbundu people living along the Kwanza valley up to Malange, Neto and the party leadership were still from a privileged social background.[14] To compensate for or gloss over their status as a privileged minority, the MPLA leadership pursued a high modernist, socialist ideology of nonracial, inclusive nation-building—"One single people, one single nation, from Cabinda to the Cunene River," in Neto's words—that shunned tribalism and everything African (national languages, witchcraft, or any other manifestation of "traditional" culture) as backward.

Classical postindependence Angolanist literature traces the formation of the three Angolan liberation movements back to three different sources of nationalism, establishing a correlation between ethnic background and protestant missionary activity: the MPLA's Luanda-Mbundu Methodist basis, the FNLA's Bakongo and Baptist roots, and UNITA's Ovimbundu, Congregationalist constituency (Marcum 1969; Pélissier 1978). Clarence-Smith, reviewing earlier scholarship on Angola's independence struggle, wrote against the simplistic reduction of the three anticolonial liberation movements to their ethno-regional constituencies, observing that "the Angolan liberation movements were all coalitions of class and regional interests, which tended to vary over time and which used ethnic ideological appeals only to a limited extent" (1980, 116). Nonetheless, the equation of ethnic background with affiliation to a specific guerrilla movement is very persistent, also in popular belief, which imparts a sense of manifest destiny on the MPLA's capture of the state after independence and undermines its rivals' claims to political legitimacy. Indeed, FNLA, the first liberation movement, did start out as the Union of the Peoples of Northern Angola (UPNA), but was de facto led by Bakongo exiles in Kinshasa, who, as its detractors claim, harbored dreams to restore the Kongo kingdom across colonial boundaries. Similarly, UNITA has been dismissed as an ethno-nationalist movement that addressed particularistic, regional, Ovimbundu grievances, as opposed to the MPLA's professed project of modern, postethnic inclusivity.

As Péclard (2015) and Pearce (2015a) argue, the MPLA and UNITA both pursued modernist projects, but both also invoked "blood and soil" nationalism, as evinced for example in Neto's poems. However, UNITA's modernist project was based on a different vision of modernity, developed by elites from the central highlands who were ascending in the ranks of the local colonial administration of Nova Lisboa (today Huambo) and who had been educated in mission schools that were careful to preserve and promote "African culture and values" (Péclard 2012, 162–3).[15] UNITA's being driven out of Huambo after independence fuelled inside the movement a "broad narrative of exclusion," which portrayed the military defeat at the hands of "Portugalized" elites from the capital as the "second colonization" of Angola and painted the MPLA as "a coastal elite who were the heirs, both genetically and culturally, of the Portuguese colonizers, and whose roots in Africa were questionable" (Pearce 2012a, 204).[16] The two nationalist projects were thus ultimately not that dissimilar. Like each other's distorted mirror image, they tapped into the two distinct African nationalist modes of "self-writing" that Mbembe identifies: a "Marxist-nationalist" project in the case of the MPLA, and a "nativist" discourse in the case of UNITA (2002, 243, 252).

After independence, the MPLA largely left to the intellectuals and literary figures the question of what *angolanidade* meant, corralling cultural production to build the new socialist nation (Moorman 2008). The party leadership pursued its high modernist, socialist project of building a new nation and a "new man," liberated from the shackles of tribalism and backwardness. And it espoused a vision of *angolanidade* that celebrated cultural hybridity, consistent with Marxist doctrine and the social background of its leaders (Henighan 2006, 135). Indeed, the makeup of the party leadership still largely mirrored colonial social privileges, with many (new) *mestiços* and whites surrounding President Neto.

Arguably, the question of what *angolanidade* meant was one of the key drivers of the 27 de Maio coup attempt (see chapters 1 and 2). Many Angolans still uphold a racialized interpretation of the *vinte e sete*. They continue to believe that Alves and his co-conspirators wanted to remove the privileged *mestiços* from power and replace them with a black African leadership, and that the subsequent purges were a means for the white and mulatto leadership to eliminate black intellectuals and leaders so that they could maintain their control of the country. Of course, many Angolans—like Adriano (see chapter 2)—reject this interpretation because it does not fit with the grand narrative of postracial *angolanidade* that the MPLA proclaimed to espouse. Such attitudes are obviously inherently positional. It might be easier or more convenient for someone who, like Adriano, is socially at the whiter end of the racial scale to deny that lighter-skinned Angolans enjoy any unfair privileges. And because of the violent repression of the 27 de Maio, the question of race and class inequality became even more of a taboo from 1977.

After Neto's death and dos Santos's ascension to the presidency in 1979, the old creole families crowded out from the leadership positions of the regime the *mestiço* parvenus who had played an active role during the liberation struggle and in the period immediately after independence (Birmingham 1988, 94–5). Birmingham's (2012) attack on the "chattering classes" of Luanda identifies their "Luso-Brazilian" mindset to explain their neglect of the population and questions whether Angola's political and financial elite feel "truly African." Birmingham's conclusion is, "Probably not. Angola is a semi-detached member of the African Union, a country which is somewhat superior to the other fifty, rather more backward members" (219). It is telling in this respect that I have repeatedly heard Angolans say they had travelled "to Africa"—usually expressed as having been somewhat of a shock—when they visited another country on the continent.

In the Angolan context, Fanon's denouncement of the "national bourgeoisie" (2004, 100) rings true: an elite that mimicked and aimed to replace the colonial rulers without fundamentally changing anything in the distribution of economic and political power. Arguably, in Angola's case, it was less a case of a mentally colonized group's self-hatred, but rather the reassertion of a previously dominant, creole, urban elite. As Barbeitos writes, "Once in power, however, like increasingly devastating metastases, an ancient evil is perpetuated, by which the former victims who once stood up against their status as victims produce new ones [victims]" (1997, 316).

Although this internal tension between old and new elites persists within the MPLA, the struggles have outwardly been solved and are dealt with within the party. According to Vallée, the ruling elite is a pact between the old and new elites, who ally according to "configurations determined by generations of access to power, cultural references according to whether they are from old families of the *assimilado* bourgeoisie (the Van Dunem [*sic*] for example) or newcomers whose reference is African authenticity" (2008, 44). But the second tension persists: because the postindependence party leadership, with its *nomenklatura* privileges, tended to reproduce previous social hierarchies—with the old creole families at the top—the disconnect between the leadership (urban, *mestiço*, and creole) and the social basis of the MPLA (the black African *povo*) has never properly been resolved.

The Cold Discourse of *Angolanidade*

Many of my informants reflected the widespread sentiment that the original MPLA reproduced the privileged elites from colonial rule. Setucula, an NGO activist I had originally met in 2007, when he was setting up civil society monitoring of the 2008 elections, told me how he felt that Neto's proclamation *"de Cabinda ao Cunene, um só povo, uma só nação!"* (From Cabinda to the Cunene River; only one people, only one nation!) was merely ideological, with little foundation in Angolan realities:

This sentence is typical for Neto, but it is a great mistake. The MPLA's first ideological motivation was that whites, mulattoes, and *assimilados* gain independence from Lisbon, but would continue to lead the process.[17] They wanted independence following the model of Brazil. The whites and mulattoes, together with the *assimilados*, would have the leadership and gradually lift up the blacks. Their first leadership were all whites: Viriato [da Cruz], Américo [Boavida]—Neto only became president in 1962. The MPLA was confronted with a problem: what would be the place of whites, mulattoes, and blacks, respectively, in a new country? Neto was married to a white woman but he came from the masses; he was able to be a bridge. Chipenda never liked this—the progression of mulattoes within the party. That's what's led to all this *confusão* in the East.[18] Neto needed a conciliatory discourse and to fight tribalism. That's why our national languages were banned in all institutions. . . . *Um só povo, uma só nação* (Only one people, only one nation) was a historic error. Ethnicity became a political thing. Today, it's a cold discourse, without politics, even though there is some recognition that we are an aggregation of nations.

Setucula referred to a "conciliatory discourse," but homogenizing might be more accurate: in search of legitimacy as *mestiço* or white nationalists in an Africa that largely conceived of itself as black, the leaders of the MPLA embraced the theses of Soviet vanguardism—because Marxism conceptualized race relations as class relations, they could justify their political leadership through their struggle for a more just society, without classes and without racism. The consequence of their own contestable cultural (or racial) identity was "the unitary, racially and ethnically homogenizing state that they developed after independence" (Venâncio 1998, 83). Independent Angola was to be built on an eminently integrationist and globalizing discourse, on a deep disdain for all things tribal, and on a disregard of ethnolinguistic realities, in favor of a unitary, fundamentally hegemonic identitary reference: the Angolan nation (Mabeko-Tali 2001a, 161).

Homogenizing Nationalism in Postwar Angola

The MPLA has recycled Neto's slogan of "Only one people, only one nation" in political speeches and campaigning. Whenever I conducted interviews with members of the administration or party officials, I tried to find out whether this policy was still being promoted or at least used in official rhetoric as part of the postwar nation-building project. I asked Dr. Manzambi, one of Angola's prominent anthropologists and the National Director of Museums, about his assessment of the role of ethno-regional identities in Angola today. Dr. Manzambi is of the generation who came of age around the time of independence and who contributed to the building of postindependence socialism in Angola. He endorsed the official position on the role of ethnicities as they are portrayed in anthropological and regional museums throughout the country (a very ahistorical, culturalist representation of "peoples and their artifacts"). According to him, ethnic diversity was never a problem in Angola because "of the different communities in the territory, 80 to 90 percent belong to the great Bantu family." Hence the museums' role is to display unity in diversity through the "cultural practices" of Angolans. In fact, he explained to me, it was the colonial regime and the Christian missions—the Baptist Mission Society in the North, the Methodists in Kessua [outside Malange], and the Congregationalist Church in the South—that had fragmented society.[19] This explained, according to him, why the MPLA pursued an official policy of atheism after independence: "Socialism needed to cut this [division]. I don't know if we managed to reach this objective. But by trying to create a unity we forgot the African cultural diversity"—a diversity that is today celebrated as a "wealth" in political discourse, though not in practice.

This rose-tinted view of ethnic pluralism in national harmony is in line with a political agenda that envisions the different museums as contributing to supra-ethnic, postracial nation-building. Similarly, a sort of "Africanness light" is promoted in public, with some of Luanda's up-and-coming fashion designers tailoring their latest collections from printed wax cloth (*pano*) in the colors of the Angolan flag during my fieldwork, for example.[20]

But the issue of regional identities is clearly still much more sensitive than Dr. Manzambi put it. Another Angolan intellectual in a leading administrative position agreed to an interview about popular memories and the role of museums in promoting national history. Despite my intentionally neutral phrasing of the introductory question, most of our discussion revolved around the unasked questions, the most sensitive and contentious issues that Angolans are very skilled at picking up and talking about between the lines. My informant happily and freely engaged with my more implicit research interests when I exposed my project to him, and it is telling how, from my first question about the function of official history writing and museums, we immediately switched to more sensitive topics in the privacy of a one-on-one interview. I was nonetheless surprised at the candor with which he spoke about the issues of race and ethnicity, touching on his biography, the history of national liberation, the 27 de Maio, and the 1992 elections in the course of the interview. He recalled a history of largely unacknowledged interethnic confrontations during the liberation struggle and the Angolan postindependence conflict—including the hostility he faced as a teenager from the remote province of Moxico arriving in Luanda in the early 1980s—which belies the official narrative of one people, one nation:

> There [in Luanda] I heard for the first time, "You killed my uncle, because of your Dangereux!" [Comandante Dangereux, a legendary MPLA commander from Moxico, was killed by the putschists on 27 May 1977. Many of the people (like Teixeira in chapter 2) who were arrested in the subsequent purges were sent to concentration camps in Moxico, where many of them were killed. Luandans then often interpreted the "fury" of the people from Moxico against the suspected putschists from the capital as retribution for Dangereux's death.] My brother was a soldier, and when he heard this, he gave me an army bayonet to defend myself, which I carried around in a Russian briefcase. Even today the *mamãs* in Sambizanga think that those from Moxico killed their men.

This knowledge of ethnic conflict in 1977 and 1992 continues to impinge on ethnic or regional relations today, which is why, in his opinion, the question of ethnicity remains a highly sensitive topic in Angola's political landscape:

> I have contributed an article to an edited volume on "Traditional Authorities and Laws" in Brazil, which should come out soon, where I write about ethnic identities. To talk about this is polemic, even taboo. *O poder* may not like it. . . . I was equidistant in my analysis, but when the book is published, I think someone is going to call me.

His statement betrays the very ambivalent, even fearful, relation to power (*o poder*) even for someone who would appear, by his professional status and party biography, very much part of the higher echelons of the administrative and social hierarchy of the city.[21] Indeed, at the end of the interview, after we finally had talked about museums for two minutes, he asked me if his contribution would appear under his name, or if it would be anonymized. I explained to him that it was part of the dialogue of the anthropologist with their interviewees to determine this, and that I would respect his preference. He told me, "This is my opinion and I stand by it. But it would be better if you simply wrote 'an author' instead of putting my name in—we will both be more at ease [*à vontade*] that way." I was again perplexed by how even people in a seemingly secure public position are reluctant to speak their mind publicly, but the politically sensitive nature of our discussion explains this.

Dra. Irene Neto, the daughter of Angola's first president, Agostinho Neto, was in a much more secure position to address even sensitive topics openly. She is a member of the MPLA's Central Committee, theoretically the party's deciding organ, and the head of the Foundation Agostinho Neto. This, together with her father's standing as "founder of the nation," affords her some independence from the official party line, even if in practice critics in the party have been increasingly marginalized. In 2010, she gave an interview to the independent weekly *O País* in which she spoke of the need to install a Truth and Reconciliation Commission for Angola to investigate the events of the 27 de Maio.[22] When I interviewed her on this, I also raised the issue of *angolanidade*:

> This [country] is an inclusive space; we have various people who see themselves as Angolans, and there is in fact still a lot of friction. The people do not accept being led by someone from abroad. The question of *angolanidade* is one of the questions that are not openly talked about. Where there are differences between people, there will be problems; it's like in Brazil. It's noticed but not talked about. The stratified society, we want to end this, but it's not easy. Like South Africa—they are now the Rainbow Nation but some residues [of racism] can still be noted.[23] And yes, you notice it when they insult you because of your color [President Neto's widow, Maria Eugénia, Irene's mother, is white, so she herself is also rather fair-skinned]. After independence, my father was accused. And eventually, *o poder* went purifying its ranks—choosing between one like that or one like that . . . It's natural, though, in a country where the largest proportion of the population is black. But proportion isn't everything; there's also the question of competence. And until today, in the elite, you will notice . . . in the air force, especially—it had to be formed (educated) people [*gente formada*], and previously they [the whites and mulattoes] had better access to education. There is a question that always remains latent, but if there is a discussion, it's right away, "Go back to your homeland!"

As the examples of Dr. Manzambi, the author, and Dra. Neto show, the fault lines of Angolan society constantly overlap, and it is sometimes difficult to tell them apart because questions of class (that is, questions of culture, education, and status) have been historically and are today intertwined with questions of racial and ethnic identity. Dr. Manzambi represents, in his official function as director of museums, the official line. Although this line has somewhat softened from the socialist paradigm of "One people, one nation," and although it now acknowledges regional diversity, it remains largely mere lip-service to the "richness of local cultures" that remain subsumed under the MPLA's homogenizing vision of nationhood. The author, by contrast, recalls a history of interethnic tensions, both between the different liberation movements and also, more crucially, within the MPLA, expressed in the disconnect between the MPLA's leadership and its social basis, which found its expression in the violent aftermath of the 27 May 1977. Dra. Neto's statement then reflects her awareness that the social background of the first MPLA leaders reproduced the social stratifications of late colonial society. Between the 1950s and the 1970s, very few black Angolans benefitted from higher education; those who did benefit, tended to come from the privileged strata of *assimilados* and new *mestiços*, or from the old creole families. Her comments hint at the pressures the MPLA was under after independence to become more representative of the black population. They also indicate how latent prejudices against "foreign" mulattoes can resurface at any time.

In a piece on the use of *angolanidade* in the run-up to the 2008 elections, Jessica Krug observes how "the everyday people of Luanda continue to identify those in power as 'other'—as mulatto, as foreign" (2011, 116) and how many Angolans believe "that mulattos actually wield the real political and economic power in the nation" (114). According to her, it is through this discourse, based on self-identification as black Angolan and the othering of a "foreign" elite, that Luandans construct an oppositional identity for themselves. Krug then posits that by recruiting Dog Murras, a popular kuduro musician representing a rough, *bairro*, urban cool in its ad campaigns, the Angolan rulers tried "to project themselves as virile, masculine, black, and wholly Angolan" (116). She describes this deployment of Dog Murras as the appropriation and defusing of a potentially subversive discourse by those in power. From this, she concludes that "many Luandans believe that *angolanidade* and political and economic power do not typically coexist, but rather are distinct and often adversarial forces" (114).

Despite Krug's carefully unpacking ideas of masculinity, music, and a history of Freyrian racial stereotypes, this last quote betrays a slippage in her analysis between the notions of *angolanidade* and Africanness. If we follow her argument, *angolanidade* is black, African, and essentially oppositional to the elite; the elite is then trying to appropriate this "hypermasculine yet politically compliant if aesthetically transgressive *angolanidade*" to mobilize voter support from the *bairros* (Krug 2011, 118). This is in my view a misrepresentation of the dynamics at play. Government ad campaigns for both postwar elections (2008 and 2012) presented a sanitized "Benetton version" of multiracial harmony that had more to do with the MPLA's original project of postracial,

"European" modernity and nation-building than it did with the appropriation of black ghetto culture.[24]

Moreover, kuduro has become part of the global music mainstream and has largely lost its subversive character in Angola. Despite the "shocking," oftentimes sexualized lyrics and videos of kuduro hits, one of the president's sons, José Paulino "Coréon Dú" dos Santos, is himself a recording kuduro artist and promotes commercial kuduro festivals.[25]

It is true that Dog Murras was instrumentalized for political purposes. Rather than focusing on his alleged marginality, however, I would suggest that he represents the chauvinist, newly assertive *angolanidade* that the MPLA's politics of *rayonnement* aim to play out on the stage of international relations: he adopts the globalized aesthetics of success (see chapter 5), such as big cars and scantily clad girls, and drapes himself in the red, black, and yellow of the Angolan (and of the MPLA party's) flag.[26] The runaway success of kuduro on global dance floors only feeds into ideas of Angolan exceptionalism—the belief in the manifest destiny of Angola to fulfill the promises of independence, take up its rightful place among nations, and assume a leadership role within the Southern African Development Community (SADC) and the African Union (AU). In its ambitions for regional hegemony, kuduro has been appropriated by the government: "Kuduro is purely internal to the system, a form that might best be thought of as . . . a kind of aspirational survivalism" (Moorman 2014, 33). However, because of the ruling class's unstable racial identity, such a straightforward instrumentalization of blackness as Krug posits is untenable, and the ruling party can only to a very limited extent mobilize identitary discourses for populist purposes.

The question of *angolanidade* has all but disappeared from the political sphere; if the term crops up at all in official MPLA statements, it is to commemorate the first president, Agostinho Neto, as the "greatest poet of *angolanidade*."[27] The issue is also rarely ever raised by opposition parties; for example, when the independent deputy and member of UNITA's parliamentary group, Makuta Nkondo, questioned dos Santos's nationality ahead of the 2012 elections, he was swiftly threatened with a disciplinary process by the MPLA bench and denounced as "unpatriotic" in the public media.[28] The sensitive nature of *angolanidade*, and its almost complete absence from politics, is partly to do with the general depoliticization of postwar nation building I address in chapter 1, which stresses unity and stability over social inequality and wartime division. More important here, however, it is difficult for UNITA "to reconcile its role as a subordinate loyal [to the system of multiparty democracy] opposition party with claims to a nationalist history that brought Unita [*sic*] into head-to-head conflict with the MPLA" (Pearce 2012a, 212). However,

I contend that the reluctance by political actors to address openly the question of national identity has to do at least in equal measure with the political elite's own unstable identity as a socially white or *mestiço* privileged class governing a black, African country.

Angolanness as Vernacular Criticism?

> The upper class are culturally lost. They don't identify with the Portuguese, nor with the Soviets, and even less with the culture of our forefathers. I can identify [myself] as an Angolan; I know what it means: I have a language and a culture.
>
> Armando, Sambizanga-Lixeira, 4 December 2010

Although race and ethnicity are largely absent from open and official political discourse, the question of who is a "real" Angolan remains a central topic of popular discourse, as the above quote shows. Contesting ideas of the nation and redefining the boundaries of inclusion and exclusion are of course processes that are not unique to Angola; they are tied to much wider processes of postcolonial nation-building and nationalism in Africa. Since African countries gained their independence these issues have regularly resulted in negotiated or violent redefinitions of belonging and citizenship (Dorman, Hammett, and Nugent 2007, 4). Arguably, the "crisis of citizenship" (Mamdani 2001), or the question of who is a real national citizen, has been a key mobilization factor in many conflicts around autochthony, ranging from Côte d'Ivoire to the Great Lakes to Zimbabwe, to name but a few examples.[29] All over Africa, "rumors of allochthony have been used throughout the postcolonial period to discredit national figures. In the DRC, for example, everyone from President Kasavubu to Mobutu himself was, at some point, dubbed a 'quarteroon,' 'son of a coolie,' 'Rwandan,' or at least accused of having a Rwandan, Angolan, or other foreign-born wife" (Jackson 2006, 103–4).

Because of its apparent naturalness, autochthony is a powerful category of political mobilization. However, this seemingly clear-cut, primordial category "hides a constant flux of redefining a kind of belonging that is equally elusive," which also makes the term vacuous (Ceuppens and Geschiere 2005, 402). As Stephen Jackson asserts, it is exactly the "imprecise overlaps with other powerful, preexisting identity polarities at particular scales of identity and difference" and the "slipperiness of scales" that make the discourse of autochthony such a powerful one (2006, 95).

For the reasons outlined above, *angolanidade* is also imprecise and slippery, and because of the MPLA's own unstable Africanness, such identity debates have largely been muted in Angolan national politics. The race card is only rarely played to discredit political adversaries—mainly UNITA—as racist and tribalist and instruments of foreign interests. However, the characterization of the ruling elite as a foreign group continues to have traction as a popular trope and moral narrative to make sense of the ruling class's neglect of the population.

The rumor that President dos Santos is not really Angolan but from São Tomé, used by UNITA in the 1992 electoral campaign, keeps resurfacing today as a popular narrative. According to MPLA history, dos Santos was born in the neighborhood of Sambizanga. When I walked with a handful of local youths across the rubble field that once was the Roque Santeiro, they found it difficult to believe the president came from such humble origins while they lived in such misery: "Here in Sambizanga, we don't even have basic sanitation, let alone adequate schooling. And this is where the president was born! Well, was born *entre aspas* [in quotation marks]; he was not really born here. How can you neglect you own home like that?"[30]

During a church service in the Bairro Operário, a parish member also explained to me that Angola was a rich country but that "our leaders are not using it so well. But that's because our president is a foreigner. He's a Santomean." When I feigned surprise, saying I thought dos Santos was born here, in Sambizanga, the *mais velho* cut me short:

> Lies. If he was born in this neighborhood, who is his grandfather, who is his father? Why would he go to São Tomé to bury his mother? You know, the FNLA and the UNITA, these are the real representatives of the Angolan people. But the MPLA? They're all Capeverdeans. Yes, Neto was a Capeverdean! Otherwise he wouldn't have betrayed us to this Santomean! I only hope that someday, an Angolan will take his place, and make it better for the country.[31]

Anger at the elite's perceived neglect of the population—more specifically, at the impunity with which the president and his family have amassed spectacular wealth—is often voiced in terms of foreignness, with people attacking "this crazy man [*maluco*] from São Tomé" as the root of all evil or suggesting to "throw him into the sea and see if he can swim back to São Tomé."[32] In the safety of a private space or protected by the anonymity of online forums, strong opinions are voiced, claiming that "dos Santos does not care about us, the autochthonous people." People feel that "because they are from somewhere else" and not originary Angolans (*Angolanos de origem*), the country's rulers neglect the country. Here we can see parallels with the distinctions made between *Ivoiriens de souche* and foreigners (Marshall-Fratani 2006) and between "autochthonous" Congolese and "foreign" Banyarwanda (Jackson 2006). Also, there seems to be something intrinsically unstable and treacherous about mixed-blood *mestiços*, who are contrasted to an imaginary more pure and authentic African identity.

Angolanidade Lived Out

To see how these ideas about who is a real Angolan and who is a foreigner are felt and expressed, let us take a closer look at the stories of two of my informants, Dona Mariana and Simão, as their biographies and experiences are a good illustration of the crisscrossing, contradictory fault lines of race and class in Angola.

Dona Mariana, with whose comments on Leila Lopes I opened this chapter, was born in Bengo province, just outside the provincial capital, Caxito. Her father was a Capeverdean who came to Angola for the construction of the Mabubas Dam (in Dande municipality) but, as she stresses, "We are from Gulungo Alto [a historic base of the early MPLA guerrilla struggle]; that's where my mother comes from." She has lived in Angola all her life and has never been to Cape Verde; yet in her speech, she often distances herself from "those Angolans."

Reminiscing about her ex-husband, a white Portuguese, Dona Mariana tells me how she recently went to visit him and was shocked at how old and neglected he looked. Dona Mariana's eighty-seven-year-old mother, nibbling at some fish and rice while staring at the dark television screen, mutters, "It's those blacks." Dona Mariana chuckles, "You hear her? 'It's those blacks.' Ah, I don't know, he was a man who loved to eat well, in the nutritional sense. And then, last time I went to see him I saw him eat boiled eggs for lunch—only boiled eggs, can you imagine? It was 2 pm in the afternoon, and his [new, black] woman was nowhere to be seen. Is that a life?"

In the discussion with Dona Gabriela after Leila Lopes's victory, the two light-skinned ladies recalled the days after independence, when there was an upsurge in antiwhite and anti-*mestiço* sentiment in Luanda. Dona Gabriela said, "*ai*, Dona Mariana, don't you remember, I was walking on the Marginal when this guy comes up to me and asks me 'Don't you want to go back to your father's country?' and I said, 'No, I choose my mother's country, do you have any problems with that?' And it's not true, by the way. Both my parents were *mestiços*, from here." Mariana chimes in: "And when I am in the street and someone calls me *latona* [female of *latón*, a derogatory slang word for mulatto], I go up to him and ask him why he is saying that.[33] These kids have to be educated. What counts is what is on the inside!" Gabriela again: "Yes, I don't care about the color of the skin; what counts is what a person is, on the inside, educated and such."

Both women claim their right to be Angolan and *mestiço*; yet they often speak of "these Angolans" and "these blacks." Despite a discourse that proclaims an aversion to racial prejudice and the value of education and individual merit, the inherent intertwining of a racial identification with "culture" mirrors earlier colonial stereotypes that are hard to root out. Indeed, as Dona Mariana chimes in: "When I am in the street and someone calls '*mulata*, go back to your father's country!' I say 'Was it me who spread my legs to the white man or was it your sister? I am just the fruit of this union; if you want to blame someone, blame your sisters!' "

Questions of race and of *mestiçagem* are quite often tied to questions of sexuality and morality,[34] and it is no coincidence that rumors about the ruling class always include a dose of gossip about the alleged marital infidelities of the political leaders. Here, Dona Mariana squarely put the blame for this *mestiçagem* on the lascivious ways of the black woman, thereby reproducing the old Luso-Brazilian foundational myth of Lusotropicalism.

Simão, by contrast, is a young entrepreneur in his early thirties, dabbling in all sorts of business. I had met him by chance in the street in the São Paulo area, when I chatted him up after overhearing him speaking French on the phone. We ended up boarding the same taxi and stayed in touch due to shared Francophone affinities, mutual sympathy, and curiosity. Sent abroad by his parents during the civil war to escape conscription and Angola's dismal education system, he had been educated in Paris and Brussels, and had only recently returned to Angola permanently, having assessed that the business opportunities here were better than in Europe (see chapter 5). He spoke French with me and with business partners in Europe, but switched into rough *calão* (Luandan street slang) when conducting his Angolan deals: "*iá, tá fixe, vou agilizar aquele mambo*," approximately translatable as "Yeah, all cool; I will put that thing in motion."

Simão is from a Bakongo family from northern Angola and cultivates a style at times more reminiscent of Kinshasa and Paris than of Luanda—sharp clothes, tailored shirts, horn-rimmed glasses, and evident pride in his blackness. Although he clearly benefitted from his uncle's connections when it came to business, he was very critical of Angolan society's systemic inequalities, which he explained as follows:

It's these *mestiços*, the sons of the Portuguese who brought us all the evil. Take this, for example [pointing at my poster of the 2010 Luanda Art

Triennial in my room]—do you know who he is? [He means Sindika Do-kolo, the husband of the president's daughter, Isabel, whose founda-tion funded the Trienal de Luanda. I tell him I know that he's Isabel's Congolese husband.]

Yes, but his mother is white [Danish]. And her [Isabel's] mother was white, too. Do you think they care the least bit about Angola or the An-golans? Not at all. They will plunder the country as much as they can because they have no interest whatsoever in the Angolans. I have a friend who is black like I am, and he applied with UNITEL [Angola's largest mobile network operator, incidentally owned by Isabel dos Santos], to-gether with two lighter-skinned girls. He had the best diploma and work experience of all three. They interviewed him for twenty minutes and then they told him the place had been occupied before. The two girls who got the job couldn't believe that he didn't get the position and told him so. But he only said, "Haven't you noticed that at UNITEL all people look like you?"[35] And we've all been conditioned like that. The Angolan men, their greatest dream in life is to have a *mestiço* wife. Not for me. I will have a Bantu girlfriend, black like me.

Both Mariana and Simão used the language of racial identity to make a larger point about perceived social inequalities. Evidently, this discourse is essentially positional: Dona Mariana blames the MPLA for the inequalities and the subsequent rise in antiwhite and anti-*mestiço* sentiment. However, her talk about "those blacks" reflects a persistent cleavage between an urban, creole elite and the people they claim to represent, stereotyped as backward people (*povo matumbo*). In the examples of Dona Mariana and Simão, we see the use of the idioms of race as essentially positional popular criticisms of the socioeconomic inequalities in Angola. However, we need to complicate again the idea of race as a fundamentally oppositional discourse by taking into account the historical contingencies of the intertwining of race with class in Angola.

Race, Class, and Urban Modernity

Following Scott (1990, 136–7), we would view such talk and practices as part of the "undeclared ideological guerrilla war" that rages in the political space between compliance and open resistance, allowing people to express ideas pri-marily not about race but about social hierarchies and power inequalities. As Scott suggests, people do indeed express opposition to a power perceived as unjust and foreign in whispers, rumors, gossip, and the liminal spaces between the public and the private (see chapter 2).[36]

As the above examples of my informants show, it is true that "the everyday people of Luanda continue to identify those in power as 'other'" (Krug 2011, 116). However, such an interpretation all but essentializes this difference and posits a clear-cut division between "everyday people" and "those in power." Although I follow Scott in his attention to the micropolitics of the ordinary, I think we need to nuance the division Krug posits. Using the language of racial identities is an inherently positional strategy to make sense of and talk about social inequalities outside politics. More important, however, I suggest that we need to take into account the ideas and aspirations that such statements and practices transport.

We have seen how the idiom of race is deployed as a vernacular criticism of socioeconomic inequality; here, I complicate the binary opposition that an analytic of autochthony posits and highlight the aspirational, relational qualities of the imaginaries of race in Angola. In his work on Eastern DRC, Stephen Jackson characterizes autochthony as a "loose qualifier, a binary operator" that, although relational and open to situational shifts between scales of meanings, possesses an "underlying polarity" and serves to "policing a distinction between in and out" (2006, 99–100). However, although practices that identify the Angolan ruling elite as foreign are often deployed in a subversive and oppositional way, they are not just a subaltern discourse of resistance. Instead, they give voice to and enact deep-seated social hierarchies and aspirations, ultimately reproducing and consolidating existing inequalities and cleavages that are, because of their historicity, construed as racial or ethnic.

In the above statement, Simão asserts his Africanness to criticize the age-old privileges of a creole ruling class, which he sees reproduced today in preferential treatment when it comes to public appointments, employment, access to education, and the like. But although he criticizes Sindika Dokolo's funding of the Art Triennial as whitewashing of both the image of the president's family and their ill-gotten gains, he also expresses a sense of entitlement, a claim on this manifestation of high culture that mirrors his own cosmopolitan background and class aspirations. By contrast, when I asked Alberto, the civil society activist from Campismo from chapter 2, if he had attended the free art exhibitions of the Triennial, he was surprised at my naïve assumptions about free access for everyone:

> It is open to everyone, yes. But not everyone will go because in their subconscious they will know that it is not for them, that it is only for the elites. Recently, I was at Chá de Caxinde [a downtown cultural center

where some events of the Triennial took place], and by chance I was there for the launch of Pepetela's most recent book; I was there for something else, but I just happened to be there. I felt immediately that it was not for me, not only because of the bar prices. It's also a question of skin color. Someone like me, who catches [*apanha*] dust all day and is more rustic, will feel out of place. Also, they have some strange ways of conversation. It is a social and economic apartheid. We want to tear this wall down. But the problem is that everyone just wants to get up, and once they are on top, they forget about the ones down below.

More than just denoting and performing class differences, talking about race is thus about asserting a specifically urban identity, distinct from the uncultivated people of the bush (*matas*). These tensions are indicative of a deeper historical urban–rural divide in Angola that is exacerbated today by Luanda's dominant position in the economy, politics, and culture. In many ways, the Angolan government's military victory over UNITA in 2002 represented a victory of the coastal cities over the rural hinterland, of Portuguese over national languages, and of urban, creole cosmopolitanism over Africanness. This is not just a structural and economic issue;[37] it is very much to do with the "modes of self-writing" (Mbembe 2002) of Luanda's citizens, who see themselves as having a different, superior culture than rural Angolans.[38] For example, the Faculty of Architecture of the public Agostinho Neto University (UAN) held a competition among its students to create new housings in the different provinces, adapted to the environment and made from locally available materials. However, nothing came out of it because *"as pessoas aqui desprezam mesmo o saber angolano"* (The people here really despise Angolan [read: indigenous] knowledge).[39] In the end, a Chinese company was contracted, as this kind of aesthetics was seen as more fitting for Angola's aspirations to globalized modernity.[40]

Among Luandans, we can observe a highly ambivalent attitude toward "national languages" and "cultural heritage," regardless of people's original ethno-regional background. Luandan urbanites will wax nostalgic about *"minha terra"* (my land, soil), speaking of their parents' and grandparents' place of origin, or lament never having learned a national language from their grandparents. Yet they feel so much more sophisticated and better than Angolans from the interior and speak derogatively of *"esse povo"*—"this people," but in the sense of uncultivated masses—thus consciously or unwittingly reproducing (racialized) class distinctions.[41] "Backward" ethnic "populations" of the interior are derided or pitied as folkloristic anachronisms, as in for example "These poor *mumwilazinhos*" (the diminutive of Mumwila, a "traditional ethnic group" from the highlands of Huíla).[42] Thus even someone like Simão, who proudly asserts his blackness and emphasizes his Bakongo roots—"The people who refused to be sold as slaves and were thrown into the sea instead!," distancing himself from the "collaborating" coastal Creoles—cultivates a distinctly urban, cosmopolitan persona and grumbles in French and Italian about the backwardness, corruption, and *"négri-attitude"* of his poorer, less educated fellow citizens.

Similarly, many—especially US American and European—expatriates posted to Luanda marvel at the wonderful mixity of Luandan society, where people of all hues of skin and other phenotypical markers of race freely mingle socially (and intimately) in a way that is often inconceivable—or publicly inadmissible—in their home countries or in the neighboring former settler republics. Members of the Angolan urban upper-middle-class stress their inclusivity and point to their own mixed ancestry to stress the country's welcoming character toward people from all over the world. But this self-indulgent, seemingly liberal attitude toward skin color masks deep-seated social hierarchies that can be traced back to the formation of the coastal creole and *assimilado* elites. Foreign newcomers and Angolan social climbers of any racial background along the normalized black/African to white/European spectrum can be viewed and are treated as civilized equals so long as they are highly educated (read: educated in Europe or the United States) and display markers of cosmopolitan sophistication. Poorer West African migrants, however, and the growing number of Vietnamese and Chinese immigrants are denigrated as backward, superstitious, and uncultured, and stereotyped as "Mamadú" and "Pim Pum," respectively.[43] This attitude feeds on and back into a sense of Angolan exceptionalism, a projection of Luso-Atlantic, cosmopolitan modernity centered on Luanda that looks on the other, "rather more backward," members of the African Union with a sense of superiority (Birmingham 2012, 219).[44]

Practicing Distinction in Luanda

Bourdieu's notion of class distinction (1979) is productive here as a point of departure, as both Mariana and Simão aspire, in their own way, to an urban, middle-class lifestyle that makes use of typically Angolan class markers that are translated into the realm of the racial.

Historically, as Moorman describes, inhabitants of Luanda's *musseques* developed expectations in the 1950s and 1960s about economic and cultural autonomy in music clubs, self-ascribing as "middle class," and occupying "a social space between Europeans living in comfort and poorer Angolans recently arrived from rural areas" (2008, 23). Following independence, however, the dominant narrative of the MPLA reduced "culture to a proto-nationalist moment of 'discovering our identity'" (2), while in socialist parlance, middle-classness was ideologically suspect and decried as petty bourgeois (despite the predominantly petty bourgeois background of most of the MPLA's leadership).

Social classes were also part of the everyday discourse of socialism in Angola, and the Marxist terminology of earlier analytics described classes as "bourgeoisie," "peasants," and "semi-proletariat," defined by their modes of production and ownership (Heimer 1979; Clarence-Smith 1980). Both due to the changing nature of capitalism—with the service industry increasingly predominating over the productive industry—and to the wholly opaque ownership structures of the modes of production in Angola, a definition of class in purely economic terms is unproductive. Following the death of class as a master narrative (Pratt 2003, 2), middle-classness is more usefully defined by aspiration and modes of consumption than it is by modes of production (Heiman, Freeman, and Liechty 2012, 21).[45] Class stratifications as "culturally and historically constructed identities" remain meaningful because they are both part of the ways in which people make sense of their lifeworlds and "always situated with respect to the forms and modes of power operating in a given time and place" (Ortner 1998, 3–4). And, as Bourdieu (1979) reminds us, class inequalities as expressed in cultural differences serve to ingrain and naturalize real power inequalities. So while the MPLA has, for reasons I outline above, always been at pains to downplay the racial character of social hierarchies in Angola, those connotations still resonate strongly today. In that sense, class is here also less of a fixed analytical category; rather, it is an attempt to describe and analyze very real and tangible socioeconomic and power differences, differences that are, for my informants, inherently positional and often refracted through the prism of race. For these social actors, then, class is an orientation and an aesthetic.

Such distinction is encapsulated in the expression *"ter uma vida mulata"* (having or leading a mulatto life), which is on the surface merely synonymous with a life of leisure, ostentatious luxury, and privilege, and is used jokingly and self-deprecatingly when commenting on a nice meal, a glitzy evening out, or a weekend with beers and barbecue lazing at the beach. Underneath that surface, however, lurk the historical privileges of a specific social group and the unabashed reaffirming of all the benefits that come with it—going abroad to study instead of being drafted to the front during the war, for example.

Distinction also becomes evident in the use of and switching between speech registers, where some people can utilize such (racialized) class repertoires situationally for their own purposes. Indeed, in Angola the mastery of Portuguese represents "not only a factor of social differentiation but also an indicator of an individual's level or urbanity" (Rodrigues 2007b, 247). Conversely, Angolan Portuguese is connoted with lesser levels of education, culturedness, and even intelligence—early nationalist attempts to legitimize and institutionalize Angolan Portuguese, for example, were derided by the settlers as *pretoguês* (blackuguese; see Hamilton 1982, 323–24).

When they addressed an audience at an official function (a parish assembly, an NGO meeting, a speech at the National Assembly), I observed, most people—at least those who had some higher formal education—would employ an overly formal language, enunciating it "more Portuguese than the Portuguese," to present themselves as cultivated and educated.[46] Such register switching denotes aspiration and an element of intimidation: as wearing a power suit does, donning the mantle of power language denotes superiority and authority.

There is a subversive flip side to this: when someone would imitate the president, taking on the suave, *aportuguisado* (Portuguesed) tone of dos Santos to paraphrase his speeches and state some utter nonsense, sending everyone present into fits of laughter. In a much-ridiculed speech about the levels of poverty being part of the colonial legacy, for example, dos Santos stated that he had already known such poverty growing up in the city as a child. Using an empty Coke bottle as a stand-in for a microphone, this was then rendered in pitch-perfect dos Santos silkiness as, "There was already poverty when I arrived from São Tomé." As these practices of joking and switching registers illustrate, choices of language registers do not only reinforce but also subvert power differences (Hanks 2005, 77). Linguistic repertoires are thus not just naturalizing stratification and exclusion, but can also serve to renegotiate claims of citizenship and rights to the city.[47]

Conversely to this "talking up," Simão would speak a rough Luanda *calão* on the phone to conduct his business, generously sprinkling in Kimbundu loanwords and "agilizing" a speech repertoire that marks street-savvy and a certain tough urban cool. Precisely because of his cosmopolitan background and multilingual education, he can assert his blackness by switching into lower-status slang and a street hustler persona, which gives him an edge in business negotiations. Because of his unquestioned Africanness, he can pull it off.

Compare his situation with the increasing number of young, upwardly mobile professionals from traditionally MPLA-affiliated urban middle-class families. Thanks to personal connections (see chapter 4), many of them escaped wartime *falta* (shortages, deprivation) and forced conscription, were raised and educated in Portugal for most of their youth, and have only recently returned to Angola. As they are more often than not *mestiço*, their Angolan-ness is much more unstable: they are Angolan by origin and nationality (although most have dual nationality), but their metropolitan accents and low tolerance for the chaos and poor service standards of Luanda betray their European upbringing; and their assertiveness with regard to their better education and job prospects is undermined by self-doubt with regard to their place in this African country, and the persistent fear that one day the blacks will revolt against the historical privileges of the *mestiços*.

Some of those I met might have condescendingly imitated the rough and uncultured Angolan accent and vocabulary of the "windshield washers in the street" or joked about the futile attempts of a waiter in a sophisticated restaurant to speak a cultured Portuguese, only to be betrayed by his lazy tongue and overlong vowels.[48] Yet they also spoke with admiration and more than just a tinge of envy of a friend who was able to deploy a more popular speech repertoire to produce a pretense of equality with a clerk at an airline company's office. Over a family dinner, one of them, Jorge, told the story of how he went into the agency to buy a ticket, but was told immediately that there were no tickets. His friend then went to the lady and [Jorge imitates an Angolan accent and repeats it several times] said, "Godmother, just type it into your keyboard, OK?" [*madrinha, carrega só no teclado, iá?*]. This worked, and miraculously she found available tickets.[49]

As Gal states, "Patterns of choice among linguistic variants can be interpreted to reveal aspects of speakers' 'consciousness': how they respond symbolically to class relations within the state, and how they understand their historic position and identity within regional economic systems structured around dependency and unequal development" (1987, 637). However, the mastery of such repertoires and the ability to switch between them, or in more abstract terms, the performance of class through repertoires of civilizedness, involves a lot of work and a certain educational background and privilege. In that sense, Jorge's mockery of uncultured Angolan Portuguese reflects his position as a member of the established urban middle-class, while his envy of his friend's mastery of the same codes of street-savvy betrays the existential insecurity of *mestiço*, Portugalized, recently returned young Angolans regarding their position in the system of the New Angola. Contrary to Simão's confident street-savvy, Jorge's use of *calão* feels, both to himself and the people who would see him use it, like playacting, and not entirely credible. Similarly, although Alberto also knows how to speak a formally correct Portuguese, he feels his roughness—the outwardly visible attributes that place him in the *bairro*—precludes him from successfully deploying the repertoires of the upper class.

These "indicators of urbanity" (language, gestures, and greetings, but also clothes, educational level, the area of residence within the city, housing type, and number of cars owned) replicate not only class stratifications but also colonial distinctions of civilizedness and urban segregation (Rodrigues 2007b, 238). Some indicators of educational status resort to older repertoires, such as the custom among men of growing the fingernail of their little finger to denote white-collar rather than blue-collar employment; more recent markers of distinction are linked to modes of globalized consumption (see chapter 5). However, the way these stratifications are naturalized in the body through racial repertoires is not simply a case of Fanonian self-hatred and mental colonization. Rather, citizens of Luanda are, in the multiple and contradictory ways of the slippery idiom of race, voicing at the same time a vernacular criticism of social inequality and, following Ferguson, asserting "their rights to the city, and pressing . . . claims to the political and social rights of full citizens" (2006, 161).

Conclusions

Two days after Leila Lopes's triumph at the Miss Universe pageant, the MPLA's women's organization, the Organization of the Angolan Woman (OMA, from the Portuguese Organização da Mulher Angolana), announced it would hold a festive reception at Luanda's international airport, saying that, "The women of Luanda, in representation of the entire female class [sic] [camada feminina] from Cabinda to the Cunene" would be present for the arrival of the newly crowned beauty queen.[50] The MPLA leadership, usually quick to accuse opposition parties of political profiteering (aproveitamento político), evidently saw no such profiteering at play when congratulating Lopes on her victory, describing her as the embodiment of Angolan virtues of dignity, intelligence, and beauty, and declaring that she had won "with the determination of Queen Ginga Mbandi," the sixteenth-century Angolan queen, elevated to a mythical symbol of early anticolonial resistance. The MPLA also expressed hopes that Lopes would continue to "give pride to and dignify the Angolan woman in particular, and the African woman in general, as with this feat the beauty of the black African woman was recognized internationally."[51]

Ideas and practices about race and angolanidade in contemporary Luanda are always about several things at once. The history of elite formation in Angola can help us understand why and how the coastal, creole elites came to see themselves as and be perceived as culturally different from the Africans of the hinterland. But rule of an African peasantry by a culturally disconnected, creole, urban elite was never a very sustainable political project. It was not a viable option to mobilize support during the independence struggle, and the perceived perpetuation of the privileges of this elite undermines the MPLA's claims to political legitimacy today.

Because of its unstable African identity, I assert, the leadership of the MPLA continues to promote a homogenizing, supra-ethnic national project and at the same time profess pride in Angola's Africanness—hence the instrumentalization of Leila Lopes's victory, for example. Under such a shallow, depoliticized conception of *"angolanidade* light,"* ethnicity and race remain, in the words of Setucula, a "cold discourse" that cannot be mobilized openly for political gains, either by the MPLA—due its inherent identitary contradictions—or by opposition parties—because it would jeopardize the national consensus of peace and stability. This is especially true for UNITA, whose wartime rhetoric was partly built on African indigeneity, but which since the end of the war has cautiously avoided any claim to nationalist "authenticity" (Pearce 2012a, 210, 216).[52]

That is not to say that a discourse of autochthony could not be mobilized by certain interest groups, especially when their own political survival is threatened. Since independence, the MPLA has portrayed UNITA as stooges (*fantoches*) of the apartheid regime, and today's contestations of the regime are quickly branded "foreign conspiracies"—the plotting of Western powers "interested in Angola's natural resources" together with "enemies of stability," who are probably not even real Angolans (see chapters 1 and 6). Equally, the large influx of African and Chinese economic migrants into Luanda portends the potential of populist anti-immigrant rhetoric for political gains in the future.[53] But the questioning of the MPLA's own Africanness makes such a straightforward instrumentalization of indigeneity much more difficult and ambiguous. As Jackson states, the autochthony discourse is "endemically nervous because many of those deploying it suffer the nagging fear that they could suddenly find themselves its objects" (2006, 115).

Popular discourses about a foreign elite continue to be circulated in safe social spaces in the form of jokes, gossip, rumors, and malicious social commentary. At first glance, these tensions and popular discourses about the elite's racial identity and their historical formation as a privileged segment of society can indeed be interpreted as a Scottian hidden transcript that subverts the MPLA's dominant discourse of a unitary nation. People mobilize notions of Angolanness and foreignness to make sense both of the inherent inequalities of the system and of the disconnect between the MPLA's populist discourse—in the literal sense, of the people—and the elite's evident neglect of the population. Thus when the MPLA recycles slogans from the struggle such as "The MPLA are the people and the people are the MPLA" or "The most important is to resolve the problems of the people," my informants used the same slogans as a frame of reference to explain Angola's problems today.

Speaking the language of race or ethno-regional identities is thus a contestation of the hegemonic, postracial *angolanidade* of the MPLA to express a criticism of real social inequalities. Looking at the gaping socioeconomic divide of Luandan society, Bayart's cynical shorthand rings eerily true: "The MPLA's great and overwhelming trouble is that it has to govern a people" (2000, 235). However, I assert that this is not only because, as Bayart claims, the elite want to concentrate on plundering the country's assets (although that might certainly appear to be the case to a casual observer), but also because of a deep, historical cultural divide between the socially white ruling elite and the socially black *povo matumbo*. Getting rich is certainly a central and valued aspect, which is part of the markers of privilege of the national bourgeoisie (see chapter 5), but that alone would not explain why the ruling class show such disdain for the uneducated (read: black) masses.

Because of this, talking the language of race is not only about criticizing a foreign elite, and any ideas of binary oppositions or race as a fundamentally oppositional discourse have to be complicated. As I have elaborated in the final part of the chapter, due to the intertwining of race and class in Angola, these ideas and practices ingrain and naturalize long-standing social hierarchies. Talking about culture is not only about asserting or aspiring to class difference; it also represents and reproduces urban–rural cleavages, the victory of the city over the bush, and a general disdain for "backward African culture," languages, and ideas, which has deep roots in the social history of Angola.

Claims to entitlements as citizens of a modern, independent African state are thus based on a nationalist (African) pride mobilized in opposition to a "foreign" elite that is seen to deny to a majority of the population the benefits of citizenship, and based at the same time on a notion of urban modernity that shuns tradition and cultural heritage as backwardness, and which in fact resembles the MPLA's original modernist project more closely than the regime's detractors would have it. Thus focussing on the aspirational qualities of identitary discourses and practices can also help us push the analytic of autochthony as a strategy of inclusion and exclusion one step further.

In chapters 4 and 5, I develop some of these ideas further. For one, "tradition" is not universally shunned as a marker of backwardness; it has a value in itself that, because of the MPLA's rejection of tradition, constitutes a terrain on which relations within the system can be renegotiated. How ideas of tradition and "correct behavior" are mobilized in everyday interactions in Luanda, and how those practices tie in with larger political imaginaries, is the subject of my analysis in chapter 4. Here I have discussed the cultural and identitary aspects of class. In chapter 5, I turn to the equally crucial issues of economic power and consumption, and how they play into the renegotiations of political legitimacy in Angola.

CHAPTER 4

Cunhas

Situational Kinship and Everyday Authority

On 16 January 2014, Angolan judicial authorities arrested a young man in Luanda's swanky Talatona Convention Center Hotel. Paulo Feijó, twenty-eight years old, had been living it up at the hotel for four months. He had commandeered an executive suite from the hotel management by presenting himself with a forged identity card as Paulo Anderson Feijó dos Santos, with his filiation given as José Eduardo dos Santos, Angola's long-time president. Preliminary investigations revealed that the president's false son had gained a 500,000 dollar credit from the Angolan Development Bank and had been holding regular meetings with investors at the hotel, promising them privileged access to the Angolan market.[1] Further revelations by the authorities in June 2014 revealed that the "false son" had, in this short time, accumulated fourteen million dollars through credits and loans.

The case of the false son is perhaps the most extreme example of the mobilization of family links, real or imaginary, for personal advancement in contemporary Angola. The vernacular term for such mobilization of a personal connection is *cunha* (literally, "inserting a wedge").[2] In this chapter, I explore the *cunhas* both as a practice and as an idea. To do so, I look at how people personalize everyday, mundane social interactions when they navigate the city, including, but not exclusively, dealings with state agents such as the police or administration. The two key elements of these interactions are familiarity and hierarchy. These are mobilized for personal purposes and linked in their collective representations of how the system works in Luanda. Around this everyday practice of mobilizing *cunhas* for one's own goals, competing ideas of hierarchy, authority, and a moral order of society are expressed.

It is around these *cunhas* that we can condense and concretize this book's central notion of the system. Angolans often perceive the way society works in the city as a big system, and express how one has to know how to navigate and use this system to make it work. This system is thus simultaneously a moral ordering device, a form of vernacular criticism, and a user manual for their everyday lives in the current political and socioeconomic environment. It is characterized by internal tensions between the blockages of administrative inertia, on the one hand, and the social mobility and speed of urban life, on the other. People spend hours navigating the bureaucracy, only to be told, once they have finally located the right department and assembled all the necessary documents, that the system is down (*não há sistema*, lit. "There is no system"), and to return the next day, the next week, the next month. This "lack of system" is often linked to power cuts or faults in the IT infrastructure, but can also be due to administrative reorganization of the service, or general unwillingness to attend a citizen, customer, or client (unless a *cunha* is mobilized or the payment of a *gasosa*—literally a fizzy drink, but in the Angolan context a small bribe—eases the way). Thus the system can be made to function for one's own purposes by turning the right wheels, as it were, which stands in stark contrast to the numerous delays incurred by administrative services for "system failure."

I believe the "lack of system" is a fitting expression of the perceived inefficiency and complications not only of the bureaucracy but also of the chaos of everyday life in the city in general: there is no system. And yet there evidently is a system to it—people mobilize *cunhas* and act out social norms of hierarchy and "correct" interactions to make the system work. These practices and discourses then reveal the tensions between what people see as the real functioning of society, and their perspectives on how society should work. A person's ability to mobilize and act out a *cunha* is inherently tied to his or her social standing, which is often mediated by social identities (see chapter 3), age, gender, and family affiliation (as detailed below).[3]

Much of my fieldwork, especially in the early phase, was spent navigating the bureaucracy of Luanda to obtain paperwork that would allow me to stay in and move around the country. This involved notarizing copies of my passport and visa, securing an affiliation letter from the national archive, acquiring an endorsement from the Ministry of Culture, authenticating translations of health certificates, supplying details of any criminal records and my home university affiliation, and last and most important, ensuring the correct and timely processing of my application for a research visa. Later in my fieldwork, I also applied for an Angolan driver's license—it took five months to be issued—and chased down an up-to-date extract of the birth register for my brother's passport application.[4]

As for most Angolans, none of this could have been achieved without the help of various friends with connections. All of this was at times extremely stressful and frustrating; yet it constituted a valuable firsthand source of data because it was, in the context of Luanda, the most *participant* observation I could make.[5]

It could be argued that my own experiences were not representative, either because they were eased or made more difficult because I was a foreigner or because I was privileged by socializing with elite-affiliated Angolans. However, my experience shares central features with numerous of my informants' accounts of mobilizing a *cunha* to navigate the bureaucratic maze (and everyday life in general).[6] People across the social spectrum generally agreed that bureaucracy was a nightmare—costly, time-consuming, and full of obstacles, especially when they needed identity papers or property documents—and many of my interviews and encounters were shaped by stories about interactions in administrative offices. Complaining about the problems of getting an identity card, Mamã Rosa, a former market vendor at the Roque, detailed:

> To get my ID, I have to go to my municipality of birth in Uíge, Negage, and ask for the complete copy of the birth register [*cópia integral*]. But even with this document, they will find a fault. And I have my birth certificate [*cédula pessoal*]. The trip both ways costs 6,000 [kwanza], the copy another 7,000. I am unemployed—how will I manage? So I will simply not go and apply for [*tratar*, literally, treat) my ID. If my passport identifies me as Angolan, why do I still have to apply for another document?

To deal with these complications, people told me, "It is always good if you know someone." This was not limited to administrative services of the Angolan bureaucracy but included everyday interactions with police agents, public utility companies, education institutions (especially with regard to access), and even services by private companies, which are also characterized by a great love for formalism and paperwork. Repeatedly informants told me how they dodged a—justified or invented—fine by a police officer by "talking very well" (*conversar muito bem*) and mentioning the name of a police commander they knew or pretended to know. Because of the similarly high levels of bureaucratization of everyday interactions in the private sector, the purchase of an airline ticket at the company's office (see chapter 3), or the payment of a telephone bill will also always be much eased by mobilizing a *cunha*. Angolan embassies abroad, too, follow this logic: at a wedding anniversary of family friends in Viana, the children of the celebrating couple, some of whom had flown in from Canada, complained to each other how Angolan embassies were no better than the administration here—*"quem não quer fazer bicha liga já pra o general"* (Whoever does not want to queue just calls the general [and jumps the queue]).[7]

Interactions with a cumbersome bureaucracy are a central, time-consuming, and expensive element of everyday life in Luanda, and the ways in which these interactions work could be categorized as corruption in the larger sense: nepotism, favoritism, and influence peddling. However, *cunhas* are not primarily about corruption. The more challenging and fruitful approach, in my view, is to see what ideas and ideals are expressed around the practice of *cunhas*, as these participate for Angolans, in the political and moral ordering of the world.

Thus, keeping in line with my interest in the affects and aspirations produced by the system, my focus is not on the administrative functionaries that represent the state agents and "make the state" at the local level; rather, it is on the experiences and ideas of power and hierarchy that people express and enact when confronted with this bureaucracy. I am interested not so much in how the state manifests locally in "street-level" bureaucratic encounters (Blundo 2006; Chalfin 2006; Bierschenk and Olivier de Sardan 2014) but rather in how in these everyday interactions citizens and bureaucrats play out and jointly create typically Angolan notions of hierarchy, decency, and legitimacy, constantly remaking and renegotiating the system. As Nuijten and Anders suggest, looking at the relational aspects and the moral complexities of a practice like *cunhas* thus allows us to overcome the state–society and public–private dichotomies (2007, 2). And as in James Holston's Brazilian example of queuing at a bank (2008, 16–17), such social interactions create micro-public spaces in which competing moral economies and notions of citizenship are expressed.

As a second point, I prefer to eschew the "Orientalist overtones" (Nuijten and Anders 2007, 3) and normative assumptions of corruption. Indeed, a "neoliberal fascination" with corruption in African studies very often perpetuates a normative, largely criminalizing diagnosis of the ills of "the African State" and fails to recognize that "forms of desire that fuel corruption are not merely selfish and private but profoundly social, shaped by larger sociocultural notions of power, privilege, and responsibility" (Hasty 2005, 271). Corruption is definitely part of the Angolan vernacular to criticize specific practices deemed illicit or immoral (see chapters 5 and 6). Here, however, I suggest that the personalization of interactions in *cunhas* is a much more fluid and reciprocal process of negotiations that is inadequately described by a term as value-laden as corruption.

Cunhas are, then, inextricably linked to the relationality of the system in Angola. By analyzing the personalization of mundane, everyday interactions we can chart the practices of creating authority and legitimacy that produce the system, and how these practices, and the popular imaginaries of authority and hierarchy that they evoke, are employed as strategies to make the system work.

To chart these strategies, I proceed in three movements: I first give a brief introduction to the symbolic of "correct" forms of addressing someone in everyday interactions, and the degrees of hierarchy and familiarity this system helps to establish. This also provides a more fine-grained analysis of very situational social hierarchies, which complicates the broader class divisions identified in chapter 3. In a second step, I then detail the material basis of the practice of the *cunhas*, the intimate knowledge people have about real or imagined family networks in Luanda, as well as the outcomes of mobilizing *cunhas* in encounters with the public administration. In a third movement, my analysis then suggests that there is a tension between two distinct but intertwined sets of values or discursive repertoires—the "traditional" ideal of the body politic as family, and the real practice of mobilizing family relations in Luanda. This tension reveals some of the system's fault lines, which can then be exploited by a varied set of actors for different purposes. Although traditional forms of familial and political authority are evoked as a form of criticism of a government failing to fulfill its obligations, real and imagined family links are also deployed as a situational strategy to make the system work through the activation of *cunhas*. The mobilization of horizontal and vertical rapport also demonstrates that, although the social hierarchies and fault lines detailed in chapter 3 persist, the system's fluidity also offers people niches and inroads for individual agency and social mobility.

Etiquette, Luanda-style

> Late afternoon, I stand at Cuca, waiting to board a taxi for São Paulo. The low sunlight filters through the dust whipped up from the road, and the traffic is hectic. We wait for the taxi to fill up with passengers, but as soon as it is full, a policeman appears and asks for documents. The driver and the *cobrador* [fare collector] start pleading: "Oh no, Kalangana, you're a relative [*parente*], don't do this to me!" The police agent is first insisting, but then he ostentatiously turns his back to more pressing matters. The driver takes the opportunity to weave between two other taxis into the outer lane, and off we roll.
>
> Field notes, Cuca, 26 July 2011

Social interactions in Luanda are informed by a set of rules and values that are played out in situational relatedness. As the vignette above shows, Angolans follow an elaborate system of how to address each other correctly in everyday situations. In this case, the taxi crew knew the police agent by name (Kalangana), but more importantly, they evoked situational kinship ties, appealing to him as a relative. This system of greetings relates directly to notions of social hierarchy and authority, which inform daily practice.

Anthropologists have long observed how, especially in African societies, as a person gets older, their rank and social status rise, and have recognized age as the "most general condition of leadership" (Wagner 1940, 234). In Angola, the opposite is also true at the same time: as a person's status rises, she or he becomes socially older, regardless of biological age. Because of this, the correct form of addressing someone is a very flexible, situational system that can express very differentiated shades of respect and deference, as well as authority and command. Put simply, people position themselves in a relation of hierarchy with their interlocutor depending on the situation, where age denotes status, and familiarity represents respect. The greater the difference in age, the greater the difference in status; the closer the family link, the greater the respect and familiarity. These relations are also shaped by gender, race, and class (see chapter 3).

The foundation of correct daily interactions is the show of respect and deference to hierarchy, which is especially true in interactions with the state administration. Nothing can prejudice the successful outcome of an encounter as quickly as a lack of respect (*falta de respeito*). In official interactions, especially written ones, people will resort to formal titles such as *Senhor/Dona* (Sir/Madam), often combining them with professional titles such as *Doutor(a)* (Doctor), *Professor(a)*, *Engenheira/Engenheiro* (Engineer), or similar—attributed regardless of factual academic or professional qualifications.[8] However, more often the key to smoothen everyday interactions is the establishment of a rapport of familiarity, even in formal environments. To create this rapport, people resort to kinship terminology: a petitioner will address a person higher in status as Mother or Father (*Mãe/pai*), or as Uncle or Aunt (*Tio/Tia*). Likewise, street vendors will call out *"Madrinha"* (Godmother) to a woman passing by to attract her attention and solicit her custom. For men, *mais velho* (elder, old one) is a commonly used form of respect, as is in Luandan *calão* the Kimbundu-derived *kota* (elder). *Pai Grande/Mãe Grande* (Big Father/Big Mother) is a further sign of respect. Originally used to denominate one's mother's oldest brother or sister (and thus in the "traditional" matrilineal Bakongo, Mbundu, and Ovimbundu societies the highest familial authority for the child), it is used as a common show of respect and deference in everyday, mundane contexts—be it a shoeshine boy (*engraxador*) calling out to a pass-erby or a banner on the windshield of a taxi praising a local soccer club: *Petro Pai Grande!*[9]

Where the speaker is in a position of higher authority than the person be-ing addressed, the form of address used will reflect this: the conductor (*cobra-dor*) in the taxi will usually be addressed as *moço* (boy, kid); waiters of either gender are usually treated as *moço/moça* or *jovem* (youth), or, for a friendlier variant, as *filho/filha* (son/daughter) or *cassula* (last-born, youngest child). A waitress could also be addressed as *mana moça* (sister girl), or a waiter as *mais novo* (younger one), which is slightly more endearing but still indicates clear age hierarchies.

Even in relations of equality, the degree of familiarity invoked denotes the respectfulness of the interaction. Among equals one knows, the address *Irmão/Irmã* (Brother/Sister) is generally deemed appropriate, or in its more collo-quial form, *Mano/Mana*."[10] With greater distance, *parente* (relative) is always a safe option, before resorting to formal modes of address (*Senhor/Dona*). One evening, for example, while I was having a beer with my neighbor João and a friend of his, João complained that the new security guards at the petrol pumps under construction in front of our house seriously lacked in respect. As he told us, "This guy called out to me, '*branco, me arranja só 200*' [White man, just ar-range me/give me 200 kwanza']. I turned to him and said, 'What, does it say BNA [the National Bank of Angola] written on my forehead?' What an utter lack of respect [*falta de respeito*]!" João's friend agreed, "That's not the proper way, calling someone 'white' or 'black' or anything." João reinforced his point, "Yes, he could have greeted me correctly, '*boa tarde senhor*,' or call me '*pai*,' '*parente*,' or '*irmão*.' But not like this!" (Jorge, B. O., 8 July 2011).[11]

However, these social hierarchies are highly situational, not fixed. For ex-ample, after Sunday service in IERA's Bairro Operário parish, lunch is usually served to the pastors, members of the parish council, and guests in the sac-risty—a small, unlit room of naked concrete walls behind the church room. The *mamãs* who prepare the meal during the service also serve the food. My friend Paulo, not much older than I am, addressed the woman who served us as *filha* (daughter), although due to her age, we would normally address her as *mãe/mamã*. If your (momentary) status confers you more status and thus symbolic age, you are expected to express this in your interactions.

The hierarchy can also be reversed within seconds, according to criteria that may at first seem impenetrable and random. In a conversation between friends, for example, two young women would easily switch between "*mãe*," "*mana*," and "*filha*" from one sentence to the next. In interactions with me, this indeterminacy was heightened by my ambivalent status. I was at the time of fieldwork twenty-nine, unmarried, and childless. So I was still a *jovem* in terms of my social weight. Being a (white) foreigner, and, more important, a *doutor* (a title freely attributed to—and regularly claimed by—anyone who has followed any form of higher education), however, gave me increased social status beyond my years. My informants, especially those who were my age, often reflected this when they said how much they appreciated my "simplicity" and willingness to spend time and discuss openly with them. Nonetheless, although I dissuaded most from calling me "Senhor Schubert," many never adopted the intimate address *"tu,"* opting for an intermediate form (*"o Jon"* with third person) instead.[12]

The flexibility of the system of age hierarchy is also apparent in the level of intimacy that marks an interaction, which is not always reciprocated. At the transit authority, a petitioner might address the policeman on duty as *Senhor agente* (Mister Officer) and be rebuked in a rather gentle way as *Sobrinho* (Nephew) when told to stand back in line. By contrast, at the public notary, a young man trying to ingratiate himself with the lady behind the counter by addressing her as *madrinha* will be warded off as a mere *Senhor*.

This system of situational kinship terms, however, combined with the Portuguese formal address in the third person, can also be a cause of misunderstanding, as the following vignette of an experience I had illustrates:

> At the UNITEL shop, a young woman in her early or midtwenties is attending the customers. While her colleague processes my purchase, several other people sidle up to me to ask for her help. An elderly man comes up to the desk with a query. In his position as a petitioner, he addresses her as *"mãe."* She tells him to come back with a copy of his driver's license, and he asks her back, "And give it to the mother?" [*para entregar na mãe?*] He means to say in a polite way "Give it to you," of course, but she is completely puzzled at first, wondering what this man's mother might possibly have to do with this transaction. . . . I cannot suppress a smile, and she gets it, and says, "Yes, yes, bring it back to me."[13]

More than a signifier of hierarchy in interactions, the use of the language of familiarity is also a marker of distinction, as elaborated in chapter 3: like the UNITEL clerk, not everybody is equally at ease in using the system, which reflects differences in age, background, education, class, and race.[14]

When applied to people's ambivalent relation with *o poder*, the risks of being too close to power are also expressed through differentiated practices of address and naming: many informants were often reluctant to directly name the concerned persons, resorting to euphemisms instead. Very seldom would they name the MPLA directly, for example, preferring to call it "the M" (*o Eme*), "the party in power," "the majority party," or simply "the party." When asked directly, some confirmed that "most people have some apprehension [*receios*] to talk about this and name them." Equally, they would refer to the rather nebulous *eles* (they), but people normally knew exactly who was meant by this.

While Savimbi was still alive, he was only referred to as "*mais velho*," in a mixture of respect and awe. Similarly, the president is today mostly referred to as "*o Presidente da República*" (the President of the Republic), or simply, "the PR." The state newspaper will always put one of his titles and full name (the President of the Republic/the Head of State/the Commander-in-Chief, José Eduardo dos Santos); more critical, independent media refer to him plainly as JES to demystify the figure of the president. Only those who somehow claim a special rapport with the president or make a point of criticizing him use his name. This is especially the case for those who fought in the independence struggle with the MPLA. Some do this in a more respectful way, either harking back to the time of socialism as "*Camarada Presidente*" or creating familiarity by using his two given names—"*o José Eduardo*"—to establish some form of equality.[15] Others, however, employ more colloquial forms of address to express their anger and subvert the president's exalted position, as in, for example, "*o Zédú* is the biggest thief of them all!" In contemporary Luanda, "the name one chooses to address [someone] establishes the pattern of the relationship between the addressed and the addressee" (Tomás 2012, 266). Calling the president by his first name, or even by his familiar nickname (Zédú, Zé Eduardo), is to lay a claim on his person and to assert one's own agency in the face of adverse circumstances and relative powerlessness.[16]

This is reflective of the power of names and naming. Naming someone gives you power over that person.[17] It is because of this that parents in Angola used to give their child a public, official name, as well as a secret name that only they and the child knew. Likewise, the practice of adopting a "war name" during the independence struggle was not only a protection from the Portuguese secret service but also a protection of one's spiritual integrity (Brinkman 2004).

As in the example of neighbor João above, my informants would situate these interactions in a system of traditional values: a respect for elders and age hierarchies, a regard for the importance of family ties, and the obligations and reciprocity expressed in those interactions. In his ethnography of the Ovimbundu, Childs asserts that in relations of familiarity and hierarchy, "the avoidance of the name . . . must be maintained: the names must not be pronounced. Many euphemisms are resorted to when it becomes necessary to speak of or to these" (1949, 52). I will return to this idea of tradition in greater detail; let us first turn to the *cunhas*.

Activating a *Cunha*

Using situational kinship terminology to establish respect and familiarity and situate everyday encounters in relations of hierarchy is only the first precondition of a correct social encounter. For the successful outcome of an interaction, a *cunha* must often be activated. The *cunha* complements or in fact supersedes the traditional forms of respectful social interaction. It is a personal relation in the largest sense of the term, but in most cases relies on some degree of family relation. Such ideas of familiarity and commensality are expressed in the forms of addressing people, as outlined above (e.g., *Madrinha, Tio*), but also in common euphemisms for *cunhas*, such as "having a godfather in the kitchen" (*ter um padrinho na cozinha*).[18]

Considering the general state of disorganization and the relatively low degree of digitalization of administrative procedures—when there is "no system"—the relative position of a specific dossier in one of several stacks of paperwork can indeed make weeks, if not months, of difference.[19] One's dossier being on top of a pile could be decisive for the positive outcome of, for example, an application for a coveted job in a bank or in the public service, or for a study place. The urban vocabulary around these processes and personalized interactions is replete with idioms of mobility and stasis; people will ask, for example, for *um pequeno toque* (a little touch), a *favor pessoal* (personal favor), a *jeitinho* (a little way), or an *ajuda* (help) to accelerate, facilitate, or *agilizar* (speed up) the *processo* (process). Unsurprisingly, many of my contacts with informants, too, relied on personal recommendations, someone who would vouch for me so that the people I met could situate me in a network of relations and thus knew who I was. Through this, they then trusted me and were willing to spend time with me and tell me their stories.

The attribution of my research visa, which finally "came out" (*sair*) three months after my arrival in Luanda, on the eve of the expiry of my final renewal of the ordinary visa (*visto ordinário*, a one-month, single-entry visa, renewable only twice), is a good example of the mobilization of multiple *cunhas* Angolans have to negotiate in their daily lives.[20] Besides a personal invitation letter from an Angolan resident, which is needed for every type of visa, the research visa required a letter of affiliation from an Angolan research institution, in my case the Angolan National Archives (ANA).[21] This entailed soliciting an audience with the director of the ANA to present my case. Dra. Aparício, the director, was, however, a very busy woman, and hard to get a hold of. When I finally met her, she was very supportive of my project and agreed to write me the letter. However, ultimately getting the letter from her on time involved the intercession of a friend of mine, who when I mentioned my problems, turned out to be Dra. Aparício's neighbor on the same floor of a colonial-era apartment block in Coqueiros.[22] Based on ANA's letter of affiliation, the Ministry of Culture then had to issue an endorsement letter to the Migration and Foreigners Service (SME, from the Portuguese Serviço de Migração e Estrangeiros) of the Ministry of Interior, requesting the issuance of a research visa. Luckily another friend had the direct telephone number of the head of the International Cooperation Office at the Ministry of Culture. Again, I could perhaps have contacted the director myself, but finding out where to direct my next steps would have taken longer, and, as my informants told me, "It is good to know someone."

At the SME, some other friends had a *cunha*—Dona Arminda, a mid-level officer in the visa department. Dona Arminda was invaluable not only in giving me the necessary forms to fill in but also to hand in my *processo* on time, bypassing on most occasions the monstrous queues that congregate every day at SME's public attendance counters near Maianga Square. Needless to say, my friends then brought Dona Arminda two crates of good wine for the Christmas festivities, as she had also helped them with their children's passport applications.

However, several complications arose with my dossier. At the SME, delays were compounded due to the switch from paper-based to digital information processing, from cash to bank payments, and yet another reshuffle of internal units after the President of the Republic had reappointed his cabinet and installed a new Minister of Interior, Sebastião Martins. Then, the Ministry of Culture erroneously requested a "temporary leave to remain" visa in its letter, where in fact I needed a "research visa." Due to looming SME deadlines and my increasing desperation I had less than a day to correct the mistake. And so I called the Vice Minister of Culture, Dr. Caley, whom I had met earlier for an interview through the intercession of a professor at the University of Lisbon, asking him to speed up the process at the International Cooperation Office. On top of these complications, because my visa request was made in Luanda instead of at an embassy abroad, my process was somewhat irregular. Luckily, a former teacher at my primary school had studied with the then Minister of Interior in East Germany and knew his chief of staff, who was willing to give my case special consideration and instruct the head of the migration services accordingly.

Most of these procedures would perhaps also have been possible following regular due process, but to have it all done in a reasonable amount of time would have been almost impossible because all these steps involved a number of authentications, where official stamps (fiscal, ink, and embossed white stamps) and signatures had to be obtained. Furthermore, in an effort to curb corruption, a decreasing number of administrative services accepted cash payments, necessitating numerous trips to bank branches, including queuing, and back to the first queue again.

I have used the story of my visa application here because it provides a wealth of firsthand data, but my experience was by no means unique. In interactions in public and para-public service, many Angolan informants and friends had to invoke familiarity with a person of influence, such as a municipal or even provincial police commander, to ensure that officials shifted from being distrustful and reluctant to being helpful and compliant. This was especially the case when they dealt with the police—not just from a position of inferiority, when being stopped for some infraction of traffic rules, but also when filing, for example, a complaint about a robbery.

The system of *cunhas* even works across national borders, as the following story attests: Mantorras, an Angolan soccer player with the Benfica Lisbon club, was stopped in his car by the Portuguese police. He had only his Angolan driver's license, which was not recognized in Portugal, and had to appear before a judge. Mantorras called President dos Santos, who allegedly ordered the Angolan police to intensify their controls of Portuguese drivers, while the Angolan Public Television announced that Portuguese licenses would no longer be recognized. However, if you are driving without driver's license in Angola (or with a foreign but invalid one), you will not just be fined, you will be jailed. Within one week, twenty Portuguese were in prison. The next week, the Portuguese Minister of Foreign Affairs came to Angola to sign an agreement of mutual recognition of the documents.

It is also worth noting that, in the case described above, I did not necessarily seek out this help. Rather, when hearing of my visa troubles in ordinary conversations, my interlocutors would immediately say how they knew someone in this or that service (*serviço*) of the administration who might be able to help, offering to intercede on my behalf. Much as Luandans often deplore a lack of solidarity in contemporary Angola, compared to the time of socialism (see chapter 5), these networks of mutual help are still very much alive.[23]

These practices have a typically Angolan slant—the cultural embeddedness of the forms of address, and the historical and social contingency of Luanda's family networks described below. The personalization of everyday interactions is a result of necessity born out of the persistent dysfunction of the public administration and shortages in the supply of essential goods. This mirrors practices of *débrouillardise* (making do, getting by, street savvy) we know from other African, especially urban, contexts (Simone 2004; Tréfon 2004).

Still, the practice of *cunhas* has a distinctly Angolan (postcolonial and post-socialist) flavor: endless paperwork colors and complicates all interactions with a seemingly all-powerful state administration. The colonial government was incredibly bureaucratic, and much of the current bureaucracy of stamps and crests and copies hails from the colonial period. State power interferes in the lives of its citizens in often inscrutable and arbitrary ways, ways that were also typical of socialist regimes. Equally, the bartering of one's own preferential access to determined goods and services for goods and services available to others at specific times, is a custom installed during the times of *candonga* of the 1980s and a direct consequence of the system of rationing cards and differentiated access to food and consumer goods of socialism. This habit still resonates in today's practices of relation-making. Such strategies to cope with a "shortage economy" are another socialist heritage—echoed in the widespread Soviet jokes about queuing for useless goods that might acquire relative exchange value later (Fitzpatrick 1999)—which continues to define the modes of interaction in post-socialist contexts.[24] At the same time, I hold that the exchange of goods is not the primary function of a *cunha*, though obtaining goods and services may well be the outcome of activating one. Rather, in their emphasis on family ties and social obligations, *cunhas* are, as Derlugiuan observes for clan networks in the Northern Caucasus, "networks of trust that are regularly invoked and activated in interactions beyond the immediate family circle of reciprocity," (2005, 47). Or, as Quayson writes for Ghana, "Bribery and corruption is what ministers indulge in with their girlfriends, but for the proverbial man on the street making a gift to an official, say at the passport office, is a means not just of getting things done in good time but also of accruing symbolic capital that may later be called back for one's own use or for the massaging of one's social networks" (2014, 241).

The Basis of *Cunhas*

More often than not, *cunhas* have a material foundation that harks back to the extended family networks that make up the upper echelons of Luandan society. Indeed, my informants often told me stories that implied very detailed and intimate knowledge of the family ties of the ruling elite. I retraced the formation of Luanda's creole elites in chapter 3 when talking about imaginaries and formations of race and class, but there is also a very concrete aspect of functioning family networks to it.[25] Depending on which informant (or author) one consults, there are four big families or thirteen, or just one assemblage of constant intermarriage. Indeed, "the powerful Angolan families claim to have ancestors among or to be related to the creole society that flourished in the late nineteenth century" (Tomás 2012, 272). The importance of being from the right branch of a family, with the privileges this entails, is expressed in statements such as "He / She is *of the* da Silvas" (*é dos da Silva*) to denote a difference from other people who might have the name da Silva (267). Leila Lopes, the Angolan Miss Universe mentioned in chapter 3, is in fact of the Vieira Lopes from Benguela. And according to Pepetela, "the President of the Republic is a Van-Dúnem. He does not use the name but he is. He's of the family" (quoted in Henighan 2006, 137). Whether the president is really a Van-Dúnem or not, people certainly perceive the influence of powerful family networks strongly and see these networks as a structuring principle of society (Tomás 2012, 267). They also perceive these families as being a foreign elite, as I discussed in chapter 3. Manuel Vieira, a journalist at Rádio Ecclésia, explained to me in greater detail how these families work:

> There are traditional families here. The [here using the plural *os*] Van-Dúnem and the Dias dos Santos, the Pinto de Andrade, and the Vieira Dias. They have bonds of consanguinity which are very strong—we are talking about African families here. These are proper clans, and the information flows among them. I will give you an example. My name is Manuel Pedro Vieira, but I have nothing to do with these Vieira Dias. Now I was invited to a dinner—as a journalist—when a certain Senhor Vieira Dias appears, a person very high up, with lots of money. He comes up to me and says, "Who is your father? You seem to be one of my nephews. . . . We could meet and talk in my office, you could be directing my marketing area." Not for technical competence, mind you, just for the name! I declined politely and left.

These family networks, in the largest sense, are not limited to the elite but cut across social strata. My friend Cristina, for example, had recently returned to Angola after studies in Portugal to work for a Brazilian construction company.[26] She told me how she once flew for free to Portugal in first-class because her father is an executive with TAAG, the national airline. First-class passengers would enter the cabin and greet each other by name and handshake, with a *"bom dia camarada"*:

> They all know each other! *Bom dia, Camarada Fulano, bom dia Camarada Fulano* (Good day, Comrade So-and-so).[27] I was sitting next to the deputy Fátima Jardim, and she did not know me. So she asked me, "Who is your mother? Who is your father?" When I told her, she was reassured: "Aaah, Camarada Bonifácio, we know him well." That's how it goes. And

sometimes, if it is full and a minister arrives, they will throw out a paying passenger to make space for him. This is shameful, a paying customer—imagine a CEO of a Portuguese company who has paid for his ticket. And they have reserved seats that are always free for members of the government.

Clearly, much like Jorge and his family in chapter 3, Cristina could also be counted as being from this new generation of foreign-educated, upper-middle-class young professionals. However, later in my fieldwork I was invited to a wake in a house on a muddy side road in Sambizanga, only to find that half of the men in the room—the deceased's relatives—were high-ranking administrators in Bengo province, and all of the same family, Azevedo-Paím, and related to Lucrécia Paím, a hero of the independence struggle.[28] When I later told Cristina about this encounter, she was not surprised at all; on the contrary, when I mentioned the family name, she only had to think briefly before saying, "Oh yes, I know them, they're my uncles."

Of course, not everyone has the same privileged, direct access to the "thirteen families," and one must bear in mind that people in different social strata mobilize different networks (including neighborhood associations, church parishes, or sports clubs). Nonetheless, even in what could be termed the lowest strata of urban society, the *cunhas* that people refer to often do have a material base. Throughout my fieldwork, I was amazed at how people normally had an uncle or a cousin somewhere. Leandro and his cousin Adilson, for example, who were running their cousin's fashion shop in the street where I lived, both dreamed of studying and claimed to have an uncle "in the service" to access a study place.

However, these family networks are very ambivalent, and, as we have seen with naming practices, overly intimate knowledge of the "glorious families" can be perceived as dangerous.[29] People often simultaneously boast of their good connections while playing them down, distancing themselves from "them." In another example indicative both of the pervasiveness of family networks and of their ambivalent status, I was invited to lunch at a friend's sister's home, when the discussion—as it so often did—drifted toward family networks. It turned out that Bernarda—my friend's sister—is also somehow related to the Vieira Dias family:

> They all always intermarry; it's like in the royal families in Europe. All Vieira Dias-Van-Dúnem or Van-Dúnem-Vieira Dias. But because of this consanguinity, they have birth defects. In all the families of our cousins, there is at least one child that is deaf-mute. The girls only, mind you, the boys are fine.

My friend and Bernarda's daughter both interjected, reminding her that one of the boys is also "a bit slow." Bernarda continued her diatribe, telling us about when she had seen her cousin with her little daughter in the waiting room of a service of the administration. The cousin saw her and sent the daughter over to greet her. The girl came up to her and said, "My father is Manuel Hélder Vieira Dias [General "Kopelipa," head of the president's military office and one of Angola's most powerful and influential figures], and who are you?" "I am your aunt" Bernarda replied, before scolding the girl: "Do not say your father's name out loud in public. If you have to say something, say your mother's name!" Surprised, I asked why: "Well, it makes her a target— it's better to keep it quiet."

Bernarda was referring to her family connection with a mixture of modesty and entitlement but she was also acutely aware of the privileged status of those who can tap into these family networks, a position that is also inherently precarious and potentially threatened because most people are excluded from such privileges. This awareness and the newfound "humility" of the children of the political leaders certainly reflect current social dynamics (see chapter 6).

As her joke about the negative effects of constant intermarriage shows, there is also an element of gossiping and mordant humor to talk about the big families. My informants often had a very familiar way of talking about the people in power and their families, demonstrating detailed knowledge of their family ties and gossiping about alleged marital infidelities or shady business investments. Repeatedly I would walk or drive around town, and people would point out buildings to me, telling me, "This is Zénú's bank," for example.[30] In the privacy of their car, people would tell me the most outrageous stories about nepotism and the misappropriation of state funds for personal enrichment. Another joke, circulating by e-mail, said, "They have no need for cabinet meetings; they just meet at weekends for the family lunch," followed by an exhaustive list of people in high administrative and political positions and how they were all related to the president.

In Africanist scholarship, such reciprocal links of influence and obligations have often been termed, in shorthand, "neo-patrimonial" (Médard 1982; Bratton and van de Walle 1994; Chabal and Daloz 1999). In Angola, Messiant (1999) and Hodges (2004) have described the privatization of the Angolan state and the distribution of oil rent through networks of patronage as being the key instrument for maintaining political power. Sogge (2011) and Power (2011) have also termed the imbrication of political and economic power in the hands of a few families a typical system of high-level patronage.

However, since its heyday in the late 1990s, when it was the privileged analytic explaining the failings of African states, the concept of neopatrimonialism has been criticized for being a loosely defined "catch-all concept" (Erdmann and Engel 2007); for being overgeneralizing, self-referential, and based on "African essentialism, functionalist explanations, . . . the discounting of rural and local politics and resistance, and the ignoring of social differences" (deGrassi 2008, 112); and for disregarding "specific historical experiences while subsuming them under the totalitarian grip of a Eurocentric unilinear evolutionist logic" (Wai 2012, 27). Being constructed as an inherent characteristic of the predatory state (Bayart, Ellis, and Hibou 1999), or as cornerstone of the "traditional" African cultural logic (Chabal and Daloz 1999), neopatrimonialism is seen as the root cause of underdevelopment and conflict and is placed in contrast with the modern, rational-legal functioning of the idealized Weberian state.[31] Beyond the often startlingly normative assumptions implicit in these approaches, such binary opposition tends to ignore the reciprocity implied in Weber's analysis of a legitimate type of authority[32] and to overlook processes of adaptation and bricolage that drawing on social imaginaries of personal relations and legal-rational bureaucracy allow for (Koechlin 2013, 93). Finally, neopatrimonialism also tends to postulate competition between different elites who need to redistribute resources to their respective power bases, thereby precluding elite class solidarity. However, in Luanda, similar to Sumich's work on urban elites in Mozambique, "despite fierce internal disagreements and internal social cleavages, members of this group tend to take a common stand and defend their interests vis-à-vis other social groups" (2008, 112).

To move beyond the largely functionalist and normative trope of neopatrimonial networks, critics such as deGrassi (2008), Wai (2012), and Koechlin (2013) have suggested investigating both the historicity and reciprocity of these relations, as well as the symbols, representations, and social imaginaries at play in constructing them. To pursue this line of inquiry, I focus in the following on the imaginaries of authority, hierarchy, and moral order expressed through ideas of tradition and kinship.

Popular Imaginaries of Authority

As we have seen, *cunhas* have a material basis in Luanda's extensive family networks and are mobilized by claims of real or pretend affiliation with these networks; familiarity and hierarchy are then expressed and acted out in situational kinship terminology. I noticed throughout my fieldwork that my informants were greatly concerned with "traditional values" and tended to connect traditional values with correct social interactions. Indeed, several of my informants explained to me that the ways of addressing someone in everyday interactions were rooted in "tradition": the important role of the uncle, for example, reflects the important position the oldest uncle traditionally has in Angolan families.[33] I do not mean to deploy a reified notion of tradition as custom frozen in time here; rather, I seek to understand what my informants were talking about when they invoked *tradição*, or the "traditional way" of doing things.

Familial metaphors were employed to express notions of just and unjust authority, as in the saying *Deus é pai, não é padrasto* (God is a father, not a stepfather), through which people expressed their faith that God would not let them down in hardship. By contrast, the government was treating the people like stepchildren (*enteados*).[34] Informants also invoked traditional social organization to talk about legitimate political authority, where the traditional ruler (*soba*) was invested by the people and seen by them as a father figure, mediating disputes, warding off evil spirits, and assuming responsible for the community's well-being. Conversely, a *soba* who failed to protect and provide for his people would be deposed by the community.[35]

> Traditional authority had its own way of criticizing the ruler. Today, this does no longer exist. There is no criticism. The *soba* never takes his decisions alone, only after conferring with his counselors. And he listens to them attentively. This man [the president] no longer does that.[36]

As in the above quote, several informants explained to me that because of the tradition of the *sobado* (traditional authority), it was impossible to criticize those in power. In contrasting these traditional ways with current practices, they made a point about the impossibility of openly challenging the *mais velho* (the president of the Republic), even if his rule had betrayed these traditional obligations of care for his people. In some cases—informants with an activist streak—it was more a lament about the inactivity of political opposition; in the words of other, more establishment-affiliated informants, it sounded more like a call to not upset the social balance or the gains of peace (*ganhos da paz*) by rash, inconsiderate actions.

Reverting to classical anthropological and historical scholarship on Angola, we could draw some parallels to such contemporary practice and see how the creation of fictitious family relationships as a show of respect and deference can be traced back to precolonial and colonial times.[37] But it would be too simple just to point out the continuities between past and present practices. It is more complex than that: as an informant explained to me, after inviting me to his younger brother's engagement ceremony, "This is a sort of genetically manipulated tradition."

Indeed, this is no simple nostalgia. Some traditional rules of social interaction still hold, even if they are contested and constantly remade. Important family rituals such as the *alambamento*, the engagement ceremony where the two families meet and the bride price is paid, are reshaped to accommodate unions across ethnic boundaries or religious denominations, and the symbolically charged contents of the list (bride wealth) are updated and adapted to the urban context of Luanda.[38] Clearly, tradition and kinship are not the same thing and should not be conflated analytically, but why and how is the notion of tradition invoked in the context of familial imagery? And how do the practice and imagery of the family tap into and contribute to notions of legitimate and illegitimate authority? As described earlier in the chapter, traditional kinship terms are deployed situationally in everyday interactions. More important, however, the idiom of tradition is also specific discursive repertoire within the system that is mobilized to make a point about the current state of affairs. Thus evoking an arguably reified notion of traditional order is also a way of criticizing the structures of power and the unresponsiveness of power to the needs of the people. When people deploy the idiom of traditional values, it is to denounce an elite that has lost all values, especially the solidarity that is present, according to them, in "traditional African," Christian, and even socialist values.

Anthropology has successfully probed the link between kinship symbolism and political legitimacy.[39] Charting the "moral matrix of legitimate governance," Michael Schatzberg analyzes how in "Middle Africa"—eight countries from West and Central Africa in his comparative study—political legitimacy derives from "an idealized vision of patterns of authority and behavior within the family" (1993, 451) and "rests on the tacit normative idea that government stands in the same relationship to its citizens that a father does to his children" (2001, 1). Despite the generalizing scope of his work, which has been criticized for reifying the concept of legitimacy (Lentz 1998, 47), Schatzberg's description of the imageries of "presidential fathers," of the nation as family, and of the parallels between food and power is very productive and has been echoed in subsequent explorations of political culture in Africa.[40] Another example, analyzing contemporary Tanzanian politics, details how the overwhelming electoral victory of the Chama cha Mapinduzi party in 2005 was based on "the production and performance of a political rhetoric . . . that turns on shifting, and sometimes contradictory, conceptions of eldership and youth, fathers and sons, and illicit eating and legitimate consumption" (Phillips 2010, 111).[41] In these cases, paternal narratives and tradition are actively invoked and reproduced by state media to tap into and build on existing conceptions of political legitimacy (Piot 2010, 6).

I suggest that this classical Africanist trope has to be extended and revisited in the case of Angola. Indeed, the familial metaphors that people employ to evoke notions of traditional and legitimate authority seem to conform to Schatzberg's moral matrix of legitimate governance: a just ruler should be to his subjects like a father is to his household. However, in contrast to the Tanzanian example, or Schatzberg's analysis of paternal imagery invoked in the service of ruling presidents, the MPLA only very rarely invokes the symbolism of paternal narratives. On the contrary—and this, I would argue, is linked to its ambivalence toward anything traditional and African—it is careful to present itself as a modern, developmental regime (see chapters 1 and 3), denying any allegations of unfair privilege.

Thus, in contrast to ordinary Angolans—who freely admit that they have to rely on their *cunhas* to get by, and often boast of their connections—the members of the big families conspicuously avoid drawing attention to their family networks. Many of them publicly emphasize their "humble upbringing" and how "normal" they really are, attributing their business fortunes to skill, hard work, and dedication—and most certainly not to familial connections. The president's children are perhaps the best example of this communicative strategy of denial: when José Filomeno "Zénú" de Sousa dos Santos was made one of the three administrators of the newly created, five-billion-dollar Sovereign Wealth Fund of Angola (FSDEA) in October 2012—at the age of thirty-four—he refuted any suggestion that he had been appointed because of his father's position, pointing instead to his superb track record in insurance and banking.[42] Equally, shortly after *Forbes* magazine hailed Isabel dos Santos as Africa's first woman billionaire in an embarrassingly uncritical article,[43] the *Financial Times* managed to secure a (only marginally more investigative) lunch interview with the elusive entrepreneur.[44] In it, Isabel stressed her normal upbringing, saying that she had inherited her business acumen from her mother and that she had sold eggs in the streets of Luanda at the age of six—a story that was immediately ridiculed widely in the Angolan blogosphere.[45] When her appointment as the new chair of the board of state oil company Sonangol on 2 June 2016 was met with some criticism, her own and the regime's first reaction on all fronts was to say she had been chosen because of her "experience in the private sector" not because of "political questions."[46] By stressing their normality and downplaying any family links, members of the big families aim, perhaps, to promote the idea of an egalitarian society— an illusory enterprise since their family connections are common knowledge in Luanda, and because their riches are plain to see.

Because the government is reluctant to employ paternalistic metaphors or traditional values, opting instead for the more technocratic, Western imagery of the Architect of Peace, popular reference to paternal and filial responsibilities is a way of invoking an idealized, traditional social contract that has been broken, and a circumlocutory way of voicing a political criticism of the current regime.[47] The idea of dynastic succession is anathema to most Angolans, expressed for example in the proverb *"o filho da cobra também é cobra"* (The son of the snake is also a snake). And because the government is failing to fulfill its obligations, the people in power are increasingly afraid of the population.[48] As Chinguito, one of my informants from the Bairro Operário, said, it is like in a village community:

> If you have a tank of water and you leave it to rot and throw it away, while your neighbors need it; if you have a thousand bananas and you throw them away so that their son slips instead of letting them eat one or two, then you are a bad neighbor. If the persons are static and want to monopolize what belongs to all—you cannot walk freely [among the people] if you have a debt toward all. If you owe nothing, you have nothing to fear [*quem não deve, não teme*].

This *"quem não deve, não teme"* was a constant refrain of my fieldwork encounters, and I often noticed my informants' concern with the "rescue of moral and civic values."[49] People invoke tradition to depict the body politic as a big family—with clear hierarchies, certainly, but also with mutual obligations and responsibilities—and to demand its rulers fulfill these obligations. Thus we must also question and extend Schatzberg's assertion that familial imagery is so pervasive that people "just unthinkingly accept the metaphors and the images they conjure up as . . . part of the diffused understanding of common sense and [that it is] thus hegemonic" (2001, 23): paternal or familial imagery has a historicity and cultural embeddedness that makes it pervasive and hegemonic; yet it is a flexible, agentive idiom that social actors mobilize consciously and situationally to position themselves in their society.

Because of the ambivalence of these family networks, and because of the MPLA's fraught relation with African tradition, paternal imagery is usually not part of the official repertoires of power—although the MPLA, perhaps rightly fearing the critical potential of this discourse about values, recuperated this popular concern with moral and civic values for its own campaigns, recycling it as a campaign slogan.[50] I argue that this leaves familial metaphors as an open, seemingly apolitical arena in which people can express their ideas of just political authority and of the ideal moral order of society more freely than they can in political contexts.[51] Ideas of family relations and notions of an idealized traditional past are actively invoked to draw attention to the disparities between these ideals and the current situation.

Cunhas and Tradition: Productive Tensions

And yet, similar to the idiom of race, it is not simply a case of tradition as an oppositional discourse that is mobilized against a system of fundamentally unequal relations of hierarchy. Because of the real, extensive family networks that make up Luandan society, people deploy not only tradition but also the practice and imagery of the *cunhas* in agentive, creative ways for their own purposes. To further nuance my analysis, I return in this final section to situational, imaginary family links as an agentive resource to make the system work. Indeed, many of my informants had a subversive *jeito* (way, manner, *débrouillardise*) and used the widespread knowledge about administrative hierarchies and family networks to their own advantage.

Indeed, the pervasive personalization and strong hierarchization of social relations, as well as the imagery that goes with it, has, according to many informants, fostered a culture of *"sim chefe"* (Yes, boss) in the administration, in which no one is willing to take any independent decision, for fear either of the *chefe's* reprisals or, indeed, of the potential consequences for one's family members: because of the ramified family networks, if you cross someone in your line of work, this person might know someone in another "service" (administration unit, company), causing, for example, your sister to lose her job.

President dos Santos has cultivated this anxiety as an instrument of control: frequent cabinet reshuffles maintain a balance between competing factions and prevent anyone from becoming a challenger. A new minister then usually nominates new heads of department, who, under the banner of efficiency or the fight against corruption, proceed to extensive promotions, demotions, and dismissals within their department. Many informants also saw the administration trapped in this deference to hierarchy, compounding the inefficiency of any urban planning, for example:

A few weeks ago, on a Saturday, we were drinking some wine, and the administrator of Rangel was there.[52] Then his phone rings, and all of a sudden he has to run. What happened? On Thursday, he saw someone starting to construct a warehouse [*armazém*] and said, "I am the administrator here, who told you to build here?" and impounded the construction materials. On Saturday, they [someone further up the hierarchy] called him and told him "give the materials back now!" This is the culture of *sim chefe*.

The spatial imagery of a vertically stratified society with the figure of the president at the top has become a central element of the imaginary of power that goes beyond these reshuffles. This is how power works, how people perceive it across the social strata. Whichever decision is taken, whichever action carried out, it is done with reference to ominous higher directives (*orientações superiores*) that may well come from the president himself. In Mozambique, Gonçalves has shown that similar higher directives circulate as provisional instructions providing "parameters for action without being precise" but in the form of actual drafts or public pronouncements by senior state and party officials (Gonçalves 2013, 610–11). In Angola, by contrast, it remains unclear whether instructions are really issued, or whether someone is only acting out what they imagine to be the will of the *chefe* in preemptive obedience (*vorauseilender Gehorsam*).[53] Merely invoking these higher directives then justifies all courses of action, ranging from police brutality to administrative and judicial arbitrariness. The vagueness of the formulation certainly serves its purpose of obscuring the lines of command and reinforcing the nebulousness of power. Even Isabel dos Santos, in the *Financial Times* interview referenced above, indirectly reproduced this imagery: "'Whatever he does is almost like some kind of cloud on top,' she says, reaching for the right metaphor and waving a hand over her head, as though her father were some celestial phenomenon."[54]

As Krohn-Hansen reminds us, academic and journalistic accounts of dictatorships tend to personalize the state, "constructing the image of nearly perfect omnipotence, projecting the assumed total power onto a mythic figure, the dictator, and demonizing him" (2005, 100). Although this idea is often actively promoted, or at least passively condoned, by a personalized style of leadership or a leadership cult, it assumes a unity of purpose that the state does not have. Analytical focus on high-level Kremlinological accounts of power plays behind the scenes then "excessively personalise[s] the workings of the state" (Ledeneva 2013, 2). Instead, the state must be seen as "a collective representation, a social fact, not a fact of nature" (Krohn-Hansen 2005, 100). The fantasy of hierarchy in Angola is multidirectional, impacting and at the same time enabling the citizens, as well as affecting those commonly identified as agents of the state.[55]

Thus the system works in multiple directions, with the need for *cunhas* sometimes quickly reversing the presupposed hierarchies of influence and power: a police officer, for example, harassing a street vendor changed from a figure of authority to a petitioner on finding out that the vendor's daughter worked in a bank, and asked for her number to "discuss the attribution of a loan." Also, despite the material basis of Luanda's extended family networks, not all *cunhas* are real. Because of the strong hierarchization of the public function, many of my informants triumphantly told me stories of how they had successfully deployed a pretend *cunha* to impress a functionary or bully a police officer.

The invocation of hierarchy was also a strategy for dealing with the notoriously unreliable public utility providers: on New Year's Day, I was staying with friends who had been without electricity for twenty-four hours, and the generator was running hot. My host called EDEL (the Luanda Electricity Distribution Company), taking on a bossy tone:

> We've been without electricity since yesterday morning . . . yes. . . . The residence of Comandante Nandó [Fernando da Piedade Dias dos Santos "Nandó," the then vice president of the Republic] in Alvalade. The boss [*chefe*] asked me to find out what is going on . . . yes . . . and how long will that take? OK, I will report that to the *chefe*. [He cut the call and turned to me:] In half an hour, you call them "from the residence of João Lourenço" [the MPLA's vice president, who lived down the street],[56] and then, a bit later, my daughter will call "from the residence of Isabel dos Santos." Ha! [making a universal gesture of insult] If you call them as a normal customer, nothing happens, you have to know these tricks.

However, the effectiveness of mobilizing real or pretend *cunhas* breaks down when conflicting spheres of influence collide or when there is no connect between the networks of relationships individuals can mobilize. For example, all parking spaces in central Luanda are organized by a host of "parking attendants," teenage boys who usually ask for small change (200 kwanza) to guard the car (see also chapter 5). There is little scope for negotiation, because they might otherwise damage your car, and there is a widespread consensus that they also need to make a living. However, when a friend of mine did not like the parking attendant's attitude, he started a rather futile argument with the kids, dropping the names of a reformed street thug he knew in Maianga (a totally different part of town), as well as of the Minister of Veteran Affairs, Kundi Paihama, and refusing to pay. The parking attendant, however, was unimpressed: he was drinking and, being very much on the margins of the law and organized society, he could not care less about the minister. Consequently, when we left, the boys were nowhere to be seen, and there were scratch marks on the jeep's hood.

Conclusion

Everyday interactions in Luanda are informed by a complex system of establishing hierarchy and familiarity through the correct forms of address. However, a successful interaction in the context of unequal power relations relies more substantially on the mobilization of personal relations, called *cunhas*. These *cunhas* are based on a detailed knowledge of and familiarity with the real family networks that make up the upper echelons of Luandan society, the powerful big families. As I have demonstrated, the knowledge of which *cunha* to mobilize in which service is vital to successfully navigating the labyrinthine bureaucracy of administrative services.

The personal networks that influence the position and socioeconomic advancement of individuals are an ambivalent resource. Much as invoking a connection to someone higher up can get you out of a tight spot, too much familiarity with those networks of power can also pose risks to those who do so. Naming practices and naming taboos reflect an individual's claim over or deference to power.

More than just a practice, however, the utilization of these social hierarchies and family networks also reflects the symbolism of authority and the popular political imaginary of legitimate power. Because political authority in Angola does not employ paternal and familial imagery to assert its dominance, this leaves the field of tradition and family open as a seemingly apolitical space to express ideas about the moral order of society. So while the symbolism of family networks, due to people's reliance on *cunhas*, does produce and reproduce authority, it simultaneously also invites transgressions, both as a means of criticism and as a subversive practice.[57]

Real or pretend personal connections are thus utilized to navigate the complexities of everyday interactions with a cumbersome bureaucracy or to deflect the disruptive arbitrariness of state agents—traffic agents, *fiscais* (inspectors), municipal administration officers. Within this system, characterized by the need to establish real or fictitious personal family rapports to make it work, people find niches for individual agency, justly because of its skewedness and its exaggerated respect for hierarchy. People subvert the authority of hierarchy to evade police controls, and use personal relationships to shortcut the maze of Angolan bureaucracy. They use *cunhas* to advance their study plans and business ventures, and, as I detail in chapter 5, to find avenues for personal betterment.

CHAPTER 5

A Culture of Immediatism
Co-optation and Complicity

Since the end of the war in 2002, Luanda has increasingly become Boomtown Africa, attracting migrants from the entire national territory and all over the world to participate in the oil-fuelled postwar reconstruction drive. Although the benefits of this record economic upturn—the much-fabled trickle-down effect of neoliberal lore—are out of reach for a majority of the urban population, this boom and the visible, fabulous gains of the Angolan elite have fostered a desire for money and quick success that pervades all social strata.[1] According to many of the city's residents, the overnight wealth and conspicuous consumption displayed by Luanda's elites have in fact promoted a "culture of immediatism" (*cultura do imediatismo*) that has displaced older values of class solidarity. And although the majority of the population live in socioeconomically difficult circumstances, the desires generated by the postwar economic growth and the idea that its benefits are accessible to all have transformed not only the urban cityscape but also the ideals and aspirations of people in Luanda, as well as the modes of expressing these.

In this chapter, I explore this culture of immediatism as an emic notion frequently invoked (or deplored) by my informants. This culture of immediatism conveys a set of assumptions about fabulous flows of money generated by oil revenues, about the instant and immediate benefits for those who are able to tap into those flows, and about the way this desire for overnight gains pervades all strata of society and changes existing ideas of sociality and the value of work. It is, for people, at the same time a moral ordering device denoting a context marked by great socioeconomic and political inequality, and a user manual to safely navigate the politics of everyday life.

A culture of immediatism is, then, a vernacular notion of contemporary Angola that enables us to think through and understand how the country's turbocharged economy is lived, experienced, and maneuvered by its inhabitants. I do not mean to reduce this culture to a set of fixed attitudes, a sort of cultural determinism that emphasizes continuity and teleology and that is then used in a reductionist way to explain the ills of society. Rather, I understand this culture of immediatism as indicative of a set of meaningful repertoires from which social actors can choose to deploy specific contexts. Immediatism further indicates a temporal instantiation produced by and producing certain social and political processes. Almost like a "trans-temporal hinge" (Pedersen and Nielsen 2013, 123), a culture of immediatism allows people to make a value judgment about these present political processes and practices by juxtaposing them against an idealized past and a time of class solidarity—here, the state socialism of the 1980s. At the same time, these practices and discourses substantiate the promise of future material gains and social ascension in the present.

Immediatism then becomes an apt illustration of a dominant ideology in the Gramscian sense, because it shows how the dominated and the dominant jointly inhabit and recreate their lifeworlds. Through this, we can explore how social actors with unequal means and access constantly remake hegemony, not as a finished or shared ideology but as "a common material and meaningful framework for living through, talking about, and acting upon social orders characterized by domination" (Roseberry 1994, 361). In this, Luanda serves as a "laboratory of the global" (Piot 2010, 18), whereby thinking through the idea of hegemony we can explore the affects of contemporary, neo-authoritarian statecraft and the unbridled turbo-capitalist economy on the people living in and with such regimes. Beyond contributing to debates about the nature and bases of political authority in Africa, in this chapter I add a further element to the repertoires that make the system work, and give a partial reply to a question that baffles many observers of Angola: why there is no greater popular contestation of the regime in a context of such evident socioeconomic inequality.

I also further complicate the standard clientelist account of Angolan politics by focussing on the micropolitics of daily life, asking what material and symbolic effects this new economic order has on people, and how it feels to live in this turbocharged economy. In this, I follow Mahmood's conception of "agency not simply as a synonym for resistance to relations of domination, but as a capacity for action that specific relations of *subordination* create and enable" (2005, 18, emphasis hers). I develop my analysis of the renegotiations of hegemony through an anthropological reading of the aspirational character of the aesthetics of power in Angola (Mbembe 2001). By looking at the aspirational, complicit, and agentive dimensions of people's subjectivities in this culture of immediatism, I aim to demonstrate how ideas of civil society engagement and corruption fall short in explaining the modalities of political engagement in Angola. It is not simply the case of an apathetic citizenry still cowed by the trauma of the war and dominated by a predatory regime; it is also about different groups daily negotiating access to economic and social resources, making values and meanings within the same discursive framework. By looking at the effects of Angola's turbo-capitalism on those who are, overall, excluded from its benefits, I also intend to balance the "Africa rising" narrative pervading mainstream media reports of postwar Angola, and overly euphoric statements about the "new middle class" in Africa in general.[2]

My argument is grounded in the stories of three young men, Leandro, Simão, and Zéca, whose experiences exemplify some of these dynamics and form the backdrop of my analysis. Like them, many of my informants could tentatively be termed emerging middle class—though we should keep in mind what this means in contemporary Angola and not, as the news reports and World Bank statistics mentioned above do, mistake impressive macroeconomic indicators for actual improvements in the everyday lives of citizens. In the *bairro*, services delivered by the state are notably absent, and any additional hardship such as an illness of a family member or unusually heavy rains is immediately an existential threat. And yet these are the people who often accumulate formal and informal jobs to make ends meet and sustain their family, and still find the energy and ambition to pursue higher education studies and improve their lives.

I first discuss the phenomenology of power. Here, I look at the aesthetics of power as reflected in consumption practices, construction work and traffic, and the swanky lifestyle of the Luandan elites, which stand in stark contrast to the economic realities of a majority of citizens. As much as respondents lamented the loss of solidarity and "traditional" and "socialist" values when describing this new culture of immediatism, they also talked about desires and aspirations and the idea that quick wealth is almost at hand for—almost—everyone.

I then look at the material effects of this immediatist economy on people's lives and explore how the people tailor their practices and discourses to deal with it. Crucially, the symbolic and material dimensions of hegemony are intertwined and mutually constitutive, and material forces and the unequal distribution of economic and political power "bring into being specific landscapes of power and mold the individual subjectivities that feel at home in these landscapes" (Crehan 1997, 24). Indeed, the high costs of living coupled with the seemingly limitless resources of the oil revenues have given the regime both the symbolic and material means to co-opt potential opposition figures and large parts of the urban population. However, complaining about the elite's cooptation of regime critics is a highly ambiguous discourse: as much as it is often presented as the corruption of "upright activists" to explain or justify the lack of opposition to the regime, it is equally an agentive strategy of upward social mobility. Thus I show how the material and symbolic power of the ruling MPLA has all but crowded out any potential alternatives, making it desirable for citizens to align with the regime.

The Aesthetics of Power

Nowhere is Angola's postwar economic boom felt more acutely than in downtown Luanda. Where in the 1980s crumbling, low, older colonial buildings stood next to the airy, if derelict, icons of 1960s Portuguese modernism, now new glass-paneled high-rise buildings and fortress-like concrete towers are rising as visible signs of the new economic powers in the country.[3] The influx of oil money, coupled with new business opportunities following the end of the war, has transformed the Angolan economy and the Luandan cityscape. Whereas in the time of state socialism, only a few battered Ladas imported from the Eastern Bloc circulated in the streets, now shiny luxury SUVs inch their way through the permanently gridlocked traffic. Unhindered by any legal or social obstacle, the scions of the elite families multiply their business ventures and openly flaunt their wealth in the city's restaurants and clubs.[4]

From a close and highly secretive network that until the end of the 1990s still upheld the appearance of a modicum of wartime austerity, it is almost as if the Luandan elite has been restored to its nineteenth-century glory, when the creole families ruled Luanda and Benguela.[5] But although there are historic roots to this modern urban lifestyle (Moorman 2008, 23), and although the MPLA's own entrepreneurial class had already developed during the "clientelistic turn" of the 1980s (Messiant 2008, 311–58), there is a new quality to this postwar economic accumulation.[6] During socialism and war, *nomenklatura* privileges were still relatively discreet; today, glossy magazines such as *Caras* (Faces) promote the glamorous lifestyles of the privileged few, while stylish music videos project a new urban Angolan confidence to a larger audience.[7]

Glinting new hotels and office towers in the city center and new, lush gated communities (*condomínios*) with all the amenities in the urban development of Luanda Sul are but the most visible signs of the increasing wealth of some citizens. The most desirable parties at the glitzy clubs on the Ilha (the peninsula forming the outer boundary of the Bay of Luanda) charge entry fees from 100 dollars upwards (450 dollars on New Year's Eve), with patrons spending at least double that amount on champagne and vodka bottles. The well-to-do rave about the new restaurant Oon-Dah—incidentally also owned by the president's daughter, Isabel dos Santos—where "waiters finally have reached European standards." A 2011 article in the Portuguese weekly *Sábado* described, with a mixture of envy and admiration, the lifestyle of the gilded youth of Luanda, spending "700 euros on a night out, and 700,000 euros for a birthday bash."[8] And business consultants Mercer rated Luanda again as the world's most expensive city for expatriates.[9] Luanda is thus not just the physical backdrop of people's daily lives; it has become synonymous with a fast, urban, moneymaking culture and lifestyle that shapes, through its raw energy and new modes of production and consumption, the lives and desires of its inhabitants.

However, there is a flip side to this boom: in contrast with the overnight gains and the ostentatiousness of the elites, the lives of a vast majority of Luanda's population remain complicated. Their experience differs fundamentally from the outside image of Angola as an investor-friendly land of plenty where economic growth and infrastructure reconstruction are healing the scars of war.[10] It is true that compared to the wartime years of penury (*falta*), everything can now be found in Luanda, but most people struggle to pay for even the most basic goods. Despite a nominal yearly GDP of 5,783 dollars per capita, unemployment is rampant, and two-thirds of its 24.3 m population live on less than two dollars a day.[11] Years of a heavily one-sided oil economy and the destruction of the local production base through war, neglect, and formal and informal "import taxes" maintained by entrenched politically connected oligopolies have sent living costs in Luanda skyrocketing.[12] About 80 percent of the urban population live in the sprawling *bairros* around the colonial core of the cement city, surviving in informal business[13] or combining formal employment in the administration with "a *negócio* (enterprise) here, a *bizno* (business) there, a little borrowing there."[14] Equally, out of sheer material necessity and the will to tap into the fast flows of money, almost no space in the city is left unoccupied by economic activity, be it a corner shop (*cantina*) built into the street-facing wall of a property, boys shining shoes or carrying wares, *mamãs* selling vegetables or fruit on the sidewalk or from a bench in front of their houses, or a private courtyard (*quintal*) transformed into a lunch kitchen.[15]

Leandro, whom I briefly introduced in chapter 2, was twenty-five, "turning twenty-six," and taking care of his brother's "fashion boutique" in the street where I lived in the central, high-density São Paulo neighborhood.[16] We met over morning coffee in the *pastelaria* at the corner—the customary midmorning break of a strong espresso (*bica*) or milky coffee in a glass (*galão*) with a Portuguese-style custard pastry (*pastel de nata*) is one of the few fully embraced colonial heirlooms, and at around 150–200 kwanza per coffee, a luxury affordable even for the only moderately affluent citizens of contemporary Luanda.[17] From his shop, a tiny, concrete annex built into the street-facing wall of a courtyard, Leandro resold European chain-store clothes with a substantial markup. The first time I visited his shop, I saw that he was selling a pair of "leather" shoes from H&M for 22,500 kwanza (230 dollars)—shoes that would hardly cost more than fifty dollars in a European shop. Leandro, however, just laconically explained that the customs agents "billed" (*facturar*) a lot.

We regularly bumped into each other, and I would often stop for a chat or a beer in the evening after he had closed his shop, with Leandro expounding on life in Angola in general, commenting on the shapeliness of girls passing by, and berating me for "always doing research" instead of using my language skills, education, and presumed privileged connections (as a foreigner) to do business. Sitting in front of his shop on rickety plastic chairs, Leandro watched an impressively coiffed young woman driving by in a shiny green Jeep Cherokee, slowly navigating the rainwater-filled potholes in our street:

> Sometimes I feel I'm not living the life I deserve. A [BMW] X6, and a house on Mussulo, is that asking too much? My uncle is a *commissário* with the PIR [Rapid Intervention Police]—but I'm not using these contacts. I hope to travel soon. You will see, things will be good. One of these weekends we'll go to Coconote or Miami [Ilha clubs/restaurants] to eat a pizza and drink beers. That's the good life!

In his *On the Postcolony*, Achille Mbembe alerts us to the ambivalence of the aesthetics of power. He sees presidential grandiosity, overt violence, obscenity, and corruption as integral to a "generalised aesthetics and stylistics of power" in sub-Saharan Africa that bind the ruler and the ruled in mutual "zombification" (Mbembe 2001, 104, 115). While these topics echo central ideas about the symbolism of power in Africa,[18] Mbembe's central point is that laughter and gossiping, far from undermining power, actually endorse and reinforce it.

However, Mbembe's focus on power *over* at the detriment of power *to*, and his pessimistic, if highly evocative account of the helpless laughter of the ruled, have been criticized for eliding the possibility of resistance (Weate

2003, 32, 36) and for omitting the utopian, affirmative dimension of African popular ambivalence toward state power, as well as the aspirations of the ruled (Karlström 2003, 63). If the aesthetics of power are dialogically constructed, it "suggests the existence of a popular political imaginary" that is partially autonomous from state domination and opens up alternative interpretations (Karlström 2003, 61). Following this logic, talking, dreaming, and scheming about moneymaking and the consumption of luxury goods are at the same time "substantive aspirations of what a legitimately constituted state could be and do *for* its subjects if properly attuned to their needs" (63, emphasis his) and the everyday performance of "creative, embodied resistance at the level of everyday praxis" (Weate 2003, 39).

Borrowing from the anthropology of consumption can bridge the gap between aspirations and practices of resistance on the one hand, and a "more subtle account of complicity" on the other (36). If goods are markers of distinction and a visible sign of social capital,[19] then displaying wealth and conspicuous consumption is one of the means for the ruling elite to assert its claim to high status (Vom Bruck 2005, 255). However, more important than just status claims, certain objects and displays of wealth are an integral part of the stylistics of power. Because of that, claims to economic betterment are also an assertion of political aspiration and empowerment. In her ethnography of fiscal disobedience in northern Cameroon, for example, Janet Roitman writes how petrol smugglers at the border with Nigeria described their activities as "democratisation," which "was in many ways an attempt to dismantle exclusionary references to 'democracy' and *la vie moderne*" (Roitman 2005, 33).

Following Mbembe's line of argument (2001, 104), Leandro's longing for the "good life" that was dangled in front of him—driving around in big, air-conditioned SUVs; travelling abroad; owning property; and eating and drinking on the Ilha—could simply be seen as helpless endorsement of the status quo, because he expects important people to drive around in big cars and admires them for that even though he is well aware that this kind of life is out of reach for him. However, his comment is also indicative of the substantive aspirations of a younger generation that simply wants a "normal life" after the end of the war,[20] aspirations negotiated on the discursive terrain of the immediatist economy. Indeed, Leandro lived in the high-density neighborhood of Rangel with his grandmother and had never taken a proper shower in his home: "At home it's just the mug-and-bucket shower [*caneca*]. I don't want much for myself. Just water twenty-four hours a day, and light. In these nine years of peace, what have *they* done? They should at least have built a college and a general hospital in each of the nine municipalities."

Leandro's mention of his "uncle in the PIR" also highlights again the importance of the *cunhas* in navigating everyday encounters with public administration, privatized service delivery, or police agents (for more on *cunhas*, see chapter 4). Mirroring the entrepreneurial elite's preference for short-term, quick-return investments over capital-intensive investments in the productive sectors (Soares de Oliveira 2015, 147), the spirit of turbo-capitalism promotes the idea that in the supercharged economy of Luanda, money is fast and there for the taking if one is cunning enough—and well connected.

Thus social ascension is not just a mirage that only operates at a symbolic level to keep the population down as they admire their rulers in helpless admiration; it also works at a material level, precisely because living costs in Luanda are so high. Although the oil boom has driven prices up, it has also injected so much money into the system that some people experience a rocket-like ascension, especially with the right connections; the masses are at least offered a glimpse of what could be theirs. The Belas shopping mall in Luanda Sul, for example, complete with fast-food court, multiscreen cinema, and elaborate window displays of clothes, electronics, and luxury goods, offers the nascent middle class a taste of luxury and of the good life.

For those who can, "consumption is a material realization, or attempted realization, of the image of the good life" (Friedman 1994, 121). Just as the powerful flaunt their wealth, so do aspiring urbanites across the social strata equally espouse these attributes of wealth to project an image of successful, connected entrepreneurs "in the know" (Geschiere 1997, 137–8). Consumption of the right kinds of goods, or "the appropriation of objects as part of one's *personalia*—food eaten at a feast, clothes worn, houses lived in" (Gell 1986, 112, emphasis his)—is crucial to fashioning an image of success and living out these aspirations. Thus, as in Leandro's lament above, aspirational consumption in Luanda includes driving expensive cars, clubbing at the Ilha, wearing branded clothes, and consuming specific food and drink at birthday and engagement parties.

Moreover, despite these complaints and the hardships of daily life, high consumer prices also mean that money circulates quickly, and there are seemingly countless opportunities to tap into that flow. Thus the exorbitant costs of living—as well as Luanda's top spot in the ranking of the most expensive cities on the globe—are at the same time a daily worry and a source of pride, confirming Angola's exceptional position in the world. Leandro, for example, had previously worked on an oil rig. Although the pay had been good, he had been unable to stand the hardships of life on the platform:

Really, thirty days out on a platform, that's a tough life. But I left it—
there's too much wind out there, causing pneumonia. You have to work

at 1 or 2 in the morning out there! You earn well, true. I earned 1,800 [US] dollars per month. But these 1,800, they don't last long. When you get home, you have to give 100 each to your siblings—my parents died, you know—and then buy some frozen food [*frescos*], a box of chicken, some oil, and give some money for schoolbooks. Then you want to buy a nice shirt, a pair of shoes. I like perfume. This perfume here, which might cost 50 dollars in Europe, that's 100 dollars here. And then my baby, she will also want something nice, a perfume, or a necklace, maybe. So what will be left of the 1,800?[21]

In a typical mixture of lament and boasting, this statement shows how the quick flow of money also feeds an idea of Angolan exceptionalism, despite the problems associated with the high costs of living, an exceptionalism that the regime happily uses and taps into. Many respondents thus denigrated immigrants from "poor African countries" who had come to Angola to run corner shops and save money for home, boasting how easily they could spend a hundred dollars in one day in Angola, while "there, in Mali, in these countries fifty dollars is a lot of money . . . it's a fortune!"[22] Replicating the dominant economistic discourse, they quoted official statistics to explain how Angola was experiencing an unprecedented period of growth and stability, which was a source of pride for them—although most conceded (sometimes after rattling off growth figures for a while) that this boom had "not yet translated into betterment of the conditions of the population."

Because of the availability of fast money for some, many people feel that the culture of immediatism has completely transformed the relation Angolans have to "honest" work and money. Similarly, several informants lamented that this culture of *novo-riquismo* (new-rich-ism) had eroded the foundations of solidarity that in popular discourse had held society together in times of socialism (and in traditional Angolan society, see chapter 4). Of course, both socialism and traditional society are idealized in retrospect, especially because wartime socialism in practice meant a time of need (*falta*) for many and *nomenklatura* privileges for only a connected few. Nonetheless many Luandans recall certain elements of socialism—the solidarity, the camaraderie, the utopian space from which to imagine an alternative to the legacies of colonialism, and the declared aspiration to build a better, more equal society—with nostalgia,[23] a nostalgia that colors their assessment of their current socioeconomic predicament.

Although the parallels to "millennial" capitalism (Geschiere 1997; Comaroff and Comaroff 2001)—fast flows of overnight money, a focus on consumption as the chief source of value, and the desires this wealth calls forth—may seem striking, there are no occult forces at work here: the fortunes of Luanda's elites have a clearly identifiable source (oil production), and gains are made possibly primarily from having the right connections (*cunhas*) to important people close to power and making the right moves in Angola's postwar economy. Thus, in Luanda, the commonly circulated explanations and moral valuations of this wealth do not, as in other contexts, resort to "old, local representations" such as witchcraft, zombies, or spirit wealth (Geschiere 1997, 135; see also Comaroff and Comaroff 1999, 239), but talk of "social justice" and class solidarity instead.

This is neither to postulate a strict opposition between "occult" and "economistic" explanations of the boom nor to juxtapose reified notions of tradition and modernity as categories of analysis in the manner of Chabal and Daloz (1999, 144–47). Rather, it is to show how social actors mobilize and modify these idioms in everyday interactions with power. Indeed, although Angolans might privilege more "spiritual" explanations such as witchcraft (*feitiço*), divine intervention, or international conspiracies in other contexts—internal family disputes, for example, or the involvement of occult forces in rags-to-riches stories around diamond extraction (Calvão 2013)—vernacular criticisms of Angola's political (oil) economy are located on the discursive terrain of the New Angola. They thus adopt and adapt a technical-political logic that mirrors the MPLA's postindependence high modernist project (see chapter 1) or deploy the repertoires of "traditional solidarity" versus immediatism.

Contrasting the idealized past of socialism and tradition with the present situation, then, allows people to make a moral judgment about contemporary society: according to them, the riches and privileges of the elites, as well as their visibility in everyday life, have "corrupted" Angolans' sense of honest work and decent standards of living. Following the example set by the country's political leadership, many believe that through the right connections, or by occupying a gatekeeper position at the right time, they might accede to these exalted spheres of economic wealth and influence. In that perspective, immediatism has destroyed solidarity and undermined the capacity of the people (*o povo*) to act collectively in class solidarity. Faced with a lack of public services, Angolans have learned to find individual solutions to collective problems. As a participant said at an NGO meeting in Luanda, "In Angola, everybody now wants to be like the boss [*chefe*]. All want to be a part of the elite; there is no class solidarity." Deploying immediatism as a vernacular form of criticism, then, is a way of making claims to inclusion in the MPLA's—in practice extremely exclusionist—project of national development and economic growth.

This perceived lack of solidarity dovetails with the rampant *novo-riquismo* of Luanda's elites, embodied in the ideal-type of the *"chefe* in his V8 [-jeep]," which has captured the popular imaginary of an entire society. While people "critique and ridicule the excesses and grandiosity of their rulers [they] also expect and even demand such grandiosity" (Karlström 2003, 61). Indeed, ostentatiousness is not just a privilege of the rich; in line with the imaginaries of power and status, it is almost their duty. And because everybody wants to be the *chefe*, they implicitly also accept the *chefe's* bending of the rules and the impunity of the elite. Or, in the words of Irene Neto, the "rather unorthodox access to wealth [*o accesso pouco ortodoxo à riqueza*] has created a mentality of 'I can do anything.' "[24]

However, while it fosters desires, this culture of immediatism also has corrosive effects on social life and has led to the inflationary commodification of all spheres of life, polluting not just politics but personal relations, too. The ubiquitous demand for *gasosa* (literally, a soft drink; in practice, a "tip" of 100–200 kwanza) by police agents, private security guards, and state functionaries has been inflated to demands for *saldo* (literally, additional credit for a cell phone; in practice, 900 kwanza).[25] Around Christmas the demands for *boas festas* (a contribution to the holidays) increase exponentially, and the customary *Cabaz de Natal* (a hamper of food stuffs that companies give, and colonial *patrões* used to give, to their employees for Christmas) has evolved into a whole industry of prepacked luxury *cabazes* filled with champagne, legs of cured ham, dried fruit, and cheese, with subordinates competing among themselves to offer their superiors the most lavish basket.[26] Petty criminality is perceived to rise around holidays because "the poor also want a part of it"; many adults also complain about the youth's unwillingness to work, preferring to take money from their parents and spending it on beer, and see this as a further symptom of immediatism.[27] Several young men also told me how their girlfriends had left them because they could not live up to the girls' demands of *saldo*, restaurants, entertainment. Leandro also echoed this sentiment:[28]

> Here, the women only want your money. See, if you were to meet a really good girl, you would be able to talk to her easily, for sure. But then, if she finds out that you have no money, no car to take her out to the Miami, the Coconote, she will no longer be interested.[29]

As Leandro's laments and wishes show, consumption and ostentatiousness are a double-edged sword: they are part of the imagery of power that reduces the regime's need for coercive measures;[30] but they also exacerbate social difference, thereby making the wealth gap between social strata more visible and giving a material base to demands of "social justice" and a "normal life." Thus moneymaking schemes and active, conscious affiliation with the regime, as I detail next, should be seen not simply as economic but also as political assertions, representing claims to the benefits of peace constantly touted in the public media.

The Stuff of Immediatism

The culture of immediatism operates not only at a symbolic level; because the fruits of Angola's boom economy seem within reach, the very real economic pressures bearing on ordinary Luandans make them much more likely to embark on what they often recognize themselves as morally or economically dubious enterprises, and open to proposals of quick money. I suggest that the population's economic vulnerability, combined with the aspiration to social betterment, has become one of the "weapons of the regime."[31]

Contrary to, for example, the Albanian (Musaraj 2011) and Romanian (Verdery 1996) pyramid schemes, which ultimately collapsed, though, the Angolan culture of immediatism was propped up by oil revenues and oil-backed credit lines, which made these fantastic gains possible and, at least until the end of 2014, more or less sustainable.[32] The seemingly limitless resources of the regime, originally based on oil revenues but today often a result of private elite reinvestment in construction, media, and banking acquired through preferential treatment for licenses and contracts, provide the regime with the means to buy off anyone who would criticize the government.

At the same time, the culture of immediatism and a desire for the good life, both so prominent, have also led to the complicity of large parts of the population and opened up avenues for individual social betterment for those willing to affiliate with the regime. I invoke this notion of complicity not to shoehorn Mbembe's ideas into the analysis; rather, it is very much a comment of interviewees on the moral order of society, and their part in it, by accepting it: "We are all guilty of the system, as we participate for personal gain."[33]

This highlights how social actors commonly seen as the dominated are not just caught in webs of "false consciousness" or "captured or immobilized" by ideological consensus, but rather seek "active or passive affiliation to the dominant political formations" (Roseberry 1994, 360). Much like in Smith's work on the "culture of corruption" in Nigeria, awareness of the joint responsibility for the reproduction of this culture of immediatism then "fuels hopes for change, even as it paradoxically perpetuates cynicism and a sense of intractability" (Smith 2008, 6). Thus immediatist get-rich-quick-schemes work both ways to renegotiate hegemony—they are as much individual, conscious strategies of social betterment as they are processes of co-optation for maintaining power.

Simão, whom I introduced in chapter 3, was also an aspiring young entrepreneur, albeit at a level slightly different from Leandro. When we met, he was learning the ropes in his uncle's business and living partly in his old family home in Combatentes, partly in a small, rented apartment in an old block on Rua dos Quicombos, on the border between the neighborhoods of São Paulo and Sambizanga-Rosa. At the time we met, he was trying his hand at the profession of *intermediário* (middleman/-woman, agent) in the booming property market, where personal connections serve as a Bourdieusian social capital that is directly convertible into economic capital. Many of these *intermediários* work at a relatively modest local level, brokering private rental accommodation for commission equivalent to one month's rent;[34] but some, like Simão's business partner Divaldo—a slick young entrepreneur complete with wraparound shades, designer jeans, gym-sculpted muscles, two cell phones (one for each operator), and a new, gleaming white SUV—play the market for higher stakes.

This line of business thrives because the construction boom, coupled with high demand from embassies and oil companies, has distorted the Luandan housing market.[35] Those who have the capital or secure employment with the state or a multinational company, as well as those who have access to privileged connections, invest in houses and flats in the new property developments to rent them out for profit. Thus the growing supply of housing has not yet resulted in significantly lower prices, making property one of the economy's most lucrative sectors (Gastrow 2014b, 7–8). Those who do not have the necessary capital, but who have business acumen, wits, and good contacts, act as *intermediários*. Divaldo had brokered the rental to French oil company Total of a new apartment building near Largo da Ingombota: from the initial asking price of the owner, 28 million dollars over five years, he had negotiated the agreement down to 16.5 million, thereby netting him (according to himself) a yearly commission of 500,000 dollars for the duration of the contract.

Simão's love interest at that time was also central to his plans: she held an entry-level managerial post at Delta Imobiliária, the company responsible for commercializing apartments in the controversial "new centrality" (*nova centralidade*: self-contained urban development) of Kilamba,[36] and Simão quite accurately ventured that this was a perfect gatekeeper position from which to build capital and launch further business ventures.

As the intermediary business was ultimately a precarious one, depending on the two parties to a rental contract honoring their unwritten obligation to pay the commission to the broker, Simão later managed to register his own company and obtain a business license for "service delivery," a catchall term that allows a company to be active across sectors. Most of these service delivery companies act as intermediaries for foreign investors keen on participating in Angola's economic boom, using their contacts within the administration to overcome bureaucratic obstacles, acquire the necessary licenses and exemptions, and win the mostly unpublished tenders for government procurement or public works. As Simão elaborated over a delicious lunch of grilled octopus and olive oil-drenched, oven-baked *batatas ao murro* ("punched" potatoes):

> Angolans are experts in complication, as they know how to block your situation in a manner that you have to pay for their help to unblock the situation. This is what we call to wet the throat (*molhar a garganta*). To get a contract for the paving of a section of pavement in central Luanda, my uncle's company had to bribe no less than twelve people before gaining access to the Minister of Urbanism and Public Works. And we're not talking about 3,000 dollars here! This contract will generate some 17 million dollars, so the guy will just send you packing if you don't offer him something between 100,000 and 1 million. But when we were there, the president's daughter arrived and made a ruckus because her construction company hadn't been paid. She did not leave until the minister gave her a check for the arrears.[37]

Leaving the restaurant, he proposed to demonstrate how, at every level, Angolans make money "out of nothing." Walking along the edge of the sidewalk, he spotted a parking space. He stepped into the gap and started waving to the cars passing by calling out *"patrão!"* (boss). He only kept the charade up for a few seconds, as several street kids engaged in that line of business were charging the drivers 100 kwanza for their services, but he was very satisfied about his little demonstration. Note also the use of bodily metaphors of food and drink (to wet the throat) to express how everybody wants to benefit from the flows of money.

From the parking attendants making money out of nothing up to the minister, developing schemes (*esquemas*) is a constant preoccupation across all urban social strata. People resort to small-scale means of supplementing their meager salaries, often based on the importing and reselling of consumer goods from China, Brazil, or Kinshasa.[38] Many dream of some elaborate moneymaking scheme—frequently linked to exploiting "mineral resources" (i.e. illegal diamond mining) or setting up a community NGO to access donor funds (I was at various points approached to see whether I might be interested in embarking on such a venture). Yet there are even easier ways to money in the immediatist economy, which further illustrates the symbolic and material imbrication of economic and political power.

The following is the quintessential Angolan story about the co-optation of critics. It is a story I heard repeatedly in slight variations, from a great number of interviewees, especially from people active in NGOs and associations to explain why their activities remained ineffective in creating a civil society counterweight to the state (Schubert 2010, 665–66; Sogge 2011, 88). Spending a relatively sheltered weekend out of the city, in a lavish house on the peninsula of Mussulo, Zéca, a Portugal-educated young professional told it so well, in great detail and with such humor and gusto that I reproduce it in large parts:

> OK, so there is this guy [*gajo*] and he is really dissatisfied with the conditions of living, the lack of water and electricity, so he starts making a big noise: "It's all shit here, and it's the government's fault!" [*eh pá, tá tudo uma merda aqui e é a culpa do governo!*] Along comes a guy in his big jeep and says [Zéca takes on a suave voice], "Hey, my old man [*eh meu kota*], what is the problem? Jump in, let's go for a ride and you can tell me all about it!" So he gets in and continues [in a high-pitched, whining voice], "It's not possible [*eh pá, não, não é possível*]; it's all fucked up, the government is not doing anything about it!" The other dude just nods and they keep driving, and he just listens and then they pass a girl on the street and he says, "Man, did you see the ass of that girl? Man, she's good [*boa*]; wouldn't you like to eat [have] her?" The first guy still continues, "No, no, it's all bad!" but the other guy says, "Yes, you are right, but hey, here is her number. Go and eat her and then we can talk tomorrow." So our guy gets out and has his way with the girl. The next day, the fellow in the jeep drives by: "Old chap [*eh, meu velho*], good to see you! Hop in!" They drive for a bit and he asks, "So what was it that you wanted to tell me? Because *my* problem is really that I have too many cars. Hey! I know something—why don't you take my keys to this car here? It's yours, really, take it." Then, the next day, he'll come again and say, "You know, you got me thinking: things are really bad here, we need to do something. We are creating an office [*gabinete*] to improve things, and I was thinking, you would just be the perfect man for the job! We really need some honest people of integrity like you, who are not afraid to say things as they are. . . ." And so it goes. The next time our man is out and about, another friend comes and says, "Hey, I haven't seen you in a while! You should come to us; we are preparing something [an

action against the government]. Things are so bad here, we cannot stand it anymore!" Ha, and then [Zéca setting up the punch line with obvious delight], our man will give him a good punch [*bofetada*] and say, "Shut up, you don't speak against the boss [*chefe*]!"

Several elements are noteworthy in this story: the imagery of someone driving up in a big jeep and whisking the protagonist away from the dust and the heat of the street into an air-conditioned, privileged space above the hustle and bustle of ordinary pedestrians; the equation of power and social standing with the capability to "eat" the girl, as well as the association between food and sex (Liechty 2005, 5);[39] the detailed further steps of roping the dissenter—a car, a well-paid position—as well as the complicity of the co-opted individual in preserving the status quo.[40] Zéca then continued his tale:

If it's one of the youths [*jovens*] who are demonstrating now it's even simpler. They will take him in. But they won't threaten him at first. First, they will take out your file. They keep tabs on everyone, so they'll have this file with all the important information. "Oh, so you're the son of Mister so-and-so [*filho do fulano Xis*]? Why are you doing this, kid? Do you want to bring shame on us?" [in the whiny voice of the intimidated youngster] "No *chefe*, I don't." "I know you don't, you're a good kid. The problem is that you're in bad company. Why don't you come to the *Jota* [the "J," for the JMPLA, the MPLA's youth wing]? There you'll find good friends, and there's always fun things to do. Hey, here, take this beer, OK?"

This last section about detained youth protesters (see chapter 6, epilogue) not only reflects again the weight of family relations; it also mentions the alcohol-fuelled camaraderie of the JMPLA to underscore the MPLA's practice of organizing political rallies (*maratonas*) where beer flows freely, cheap food is offered, and, more often than not, pop stars perform to keep the audience happy.[41]

More interesting, however, is that Zéca himself is well connected and from a good family, a family whose members are on the boards of state companies or in politics. Although he has clearly benefitted from his family's standing—he and his cousins studied abroad during the war and he later went into business with a well-connected individual—he has returned to Angola with "European" values and observes the system, of which he is very much a part, with some unease. Joking about stories of co-optation is as much a form of objection as it is an expression of helplessness.[42] It is also, partly, boasting—to show off how he is in the know.

This tale of co-optation is not only a comment on the perceived ineffectiveness of political or civil society opposition, as when people active in associations tell it; it also reflects a widespread sentiment that many who are active in some kind of social, NGO, or political work are not doing so because of a social commitment, but only *"para fazer graxa"* (literally, for shoeshine; in other words, bootlicking). In that sense, the idea of co-optation alone falls short: the expression of political dissent can be, and routinely is, an economic resource, transformed into an avenue for social betterment. Furthermore, in Zéca's story, as in Simão's example above, the importance of personalized relations stands out again.

Even if not everyone can mobilize the connections of a Simão or a Zéca, the idea that with the right *cunha* the same gains would be possible is thus omnipresent. And one of the most straightforward ways of creating these connections is to join the MPLA and become "one of ours" (*um dos nossos*). The daily grind of Luanda is exhausting, and open opposition to the regime is a recipe for trouble and obstructions at every level: unpaid salaries, no school or university places for children, police harassment, windows smashed in at night, and so forth (Schubert 2010, 665). Or, as Leandro explained:

> If you want to have a successful business, it's better to follow the MPLA and not talk much. That's why so many youths are frustrated. They just want to drink and have fun. What can they do? If you start talking, imagine, someone comes here to your shop and puts up a sign, saying "Closed." Then you ask, "What is the problem? Why are you closing my shop?" [switching into the voice of the *fiscal*/municipal inspector] "What is this back there [points at the broom with which he just swept the floor]? Lack of hygiene!" "Noo, Sir, that's all fine." "Where is the bathroom? Why has it no door? Improve that!" And that can easily be a thousand dollars. But if you do that, they will look at the prices and say "speculative prices!" If you argue with them, saying that it is because the customs charged you so much, they will ask you to prove it. Prove it—how? They know very well how much they charge there, but you will have to prove it. See, so it's better to follow the MPLA. That's why the MPLA is the strongest party in the world, stronger even than the U.S.!

Compared to this, aligning with the regime opens doors and economic opportunities and smoothens and eases business. With its continued claim to being a mass-based party, the MPLA has made it easy for people to join. It contends to have four million card-carrying members and, when its dominance is contested, trots out Agostinho Neto's adage from the liberation struggle: "We are millions, and no one can fight against millions" (*somos milhões e contra milhões ninguem combate*). Neto, of course, expressed the desire of thousands of

Angolans to be free from colonial dominance, but this reinterpretation of the saying seems to suit the current situation better.[43]

The benefits of joining the MPLA range from a free lunch at a party rally to multimillion-dollar procurement deals. As Sogge writes, "There are no Angolans making money on a *substantial scale* outside the purview and participation of the political class" (2011, 87; emphasis his). Aligning with the ruling party, then, opens up avenues for new schemes for enrichment through semilegal or illicit means. Be it the undeserved drawing of military pensions, salaries for phantom teachers, the eating of commissions, the embezzlement of state procurement money, the over-invoicing for services, or the nonpayment of custom duties, as long as you are "one of ours," you are likely to get away with it. In that sense, the state's failure to deliver services to the population serves an economic purpose, in addition to expanding the regime's control through "private indirect government" (Mbembe 1999). Stories abound that electricity provider EDEL is colluding with generator importers to cause blackouts to increase sales; that there is no sanitation in the *bairros* because the generals own fleets of water tankers (*camiões cisternas*); and that domestic production is low and expensive because some ministers have partnered with food importers and rented out previously profitable factories to them as warehouses (*armazéns*).[44]

Many informants were open about the benefits of aligning with the MPLA and harbored no illusions about the political commitment of those who did. They also had little confidence in the political opposition's ability to change the system, confirming the tentacle-like grasp of the MPLA on the national economy.[45] One informant explained how ministers who close a contract for the state routinely take 10 percent of the contracted sum, and that MPLA members have stakes in all oil platforms, and most farm estates (*fazendas*) in the interior. Contrary to this, he said, "UNITA doesn't have any entrepreneurs—whoever does business and is associated with the opposition, it's a guaranteed failure [*fracasso*]."

However, while this is indicative of the increased, intentional blurring of the lines between party, state, and government, as well as of the symbiosis between economic and political power, the MPLA itself is far from monolithic. For older members, who had joined the party during or shortly after the independence struggle, or had grown up during the time of socialism, the mass recruitment of yes-men and flatterers (*bajuladores*) into the party was a source of resentment. They had a different perspective on what the party once was and should be. They complained about the party's practice of organizing political rallies (*maratonas*) and parties (*festinhas*), distributing cheap alcohol, and playing loud music to dazzle the urban population and distract them from their plight. Having only joined the MPLA to get a good job, new members were ready to applaud and please the *chefe* instead of being real committed members (*militantes*). In the view of those old members, the MPLA had completely lost sight of its former values, existing only as a vehicle for social climbers—often forgetting that it was their generation of former independence fighters who had installed the current dispensation for their own economic profit.

To explain hegemonic domination through a story of vote-buying, influence-peddling, and large-scale corruption, however, is too one-dimensional. Because of the pervading immediatist spirit, I contend, the MPLA's symbolic power as the "strongest party in the world" is equally central: despite often relatively transparent and crude use of the state's resources, the MPLA's image as the party of the successful entrepreneurs, and its very real command of economic means, induces people to support it. Politics, in such a context, is not a question of programs; it is, rather, a question of control over, and distribution of, material and symbolic state resources. The MPLA asserts its position of superiority relatively bluntly in its posters, stating, for example: "MPLA 1956–2010. We are Angola's largest party—the most representative, the strongest, and the most capable" (see figure 5). There is a material dimension to it, of course: in the run-up to the last elections, by suddenly tarring long-neglected roads or

FIGURE 5.   MPLA campaign poster, "We are Angola's largest party: The most representative, the strongest, and the most capable." The left-hand part of the poster says, "MPLA, 1956–2010: 54 years in the service of the ideals of the Angolan people."

improving the water supply, by publicly handing over a few new social houses to grateful residents, and by multiplying the inauguration of public buildings such as schools and hospitals, "the state made itself apparent to citizens in ways that could only serve to remind them of how absent it usually was" (Wedeen 2008, 68).[46]

However, although this promise of betterment, and the mass political rallies of the MPLA with their flows of cheap beer, had worked for the last elections, citizens were wearying of the old tricks. They remarked how, already one year ahead of the 2012 elections, a flurry of infrastructure projects were again being undertaken to underscore the party's image as the party of reconstruction and peace; but they were increasingly skeptical about the sustainability of such measures and joked about Chinese-built disposable roads (*estradas descartáveis*) that would wash away after the first rains. The macroeconomic consequences of this immediatist spirit, which is being acted out as the model starting from the very top echelons of Angolan society, is that there is no long-term, sustainable economic policy for the country, the consequences of which have become evident since the drop in world oil prices in late 2014 (see epilogue).[47]

Conclusion

The rapid growth of the Angolan economy following the end of the war, and the associated, spectacular gains for some, have transformed not only the cityscape of Luanda but also the modes by which wealth is accessed and publicly displayed. The desire for such fabulous overnight gains and the attributes of a successful lifestyle—specific kinds of clothing, cars, food, and housing—pervades all social strata to the extent that citizens of Luanda describe it as a culture of immediatism. The idea that material betterment and social ascension is almost within reach, and there for the taking if one is only cunning enough and sufficiently well connected, has, according to many, had a corrosive effect on class solidarity and the work ethic of Angolans.

Combined with the astronomic costs of living in Luanda, this makes ordinary citizens more vulnerable to embarking on schemes that offer easy and quick wealth. And because of the regime's control of private economic and state resources, it is ultimately easier for many to align with the ruling party than it is for them to face endless administrative and financial obstacles, even if they have moral reservations about associating too closely with the regime. This moral unease is often expressed in deploring such schemes as a co-optation strategy of the regime; but such complicity is equally an agentive strategy for material betterment that people actively pursue.

We can read this culture of immediatism as one of the terrains on which hegemony is renegotiated within the system. The immediatist spirit works at a symbolic and a material level, and draws the outlines of the shared discursive field in which people negotiate access to economic and political resources. As many informants said, "Everyone is guilty of the system." Because all elements of society are tangled up in this spirit of turbo-capitalism, by aspiring to its benefits they willingly or unwittingly participate in creating and perpetuating the dominant ideology.

However, despite a very real gap in economic, social, and political means, ordinary citizens are not helplessly caught up in webs of false consciousness imposed by a dominant system of thought. As Crehan notes, Gramsci "never solely focused on the economic conditions of power but is always centrally concerned with the ideological forms in which people become conscious of these conditions, and within which they struggle" (1997, 24). The promise of overnight success and a piece of the pie for all—as echoed in the MPLA's 2012 electoral slogan, "Angola: Grow more to distribute better"—is a very ambivalent common discursive framework that is constantly renegotiated, which "allows us to examine both the power and fragility of a particular order of domination" (Roseberry 1994, 363).

On the one hand, ideas of a better life are not just limited to overnight wealth and flashy cars but also include desires for the state, its services, and a normal life,[48] cultivating the consent of large parts of the citizenship. On the other hand, however, the material limits of this immediatist lifestyle are becoming increasingly evident. Despite the visible, enormous benefits of aligning with the regime for some, a growing number of people recognize that the promised improvements of their daily lives at a much more modest level have not been delivered. This, then, opens up the culture of immediatism as a terrain of political contestation, sketching out the limits of the MPLA's hegemonic domination. The question of what happens then, when the system begins fraying at the seams, is the one I address in chapter 6.

CHAPTER 6

Against the System, within the System
The Parameters of the Political

32 é muito (32 is too much)

Rallying call of 2011/12 antigovernment demonstrations

In this chapter, I explore the multiple reactions to a first call for an antigovernment demonstration, planned for March 2011. In previous chapters, I focused on different facets of the micropolitics of ordinary life and on how people in Luanda position and project themselves in relation to power through "inventions of the everyday."[1] Here, I follow a slightly different tack. Empirically, I pursue the question of what happens when the normal course of social life in Luanda is disrupted by open defiance and more explicit resistance to the dominant social and power structures. Analytically, by disassembling the discursive and performative reactions of various social actors to those events, I draw together the different elements that make up the modalities of power in Angola—analyzed in greater detail in the previous chapters. As I show, even the most oppositional of the manifold social actions taking place around these events, and even the most novel vectors of communication, resorted to existing, culturally significant discursive repertoires to make sense of the situation and articulate their interests. However, by tapping into and manipulating these repertoires for oppositional purposes, this call for protest significantly impacted on the dynamics of Angolan political culture, triggering strong reactions by a vast array of social actors and sketching out the possibility of change.

I begin by giving a chronology of events around the first call, in February 2011, for an antigovernment demonstration in Luanda scheduled for

7 March 2011. This allows me to make two minor points—one about the importance of social networks and one about the issue of youth and class—before exploring how these events were received and commented on. By disassembling the various repertoires mobilized by different social actors around this call for demonstrations, I will show how they relate to the different facets of the system. Thus I make a somewhat Gramscian argument about the reproduction of hegemony, arguing that even explicitly oppositional political action has to tap into the repertoires of dominant ideology to be effective. I end the chapter with the 2012 elections, posing the final cornerstone for the overall conclusion of the book. I contend that despite widespread resignation about the effectiveness of elections to bring about change, the impact of these demonstrations is insufficiently captured by the small number of people attending them, or the limited success of such political activism. Rather, through the lens of practice theory, we can think about what it means to push the boundaries of hegemonic dominance, and what this might imply for our understanding of neo-authoritarian regimes.

Luanda Calling

In February 2011, a call for an antigovernment demonstration on Luanda's Independence Square on 7 March was published on the Internet. The call explicitly referred to the then ongoing Arab revolutions in Tunisia, Egypt, and Libya, drawing parallels between the long-standing dictatorships of North Africa and the situation in Angola. It demanded the resignation of President José Eduardo dos Santos. Such open defiance of the government was an almost unprecedented event in Angola's postindependence history.[2] First sent out in an e-mail titled "A New Revolution for the Angolan People," it was soon also published on a website and circulated through social networks. It was issued by an ominous Revolutionary Movement of the Fighting People of Angola (Movimento Revolucionário do Povo Lutador de Angola, MRPLA) and signed with the pseudonym Agostinho Jonas Roberto dos Santos, thereby name-checking the historical leaders of Angola's three independence movements and including the family name of Angola's current president, dos Santos.[3]

The first reactions to the announcement of the demonstration were muted, marked by skepticism and disbelief, and limited to circles with access to the Internet and social media. A popular demonstration explicitly criticizing the government and the president was completely unthinkable in the recent history of Angola, given the ubiquitous fear that any form of dissent would be met by state violence (see chapter 2). One widespread assumption was that it was a hoax orchestrated by the government to flush out and identify the troublemakers. Although many said, quietly at first, then more openly, that they agreed with the demonstration's aims and arguments, the fact that the demonstration had been anonymously convoked over the Internet by this unknown organization, MRPLA, which in all but one letter shared its acronym with the ruling MPLA, only reinforced people's doubts about the intentions and authorship of such a call. Opposition parties and civil society associations were quick to distance themselves from the organizers of the demonstration, although some smaller parties tentatively agreed with the demonstration's objectives. My own immediate reaction, too, was one of disbelief, paired with curiosity to see how events would unfold.

The call only started to gain a wider prominence when the government reacted, with visible nervousness, two weeks after it was first announced. State media denounced the demonstration as an attempt to destabilize the country and threaten the gains of peace (see chapter 1). Government officials and high-ranking MPLA members publicly spoke out against the demonstrations, arguing that people did not need to protest, because things were fine; moreover, it was dangerous to create confusão and instability ahead of the 2012 elections. Those who were dissatisfied with the government's performance could always express their preference at the ballot box by voting for a different party. They further argued that attacking "our Comrade President" was a severe show of disrespect against the dignified institutions of the state, and that whoever committed "acts of disobedience" would feel the full force of justice. MPLA Secretary-General Julião Mateus Paulo "Dino Matross" warned all Angolans in a National Radio (Rádio Nacional de Angola, RNA) broadcast not to mistake Angola for the Arab world, and reminded them of the war as he exhorted them "not to get mixed up in any adventures."[4] Although the right to demonstrate was enshrined in the new constitution, one "should be very careful not to confuse things," and under these circumstances, "serious measures" would be taken against anyone who demonstrated, because after all, "Power cannot be [held] in the streets. We have a new constitution and we have laws, and it is according to the laws of the country that we have to act."[5] All MPLA militants should "maintain a high level of vigilance" during the weeks ahead and "abstain from any type of activities that would threaten the democratic and peaceful harmony of the country."[6] In parallel to this warning, the MPLA's then secretary-general for the province of Luanda, Bento Sebastião Bento, denounced the demonstration as an attempt by foreign powers to destabilize the country and said that those who called for the resignation of the president were not real Angolans.[7] He then announced a nonpartisan rally for peace and stability on Saturday, 5 March, two days before the planned demonstration.

The popular reactions to this barrage of bellicose rhetoric and hostile media coverage were twofold. Many of my younger informants were cautiously euphoric about this new message of open defiance, saying, "We should have gone out into the streets long ago. But we needed them [the North Africans] to show us that it was possible."[8] Beyond connecting their situation with wider global events, they also emphasized that they were no longer "the Angolans of twenty years ago" but a new generation, not afraid to protest for their rights, and pointed out the right to demonstrations without previous authorization enshrined in the new 2010 constitution.

Finally, one week before the planned demonstration, two minutes of video recorded at a rap concert at the Cinema Atlântico (one of Luanda's more established concert venues) went viral on YouTube, sending shock waves through Luanda: Luaty Beirão, a rapper variously known as "Ikonoklasta" or "Brigadeiro Matafrakuzx" (from *mata fracos*, i.e. 'Brigadier Kill-The-Weak') called out the "son-of-a-bitch government," saying, *"32 é muito"* (32 [years] is a lot, meaning that the thirty-two years dos Santos had been in power were too much). He then shouted the names of those high-ranking members of the MPLA who had threatened a crackdown on demonstrators, to which the audience replied with enthusiastic yells of *"fora!"* (Out!).[9] Interestingly, as it shows his insertion within a historical precedent and musical tradition, this *fora* was lifted from an earlier semba hit "Serenata a Angola," in which the overall much less controversial popular singer Paulo Flores sings: *"Explorador dos oprimidos: fora!"* (Exploiter of the oppressed: out!).[10]

The more widespread reaction, however, especially among residents of Luanda in their thirties and upward, was the warning to stay at home for the weekend (5–6 March) and the start of carnival (7–8 March). Although many agreed that the situation had to change somehow, they abhorred the idea of radical change and *confusão* and expressed fear or even anger at the prospect of upsetting the social order violently. Thus many people expressly advised me to buy rice, water, salt, cooking oil, and gas, and to stay inside for three days.[11]

After the buildup of tension ahead of the demonstrations, the long weekend of 5–7 March that preceded the carnival was strangely anticlimactic. Although the final days saw frantic last-minute shopping in supermarkets and on the markets, an eerie calm descended on Luanda on the weekend, with almost no traffic in the streets, and a strong presence of heavily armed police at strategic points in the city center.

Besides the media overreaction and the buzz on social networks ahead of the demonstrations, mobile internet services were cut for two days on Thursday,

3 March. Due to the lack of cable or fixed-telephone infrastructures, most people in Luanda access the Internet through the cell phone network (cell phones or USB dongles). The providers claimed some damage to the main fiber-optics cable was responsible for the breakdown of services, but as both mobile network operators UNITEL and MOVICEL are owned by individuals affiliated to the regime, most people suspected that the government had ordered the shutdown to prevent social networking sites being used.[12]

On Saturday, 5 March, the MPLA held its nationwide "nonpartisan" pro-peace rally. According to the official press, four million people came out onto the streets, wearing white shirts (often printed with the face of the president) and marching for peace, stability, unity, and the current leadership. The aptly named Spontaneous National Movement (Movimento Nacional Espontâneo, MNE), one of the civil society organizations created to whitewash the government's image, stated that the march clearly demonstrated that "all the Angolan people held peace as a value for development in all sectors"; other personalities from across the social spectrum also highlighted the gains of peace—mainly infrastructure reconstruction.[13]

"It is regrettable that some persons could still think of the instability of the country in a time when the policies of the executive are aiming at the education of the youth, the creation of jobs, the fight against criminality and drugs, and the rescue of moral and civic values," stated Phatar Mack, a pop musician and "ambassador of the fight against criminality" of the National Youth Council.[14] Church and "organized civil society" leaders sided with the ruling party, calling on all social actors to abstain from "uncivil" behavior and further emphasizing the message of stability as the supreme value of postwar Angola. The provincial governor, Bento Bento, "guaranteed" that the antigovernment demonstration of 7 March would not be realized and said that the countless marchers confirmed that the people wanted peace, not confusion, and were backing democracy, not subversion or adventurers: "Political adventures, here in Angola, never again. This is what the people here said, that they are with the MPLA, and with him who fought so much for peace, the Architect of Peace."[15]

Commenters in the street, on internet forums, and in the few independent weeklies immediately questioned Bento Bento's sanity, saying there were at most 100,000 people, and that four million was more likely the sum in dollars he had received from the president for such a blatant lie. Associated Press reported an even lower figure of 20,000 demonstrators in Luanda.[16] More important, this was hardly the spontaneous display of support for the government that official media portrayed: a week after the demonstrations, my friend Isabel told me, "Do you know they went to the market places [*praças*] and forced people to attend the rally? They took them away in vans and brought them to the march, where they gave them shirts and drinks to participate in the march."[17] Other informants confirmed that schoolchildren and teachers, as well as state employees, were forced to participate in the march for fear of losing their jobs. As at other mass party rallies [*maratonas*], alcoholic drinks and money (allegedly 100 dollars per person) were used to persuade people to participate.[18]

Most opposition parties reproduced the official discourse of equating demonstrations with a return to war. Under attack from the MPLA for "inciting disorder," UNITA and the Bloco Democrático publicly proclaimed that they, too, were for peace and stability, and against *confusão*, thereby reinforcing the government's message of stability. The 27 de Maio and the 1992 violence were also widely cited as reasons why it would be foolish to go out and demonstrate.[19] In an attempt to show endorsement of both the planned demonstration and the call for peace without affiliating themselves to either of the two camps, several smaller parties united as Parties of Civic Opposition (POC, from Partidos da Oposição Civil) and called for a peaceful candle vigil on Independence Square on the night of 6–7 March. However, the Government of the Province of Luanda announced that any demonstration on Independence Square was impossible, citing security concerns because of the carnival as the reason. Afraid of a violent reaction, the parties cancelled the vigil. On the morning of 7 March, only around twenty people appeared at Independence Square. All of them, including four journalists, were immediately arrested by the police. They were released later in the evening. The police stated that the demonstrators had been taken into custody to protect them from being beaten up.[20]

Networks, Youth, and Class

Since the 2009 "Green Revolution" in Iran—also dubbed the Twitter Revolution—and even more so since the so-called Arab Spring, Western media have hailed the transformative and revolutionary potential of Internet-based social networks. Needless to say, this often springs from wishful thinking, which is disappointed when these supposed vectors of idealized political liberalization are used for antiliberal means.[21]

True, the Internet, along with Facebook, YouTube, and Twitter, did and does play a considerable role in evading state control of information in Angola and in transmitting alternative information. However, authors such as Diani (2011) and Salvatore (2013), writing on the Egyptian revolution, have cautioned against an overly euphoric assessment of the role of new media in the revolutions, saying that the social networks that mattered most were not Twitter or Facebook, but universities, mosques, and football clubs. Similarly, although the Internet played a central role in propagating the first call for a demonstration in Luanda, we should not see it as the determining factor: the medium is not the message here. What it did, however, was to create a sense of global interconnectedness: awareness of what was happening in North Africa, facilitated by digital media, did impact on how the call for demonstrations was framed. The demonstrators in Luanda referred to the Arab revolutions as a model, highlighting the similarities of the situation in Angola with the long-standing autocracies of Tunisia, Egypt, and Libya. Likewise, the regime's overreaction was also informed by the upheavals in the north of the continent, and when the MPLA's secretary-general warned publicly that "no one should mistake the reality in Angola for the one in the Arab countries," it spoke clearly of how nervous the regime was about suffering a similar fate.

Focusing on the network aspect of the protests, however, somewhat occults the demonstrations' social context. More important than the vectors of information were other factors that made the demonstrations possible. As my analysis of reactions to the events will show, this younger generation did use new vectors of transmission; but they resorted to culturally meaningful, established repertoires of the system to craft their message. The Internet and cell networks as such may thus perhaps only stand metonymically for the immediate fate of youth activism as a whole: due to the regime's control over the network infrastructure, it was relatively easy to just shut the networks down. Similarly, because of the youth activists' lack of social weight and reach, demonstrations were easily contained.

This brings me to my second point: we should be cautious about lumping together a very heterogeneous assemblage of social actors under the homogenizing label of the "disaffected urban youth." In fact, a multiplicity of interest groups started expressing their opposition in the roughly one-and-a-half years between the first antigovernment demonstration and the August 2012 elections. In addition to the war veterans and fighters demobilized in 1992, and the organized political parties, "the youth" comprised a great variety of backgrounds and motivations.[22] Some were the scions of the MPLA revolutionary bourgeoisie, the urban, upper-middle-class families traditionally affiliated with the regime; others were neighborhood activists from the poor *bairros* of Cazenga, Cacuaco, and Sambizanga. Some were university students; others, street vendors. And, as in other African contexts, the label "youth" (*jovem*) is a very fluid marker of identity in Angola, encompassing—also at the demonstrations—people ranging from their teenage years to their early forties.

Many of my younger informants who could tentatively be termed part of an "emerging urban middle class" lived in the peripheral, informal neighborhoods of Luanda under the direst material circumstances. It is thus crucial to remember what "the emerging middle class" means in Angola. We are not exactly talking about the euphoric "Africa rising" narrative touted by international financial institutions and some media, which mistakes impressive macroeconomic indicators for actual improvements in the everyday lives of citizens. In the *bairro*, services delivered by the state are absent, and any additional hardship—the illness of a family member or unusually heavy rains, for example—is immediately an existential threat. And yet these are the people who often accumulate jobs to make ends meet and sustain their family, and still find the energy and ambition to pursue higher education studies and improve their lives—friends and informants like Paulo, who, with three children at home, taught history in middle schools, volunteered in his church's youth department as an HIV/AIDS activist, and still made time to study law in the evenings; like Nelma, who lived in a compound of crooked wooden shacks populated by constantly drunken men in the heart of the Bairro Operario, raising and feeding her younger siblings and cousins and trying to keep them out of trouble, and who studied international relations in a private university in Luanda Sul in the evenings; or like Walter, who at thirty, had eight children from three different women, but had now "given a new direction to his life." Having started out as a stevedore (*estivador*) at the Cuca brewery at eighteen, he now worked as an independent handyman in Sambizanga and had just bought a plot of land in Luanda Sul to "create the conditions" and build a house for his family.

The normative expectations of democracy that those *jovens* expressed differ from the current dominant Angolan norm, influenced by substantive expectations of what a state could be and should do for its citizens. These alternative demands are voiced in comparisons with an idealized, earlier time of solidarity (socialism) or with other political spaces, which are seen as more responsive to citizens' needs.[23] They become especially salient in the context of Angola's record postwar macroeconomic growth and persistent social inequalities. Although Angola's political leaders constantly repeat the message of the miracle of reconstruction, the gains of stability, and the progress made since the end of the war, a majority of the population remains excluded from the benefits of peace. Peace then adds insult to injury: war gave the suffering a sense (or was at least used as a justification for hardship and sacrifice in official discourse); now, the frustrations of being excluded from this miracle of reconstruction are felt even more acutely.[24] When President dos Santos, in one of his rare public interviews, dismissed the protesters as "no more than three hundred frustrated youths who never managed to integrate into education or work," he betrayed either boundless cynicism or a deep misjudgment of Angolan realities.[25]

And yet in contrast to Egypt or Tunisia, where mass demonstrations and protests eventually swept away the sclerotic regimes of Mubarak and Ben Ali, these nascent articulations of citizenship—in the sense of politically conscious demands on the state—have so far failed to result in a substantial redefining of Angola's political and social order. Partly, I would argue, it is because this new middle class that was the driver of upheaval in other countries has not yet reached a critical mass in Angola; partly, it is because of its inherent precariousness: these acquisitions are still so recent and fragile that it is better to hold on to the little gains you have made than to risk everything in yet another *confusão*. Moreover, due to the partisan nature of the economy and limited access to education and jobs, social advancement very much depends on keeping a low profile politically and not challenging the system openly.[26]

More important, and beyond this slightly old-fashioned (and somewhat patronizing) argument that people need bread before they can care about politics, I contend that it is because the existing repertoires of political expression in Angola (i.e. the "culture of fear") that delimitate the parameters of the political in the system are deeply entrenched and hard to change overnight. More interesting than the nonevent of the demonstration are thus discursive and performative strategies deployed around it. As I demonstrate in the following analysis, the reactions of a vast array of social actors to a seemingly minor, but in the context of Angola momentous, event such as the announcement of an antigovernment demonstration follow a pattern of culturally significant discursive repertoires shaped by the experience of Angolan history, especially since the beginning of the independence struggle. So let us return to the question of hegemony, and what practice theory can tell us about pushing the boundaries of a hegemonic system.

Unpacking the Repertoires of Political Culture

In the following I explore how this call for demonstrations was framed and interpreted by a variety of social actors, and what that, in turn, can tell us about Angolan political culture. I focus on only three key repertoires here: the reference to political killings, the insertion into a revolutionary history, and the dominant discourse of peace and stability.

The Long Shadow of the 27 de Maio

The warning to stay at home and stock up on food was for most people linked directly to the experience of previous government repression of political dissent, notably the internal purges of the MPLA in 1977—the infamous 27 de Maio—and the mass killing of suspected UNITA supporters in Luanda after the 1992 elections (see chapter 2).

When the organizers of the demonstration defiantly stated that "They might kill some of us, but they cannot kill all of us," they consciously inserted themselves into a narrative framework of possible political martyrdom that referred to the purges of 1977. Government figures also used the specter of 1977 to allude, in only thinly veiled threats, to the regime's willingness to use force, when they warned that whoever went out into the streets to protest "would get some" (*vai apanhar*). Rather than criticizing and undermining the regime's authority, referring to the 27 de Maio was a memento of the regime's capacity to make people disappear and thus contributed to reinforcing the dominance of the MPLA.[27]

Among the population, the assumption that the government would simply kill the demonstrators predominated. During the weeks before the planned demonstration, many people echoed these sentiments of caution and fear, and several of my informants expected that some demonstrators would be killed. For example, in the week preceding 7 March, I met with three *mais velhos*, Armando, Martins, and Pereira, all in their late fifties. Armando and Pereira had both served with the FAPLA (the Popular Armed Liberation Forces of Angola, i.e. the National Army 1975–1991, from the Portuguese Forças Armadas Populares de Libertação de Angola) after independence. Armando, whom I had met in Sambizanga, had an impressive mustache and the easygoing causerie of a natural entrepreneur; Pereira was more guarded and had the bearing of a military man, always keeping his shades on; Martins, a white Angolan from Moxico had been, in his own words, "a member of the MPLA since I was five. I fought in the guerrilla for fifteen years—fifteen years, *sim senhora* [Yes Ma'am—a very Portuguese, slightly old-fashioned figure of speech to reinforce a statement], not fourteen years like the others: I started in 1960. The UPA [later FNLA, Angola's first liberation movement] and the others started in 1961, but me and my father, we started much earlier, that was the real guerrilla!" He thus asserted his authority through claims of active participation in the armed struggle and, despite his long affiliation with the MPLA, claimed an independent, earlier involvement in the anticolonial resistance. Like a running gag in a comedy of errors, these three gentlemen were always trying to pitch me their newest business ventures (a new diamond concession in Uíge; a surefire agricultural project in Lunda Norte; an NGO for community development) whenever we met, but they also always freely shared information and their opinions and, as Armando said, they knew "the dirty tricks [*malandrices*] of the MPLA very well."

When I asked them about the demonstration and the MPLA's counter-demonstration the following Saturday, Pereira just laughed and said: "This *manifestação pela paz* [the MPLA's demonstration for peace], that's just a case of a lot of wine," intimating quite accurately that the MPLA would, as usual, give out free alcohol, T-shirts, and other financial incentives to the population to participate. As for the antigovernment demonstration proper, he said, "The MPLA will kill ten, twenty people, and that will be it." The men then referred to the then ongoing events in Libya and remarked that there, Muʿammar Gaddhafi's fighter pilots preferred to desert to Malta rather than bomb their own population. In Angola, however, Pereira mused, "The pilots are idiots [*matumbos*]; they will really bomb them!" Armando concurred:

> I know this very well. It's better not to go out on that day. Before the 27 de Maio, they came from the 1° de Maio [Independence Square] to round up all those who were on their balconies. On the twenty-seventh I was in a building on [Avenida] Combatentes, on the fifth floor. They came and ordered us to come down. We did not go—we went down but left through the back entrance. They had posted the cannons of the Futungo [the president's residence outside the city in the 1980s, now a residential area of Luanda Sul] there—those who went there returned [*sairam*] as cadavers.

On the day of the demonstration, the fear of reprisals, fed by previous experience, kept most people who had previously voiced their support from appearing. As Lucas Pedro, a political activist and independent online journalist, explained, "On 7 March [2011] we did not go out into the streets, because all political leaders received death threats. There were sharpshooters positioned outside their houses. They used the same trick in '77 and in '92, but we could not risk losing all our cadres."

Conversely, this fear of reprisals served as a point of reference for younger Angolans to distance themselves from the generation of their parents, who were still afraid of protesting because of the memory of the purges: "We are no longer the Angolans of twenty years ago." Thus for many of the young activists, the 27 de Maio, long a portent of the closure of space for discussion and the crushing of the hopes of independence, has become a symbol of the broken promises of the liberation struggle. By using it, they subvert the dominant discourse of the end of the war as the Year Zero of independence. Whereas the government emphasizes economic growth, stability, and development, the 27 de Maio is used as a signifier for equality, social justice, and "people's power."

The Fighting People of Angola

It is therefore no coincidence that some of the youth demonstrators, like their grandparents and parents who fought for independence from Portugal, have assumed aliases or war names.[28] Some of these names are rooted in urban hip-hop codes (e.g., "Hexplosivo Mental" and "Brigadeiro Matafrakuxz"); others refer more directly to the independence struggle and to 1977—"Libertador" (Liberator), "Monstro Imortal" (a famous martyr of 1977), and indeed, "Nito Alves"—to symbolize that they are fighting for the "real independence" of the country, against the dictatorship of the old (*ditadura dos kotas*), the ossified leadership of a monopolistic party out of touch with their lived realities.[29]

I asked "Mbanza Hamza," one of the most visible youth activists and one of the "15+2" imprisoned in June 2015 (see epilogue), about their naming practices, to guard myself against over-interpretation. He explained how he chose his name:

> The name was born in a conversation with Mangovo Ngoyo and Lindomar Fregona, when we prepared the 7th of March [2011]. Mangovo wanted me to adopt a war name; I already had one but he said I needed another, more discreet or what! That's when he started suggesting a mountain of European, and some African names, Adão, Pedro Manuel, Hossi, Kanga, Castro, etc, etc. I thought of Mbanza Kongo [the historical seat of the Kongo kingdom] and said I would call myself Mbanza Manuel. Then I changed and said I wanted to be Mbanza va Nza, which literally means "a place in the world" ("Mbanza" in Kikongo means palace, place, soil, land, state, *sobado*, etc.), but it could also be interpreted as "remember me in the world."
>
> The word "ma Nza" reminded Lindomar—who is a Muslim—of the Arab warrior Hamza, brave and fearless, who was only defeated when his own comrades stabbed him in the back. So Hamza ended up a corruption of the Kikongo word va Nza—and not even just my own corruption, as in some versions of Kikongo the preposition "va" becomes "ha"—and so I continue to pay homage to the Arab warrior without

departing from the real meaning of the Kikongo phrase, "a place in the world."

This place would be our Angola, rescued from the clutches of oppression, dictatorship, the thievery and all other evils! This one place is the one that is reserved for us, where we will go and benefit from the pleasures of this blessed soil where we were born; where we will feel complete! And we will help the other peoples of the world to build their place, too, until we all finally have OUR PLACE IN THE WORLD![30]

This is precisely the kind of memory work, tying personal biographies to national narratives of destiny, that fills in the blanks in the master narrative that I described in chapter 2. Beyond inserting themselves in a revolutionary tradition, we can see in the use of a "real Angolan" name—a Kikongo name in Mbanza Hamza's case—how the question of *angolanidade*, which arguably was one of the motifs of the 27 de Maio, also plays into it. Although the call emphasized the nonracial character of the planned demonstration, assumptions about Angolanness and the ruling families—and about entitlement, legitimacy, and belonging—underpinned the call itself, as well as the reactions to it. In reactions to the call, people railed against the creole or Santomean cronies of dos Santos and his family and called on "real Angolans" to free themselves from this foreign domination. Conversely, MPLA leaders portrayed the demonstrators as "not real Angolans" and as stooges of foreign powers such as France.[31]

The Discourse of Stability

Beyond the ominous reference to the crushed demonstration (or coup attempt, according to the different interpretations) of 1977 and the claims to Angola's original revolutionary spirit, another leitmotif of Angolan politics recurs in these reactions, which is the discourse of stability I detailed in chapter 1. State media, especially *Jornal de Angola*, successfully equated a demonstration with an automatic return to war. The MPLA again highlighted its own central role in bringing peace and reconstruction and attacked opposition parties, claiming that they were secretly instigating the demonstration and thereby threatening to plunge the country into armed conflict again. Conveniently, in the week before the planned demonstration, news broke that a US vessel had been seized in the port of Lobito because it was carrying arms allegedly destined for Kenya.[32] The subtext was clear (and implied less than subtly by Rui Falcão, the then MPLA spokesman, at a press conference): UNITA was smuggling arms into the country to restart the war. Very skillfully, the impression was nurtured that any kind of protest meant a return to war, which of course resonated with widespread popular anxieties. Opposed to this possible *confusão*, the MPLA, especially in its personification of José Eduardo dos Santos as the Architect of Peace, was portrayed as the only guarantor of stability.

Whenever the political opposition accuses the government of something like electoral fraud, broken election promises, inactivity, policy failings, or the like, a common tactic (mentioned earlier) is for public media to give ample space to actors across the spectrum of "civil society" to decry the "lack of political maturity" and the "irresponsible positions" of the opposition that "jeopardize stability" and threaten the gains of peace. However, this discourse of stability opened up an arena of contestation in which the government could be challenged. By using slogans like *"Não há pão, só há paz!"* (There's no bread; there's only peace), mocking the omnipresent executive (see chapter 1) as *Zécutivo*—a pun on the president's first name, José/Zé—and calling dos Santos the Architect of Hunger (*O arquitecto da fome*) rather than the Architect of Peace, youth activists picked up and subverted for their own aims the dominant discourse of stability and peace, expressing their anger at how the postwar economic boom and reconstruction had passed most Angolans by. An MPLA campaign poster—itself recycling a slogan from the liberation struggle—that claimed, "We are millions, and no one can fight against millions" was photoshopped and circulated online as "We are thieves of millions, and whoever tries to steal from us will be caught."

As I have shown in previous chapters, relations of power in any society are diffuse and ubiquitous, and never as totalizing as power (*o poder*), embodied in a party, government, or individual political leader would have it. "Even in the most repressive regimes, political power is far more dispersed and transactional than is most often assumed" (Krohn-Hansen 2008, 8). However, mirroring the personalization of President dos Santos as the Architect of Peace, youth protesters in Angola focused their accusations on the president and his children. For them, the dos Santos family had come to embody all that was not well in Angola: the accumulation of economic and political power in the hands of a select few, the partisan nature of the judiciary, and the persistent social inequalities and socioeconomic misery in which most Angolans still lived (see chapters 4 and 5).

Despite the diversity of social actors that made up these youth protesters, the slogan *"32 é muito"* (32 [years in power] is too much/enough) thus galvanized the imagination of a very diverse range of actors. Real inequalities, contrasted with the perceived "new-richism" of the elite, served as rallying points: an insufficient number of study places, a lack of employment and affordable housing, an absence of services such as water, electricity, health, and schooling. "They say the war ended eight years ago; we just want to have a *normal* level of living and be able to buy food in a shop, and raise our children."[33] That kind of normality is increasingly out of reach for a majority of Angolans.

The 2012 Elections: *Batota* and Browbeating

Although the first demonstration (of 7 March 2011) was unsuccessful, commentators saw it as the start of more open criticism of the government. As a statement by "the Youth of Angola" published on the Internet on 4 March 2011, said, "We lost our fear, mother."[34] Two further demonstrations in May 2011, one of which was a memorial march for the victims of the 27 de Maio, gathered between two and three hundred people each, while the police stood by. Emboldened by this relative success and the absence of violence, several loose, nonpartisan associations of students and artists—the Revolutionary Movement for Social Intervention (Movimento Revolucionário de Intervenção Social, MRIS), the Revolutionary Student Movement (Movimento Revolucionário Estudantil, MRE), and the Associative Revolutionary Movement (Movimento Associativo Revolucionário, MAR)—called for another, larger demonstration against poverty and the rule of President dos Santos. Some of the activists established an Internet presence under the name Central Angola 7311, in allusion to the date of the first demonstration. The MRIS later reported that Bento Kangamba, the MPLA's "entrepreneur of the youth" and owner of Kabuscorp do Palanca soccer club, had offered them money in return for cancelling the demonstration.

On Saturday, 3 September, a few hundred protesters gathered on Independence Square. Under the watchful eyes of the Rapid Intervention Police (PIR), the protesters decided to walk downtown toward the National Assembly and the presidential palace. They had advanced less than a kilometer down Rua Joaquim Kapango when unknown men in civilian clothing started shouting abuse and throwing stones at the police, passersby, and cars. The police intervened quickly and started to beat up the demonstrators. Journalists were also attacked and taken into custody. A foreign reporter of Deutsche Welle was assaulted by plainclothes security agents who confiscated his cell phones, camera, and recorder. Fifty demonstrators were arrested, taken away to unknown destinations, and held over the weekend without contact to their families or lawyers.[35]

On Monday, 5 September, twenty-one of them were scheduled to appear in front of the Police Tribunal of Luanda for a summary judgment; the others detainees were released. However, the process was postponed to Thursday, 8 December, on which day a number of demonstrators, including the then secretary-general of JURA (UNITA's youth wing), Mfuca Muzemba, appeared in front of the tribunal to argue for the release of the accused. The police—the rapid intervention and canine brigades, who were deployed en masse downtown—drove the demonstrators away on the pretext that they were impeding the traffic. The demonstrators then walked down to the Marginal, the main road that lines the Bay of Luanda, and proceeded toward the US embassy to hand in a letter of protest there. Before they came anywhere near the US embassy, however, they were taken away by the police. These detainees later reported that the questioning aimed at proving that France had orchestrated the protests. The process against the demonstrators of 3 September, meanwhile, was adjourned to the following day, when witnesses were heard. Several of the witnesses later reported intimidation attempts or physical aggression in front of the court, and the judge refused to admit video evidence from the defense.[36]

On Monday, 12 September, seventeen of the accused were sentenced to jail terms of between forty-five days and three months. Denying any wrongdoing, the police argued at the hearings—unsuccessfully, because their statements contradicted each other—that the students had started the violence and disorder. They also claimed that they had arrested the second group of demonstrators en route to the US embassy because it been the anniversary of 9/11 and there had been terror warnings.[37] The judiciary demonstrated its subordination to the executive—the judge, Simão Bento, was still studying for his law degree at university at the time of the trial and, instructed "by superior orientation," refused to admit several video recordings that would have disproved the police's statements. The MPLA declared that the youths were being misled by unscrupulous adults and should focus on the reconstruction of the country instead, "as there is much to do."[38] They also denounced the political profiteering (*aproveitamento político*) of the irresponsible opposition, after the main opposition party UNITA protested against the detention of the UNITA youth leader. The state media also decried international interference and displayed its staunch support for the government: on 9 September 2011 the director of *Jornal de Angola*, José Ribeiro, said the Portuguese had "lost their minds" to say that dos Santos should leave power, suggesting that "they, more than anyone else, should put forward his name for the Nobel Peace Prize."[39]

From then on, the rhetoric of peace and stability versus war and chaos that was deployed in speeches and the media was complemented by more repressive tactics and the increasing use of force, a pattern that continued unabated until the time of writing (see epilogue). Despite this repression, protests intensified in the period immediately preceding the 31 August 2012 elections.[40] Emboldened by the youth protests, war veterans, mainly those demobilized since 1992—former MPLA and UNITA soldiers—marched on the presidential palace of Cidade Alta on 7 June 2012 to demand the long overdue payment of pensions from their "commander-in-chief," dos Santos.[41] They were impeded from accessing the space in front of the palace, but the Army's chief of staff, General Nunda, promised to look into the issue. A second veteran demonstration, on 20 June, was violently dispersed by the police using tear gas and live ammunition, leading to the deaths of two protesters.[42] The government promised to address the grievances of the ex-soldiers, although the Commission of Angolan Ex-Soldiers later stated that their demands had not been met.

Youth demonstrations in Luanda and several provincial capitals continued regularly but were met with increasingly violent repression, with protesters being abducted and tortured or intimidated.[43] Demonstrations were systematically broken up by police squads and plainclothes thugs armed with homemade pepper sprays and iron bars, who assaulted demonstrators with complete impunity under the eyes of the police. The houses of organizers were raided by these heavies (*caenches*), who later defended their cause on prime-time national television posing as "Association of concerned citizens for peace and stability." To the degree that demands for change turned more vocal, the regime became less tolerant of criticism and resorted to increasingly violent measures (HRW, 2012a; 2012b; 2012c).

The two major opposition parties, UNITA and PRS, successfully lobbied in parliament for a more independent composition of the National Electoral Commission (CNE). However, the Magistrates' Tribunal then appointed Suzana Inglês, a veteran member of the MPLA's female wing OMA (Organização da Mulher Angolana), as head of the CNE. The opposition rightly argued that Inglês's appointment failed to fulfill four of the five requirements, especially those of being an active judicial magistrate (Inglês had not been active as a judge since the 1990s) and politically independent. The Magistrates' Court reiterated the legality of her appointment, and Inglês stayed on, passing regulations such as allowing police and armed forces to cast absentee ballots ahead of the voting day and excluding opposition parties and the media from attending CNE meetings. However, as Inglês's appointment increasingly became a focal point for protests, the Supreme Court finally overturned her nomination in May, allegedly after having received the presidential placet, and appointed André da Silva Neto, an acting judge loyal to the regime in her stead.[44]

Opposition parties, initially cautious in supporting the youth demonstrations, also started finding their voice, echoing the protesters' calls, attacking the executive's track record, and demanding social justice, a fairer distribution of wealth, and the holding of transparent elections. UNITA successfully mobilized two hundred thousand people for a rally in Luanda in May 2012 to demand fair elections. In parallel, the newly formed CASA-CE (Convergência Ampla de Salvação de Angola–Coligação Eleitoral: Broad Convergence for the Salvation of Angola–Electoral Coalition), led by UNITA dissident Abel Chivukuvuku, attracted candidates from across the political spectrum and energized the debate, aiming to break up the entrenched MPLA–UNITA duality. Chivukuvuku toured municipalities and *bairros* on foot or on the back of a moto-taxi (*kupapata*), a rare sight in a country where politicians usually travel behind smoked car windows. However, smaller opposition parties, which might have attracted support in urban areas, faced administrative obstacles and discrimination: the Constitutional Court excluded eighteen of the twenty-seven registered parties from running, including the outspoken Bloco Democrático and the Partido Popular of the "people's lawyer" David Mendes.

Although party funding was reduced compared to the 2008 elections, the MPLA, thanks to its access to state coffers and the public media, mobilized its powerful public relations machinery. It cannibalized opposition demands for more equitable wealth distribution, running under the slogan, "Angola— growing more to distribute better" and promising to create a million new jobs and construct two million public housing units. The latter sounded to many Angolans like a vacuous promise considering the government had failed to build anything near the million houses it had promised to build ahead of the 2008 elections.[45] In an attempt to present himself as a man of the people, the president toured the country to inaugurate bridges and schools wearing short-sleeved African shirts or the red-and-black party garb instead of his usual dark business suits. *Jornal the Angola* editorials singing the praises of the executive read increasingly like fiction or accounts of a parallel universe.[46]

Domestic and foreign observers braced themselves for widespread protests around the elections, but the weeks leading to the elections were strangely calm, and polling day itself was a remarkably muted affair. In major cities, the day was marked by widespread abstention, which reached 40 percent nationwide including the invalid or empty bulletins (compared to 12.6 percent abstention in 2008). Some interpreted this as a sign of the population's dissatisfaction and justified distrust in elections to actually change the distribution of power in Angola, but opposition parties and youth activists complained about severe irregularities. In Luanda, where more voters were registered than in 2008, abstention reached 44 percent but was concentrated in those municipalities that had seen the most protests in the previous year, and where the opposition vote was expected to be strongest. Voters complained about being turned away at the polling stations and about the presence of MPLA delegates to oversee the process; later in-depth analyses of the elections spoke of targeted voter disenfranchisement (Roque 2013). Rumors about dead voters on the electoral register and the impossibility of verifying the electronic counting of the votes were further possible sources of errors; domestic observers were excluded—the African Union and Southern African Development Community observer missions approved the electoral process. Local human rights organizations also reported the disappearance or arrest of several activists just ahead of the elections, which effectively muted popular protests.

Activists of the Central Angola website successfully ran a parallel monitoring system, allowing citizens to send text messages about the voting process that were published in real time on a website. Based on parallel counts, opposition parties UNITA and CASA-CE lodged a protest with the CNE immediately after the elections, which was dismissed equally swiftly for procedural reasons. A subsequent appeal to the Constitutional Court was also turned down.

The elections resulted in a strong victory for the MPLA, which took 71 percent of the vote, or 175 seats of the 220-strong national assembly. Due to the constitutional changes of 2010, José Eduardo dos Santos was automatically elected president and sworn in at a relatively low-key ceremony two weeks after the elections. Despite the indications of fraud, UNITA doubled its number of representatives to thirty-two, and the newly formed CASA-CE took a respectable eight seats. PRS and FNLA were reduced to three and two seats respectively. The ruling party and state media unsurprisingly interpreted the MPLA's electoral victory as a plebiscite on President dos Santos's continued thirty-three-year rule and lauded the mature vote for peace and stability.

Conclusions

Some Angola scholars said the demonstrations represented the first "breaking of the fear barrier" (Roque 2013, 2) and "the awakening of a counter-public and the dawning of a citizenship revolution" (Faria 2013, 293). I agree that neither the significance nor the impact of the youth demonstrations on Angolan political culture can be overstated, far exceeding the small number of people who actually protested. In Angola, where citizens and foreign observers have long seen any expression of independent political opinion stifled by a culture of fear, the hitherto unthinkable antigovernment protests had a liberating effect on public political debate. It is thus understandable that long-time observers of Angola started to harbor high hopes for political change (and I will not exempt myself from such feelings). However, in terms of analysis, it is important not to lapse into activist or policy mode when analyzing developments that could be romanticized as "the dawn of a citizen revolution" in Angola.

So why were the demonstrations important, despite their relative lack of success at the 2012 elections in bringing about change? In this chapter, I have shown how younger social actors in Luanda tapped into existing, culturally significant repertoires of Angolan political culture—such as adopting war names and revolutionary rhetoric—to make sense of, and try to change the situation. They manipulated and subverted these established codes to articulate their interests and, in doing so, modified the parameters of the political. Identifying the repertoires of Angolan political culture that were mobilized is, I think, an apt illustration of ideology in the Gramscian sense, as it shows how the dominated and the dominant jointly inhabit and recreate their lifeworlds.

In this perspective, even the most explicitly oppositional positions (i.e., those that claimed readiness for martyrdom) contributed to the social reproduction of hegemony by reinforcing a belief in the regime's nefariousness, omnipotence, and capacity to destroy lives. However, if we look at it from the perspective of practice theory, the adoption and subversion of dominant codes was also successful in pushing the boundaries of the field: by speaking out against the culture of fear, youth activists shifted the confines of what was thinkable and sayable in public. The impact of these youth demonstrations, I would suggest, is insufficiently captured by the limited number of actual demonstrators; as in the tale of the emperor's clothes, it has more to do with the public questioning of the postwar consensus of peace and stability. This in itself was disquieting enough for the regime that it increased violent repression and judicial prosecution of demonstrators ahead of the 2012 elections, and was continuing to do so until the time of writing (see epilogue).

Because, at least for now, elections in Angola (and in many other Southern African postliberation regimes) have entrenched the status quo rather than changed it, I suggest that instead of focussing on extraordinary events like elections and the violent repression of protests, it might be more fruitful in the long run as anthropologists to observe how ordinary citizens tentatively articulate political demands and how they negotiate these demands within a socially established framework of political culture. That citizens express such substantive aspirations even though they fear violent repression and still remember government violence and crackdowns challenges the one-dimensional idea that a culture of fear pervades Angola, impeding any form of talking or even thinking about politics.

Conclusion

Making the System Work

       I postulated in the introduction that Luanda serves as a "laboratory of the global" (Piot 2010, 18). In several Southern African countries—Mozambique, Zimbabwe, Namibia, and South Africa—a generational shift is replacing the historic leaders of the independence struggle. At the same time, the hegemonic strategies of developmental, postdemocratic regimes are reaching their limits; the hitherto successful combination of financial largesse for a select few and repression of dissent for the many is no longer sufficient to mitigate growing popular discontent over the broken promises of economic improvement for all. Also, with widening access to global information and a new, educated generation coming of age, many sub-Saharan African countries bear strong parallels to prerevolution Arab countries. As most recently in Burkina Faso, DRC, and Burundi, the perpetuation in power of long-serving presidents further heightens these growing social tensions. And finally, the monopolization of economic power for the benefit of a small, tight-knit circle, more often than not articulated around family ties, is evinced in exemplary ways in Luanda, but by no means unique or specific to African states only—indeed, it has been argued that the seizing of positions of command and control by a "red aristocracy," a coalition of elite families, is increasingly the norm in nominally socialist nations and a proven means of regime survival (Monday 2011).[1]

More worryingly, the authoritarian tendencies inherent to the very nature of globalized late capitalism can also be seen and felt more acutely in the hitherto protected, liberal Western democracies: the onslaught on the welfare state and workers' rights in the name of austerity, the subservience of public politics to private economic interests, the curtailing of civil liberties for the sake of security, the resort to facile populist reflexes and the scapegoating of foreigners, and the increasingly militarized restrictions on the free movement of people. Following the argument of Jean and John Comaroff (2012), we should see the global South, and Africa especially, as precursors of global dynamics of stateness and capitalism, and accordingly start building our "Theory from the South."

Seen in that perspective, living in Luanda often feels like being in a dystopian science-fiction movie.[2] Because of the turbocharged economic growth of the postwar years and the MPLA's nearly unparalleled hold on political and economic power during this time, Angola is in many ways ahead of the curve. It exemplifies and magnifies societal and political developments that find their parallels, in local and attenuated ways, not just in the subregion but across the globe.

Rather than simply engaging in a symptomology of neo-authoritarian rule, I have made in this book the case for an ethnographically grounded, critical analysis of the coproduction of hegemony. Working through the emic understanding of contemporary Angolan society as a system that needs to be understood, mastered, and managed to successfully navigate daily life, I have discussed both the symbolic and material affects of power in people's lives. By focusing on the relational, sensuous, and reciprocal dimensions of the relation between people and power, I have charted the transactional elements of the system.

It is by looking at how and why certain discourses and practices are mobilized, and why they resonate in specific contexts and at certain moments in time, that we can discern the contours of hegemony. By revealing the multiple linkages between social actors commonly understood as the dominant and the dominated, we can then think beyond the binaries of resistance and complicity, drawing out a more subtle account of the shared webs of meaning, beyond the cultivation of consent by the dominant. This allows us to analyze both the everyday practices and the popular imaginaries that make up this common framework.

I started my analysis by examining, in chapter one, the master narrative by which the nation "seeks to govern the production of all other socially constructed meanings" (Primorac 2007, 434). As I argued there, memory politics in Angola take on a slightly different form than it does in its neighboring countries. Because the MPLA's claim to historical legitimacy is tenuous because it was one of three competing anticolonial liberation movements instead of the sole representative of the Angolan people; because of its ambivalent role as one of the parties to the Angolan conflict, its instrumentalization of the past is perhaps less straightforward than it is in other contexts.

After conquering peace in 2002, the long civil war—a period of ambiguity and destruction—has been firmly relegated to the past, and the government has set out to rebuild the country and finally fulfill the promises of development, progress, and modernity of independence. This has led to the creation of a very forward-looking narrative of reconciliation through national reconstruction, and the reconfiguration of the MPLA as the party of peace and stability, with President dos Santos as the Architect of Peace.

The project of reconstructing the New Angola is then materialized in the amnesiac narrative of the urban reconstruction drive, by which disturbing reminders of the *confusão* of wartime—including the masses of urban poor—are driven out of the city center to make way for the vision of a new, shiny, African Dubai.[3] However, the elimination of the Angolan conflict in public debate, as well as the destruction of its physical remains in the cityscape of Luanda, cannot erase the "vernacular memories" of that period (cf. Silverstein 2002), which become more important exactly because of this silencing and people's individual emotional attachment to them.

In chapter 2, I explored the entanglement of subjectivities with place through the affect that places, or rather visible absences—holes in the cityscape, gaps in the narrative—provoke. By exploring the affective space of Sambizanga through the eyes and narratives of its residents, I argued that because history in a postconflict environment like Angola is "liminal and incomplete" (Bryant 2013), and healing scenarios are inapplicable due to the reduction of reconciliation to a technical issue, certain places and events intrude in and unsettle people's experiences and biographies. The visible absences and holes both in the physical surroundings and in the official narrative become intertwined with and impact on people's subjectivities, with specific places exuding affect and evoking "spatial melancholia" (Navaro-Yashin 2009, 15–16). Place ties together those very disparate and unsettling memories of key events, which are then stabilized in narratives or though "discursive somatization" (Oushakine 2006). These emblematic memories serve as an anchor for the self and as a moral compass by which to assess the present situation. The way people position themselves within the system is shaped by affects like fear, spatial melancholia, or nostalgia for the modernity promised at independence.

Thus although the discourse of stability and reconstruction that I disassembled in chapter 1 is clearly a master narrative that serves dominant political and economic interests, it is not simply hegemony imposed from above; it would not work if the call for peace and tranquility did not also resonate deeply with a population wary of a return to war. In many ways, the high modernist project of national reconstruction and the amnesiac idea of 2002 as the Year Zero of Angolan independence, where promises of progress, growth, and international influence are finally fulfilled, thus feeds from and back into the nostalgia for the promises of independence expressed by my informants in chapter 2.

Because the gaps in the narrative are enmeshed with people's subjectivities, the work of the past in the present is also sedimented in the body. For example, the experience of the ubiquity of the security service (*segurança*) shapes habits, modes of public behavior, and the limits of what can be said about politics in the open, and leads people to speak in allusions only and to skillfully read between the lines. As such, many people very adroitly use the language of officialdom, deploying a technical vocabulary of economic growth and often hyper-formalized phrase-mongering and newspeak in certain public contexts. Although they formally toe the line of the publicly acceptable, they still manage to convey their sense of dissatisfaction to an audience attuned to the subtle shifts of meaning that political buzzwords such as "distribution," "social justice," or "economic growth" can assume.[4] Or, in the case of the youth demonstrators in chapter 6, they redeploy the MPLA's historic vocabulary of the anticolonial liberation struggle to criticize the ruling party's hegemonic project, adopting war names or referring to political martyrdom, which, because of a very forward-looking dominant perspective on national history and reconstruction, assumes added importance and impact, both as an explanatory model for the present and as a strategic tool for mobilization.

If we take hegemony as a lived, constantly remade shared culture, it is by looking at the production of the political not in institutions but in its "multiple metamorphoses" (Navaro-Yashin 2002, 3) that we can understand how people's actions and discourses can at the same time be subversive and participate in and perpetuate existing power structures. In a context where politics is still often too sensitive a topic for open discussion, rumors quickly gain traction and currency. Although these often express a vernacular criticism, they also reinforce the idea of an omnipresent power that can disrupt people's lives.

At the same time, political claims and ideas are translated into the realm of the apolitical, and expressed in circumlocutory ways, through seemingly innocuous, or less charged idioms—in Angola, through notions of race, family, or social ascension. The next two chapters thus looked at how and why people make specific claims or mobilize certain repertoires at particular moments, and why these claims work in the context of Angola (Hangen 2005, 52; Kaarsholm 2012, 357). Any such analysis must take into account the historicity and cultural embeddedness of such claim-making. In chapter 3 I examined the ways in which the idea of *angolanidade* is deployed by different actors. As the analysis shows, *angolanidade* can be seen a subversive discourse and a mode of criticizing an elite historically connoted with foreignness to make sense of and denounce its apparent neglect of "the Angolan people." Because race and class are intimately interlaced, however, people shift in and out of different categories situationally; thus Angolanness is also a way of reinscribing through modes of speech and bodily habits existing cleavages between the "urban, educated, cosmopolitan city" over the "stupid natives" (*povo matumbo*) of the bush. This complicates a one-dimensional reading as oppositional discourse. Similarly, in chapter 4, the language of family and tradition is invoked for multiple, simultaneous, and contradictory purposes: although traditional forms of familial and political authority are evoked as a form of criticism of a government failing to fulfill its obligations, real or imagined family links are also deployed as a very situational strategy to make the system work through the activation of *cunhas*, or personal relations. This allows us to nuance and complicate mechanistic and one-dimensional readings of such social relations as patronage.

The *cunhas* also bring us back to the symbolic and material dimensions of the system. These links of familiarity have a material basis in the family networks that make up Luandan society. They also have a material impact in the sense that their mobilization directly affects the outcomes of people's administrative procedures. At the same time, this only works because of the symbolic dimension of intimacy and hierarchy. As such, the symbolism of family networks, due to people's reliance on *cunhas*, does produce and reproduce authority; but it also invites transgressions, both as a criticism of power, as well as a subversive practice for, personal betterment (cf. Wedeen 1999, 4).

The intertwining of the symbolic and material dimensions of the system was also the main concern of chapter 5. There, I analyzed in greater detail practices and imaginaries of moneymaking, social ascension, and success, as well as the notions of justice and legitimacy that are expressed through these. This, I argued, allows us to look at the aspirational, agentive character of the aesthetics of power in the New Angola and how these imaginaries of success and social status are dialogically constructed. By looking at how people actively seek out and employ avenues for social mobility, I further nuanced the idea of hegemony as something under which people are acted upon. Indeed, as I showed in the chapter, the dominant and the dominated inhabit the same normative worldview and discursive space, and engage in the reciprocal manipulation of discourses. The immediatist spirit works at a symbolic and a material level, drawing the outlines of the discursive field in which people negotiate access to economic and political resources. Strategies of affiliation with the "party of successful entrepreneurs" are in that sense not just economic; they are also political statements, representing claims to inclusion in the MPLA's dominant, exclusionist nation-building project.

However, as I argue in chapter 6, there are also limits to the system and to the hegemonic ideology, in the Gramscian sense, of stability and economic growth that underpins it. Here, I looked at recent events that disturbed the ordinary working of the system, by actively criticizing the socioeconomic circumstances of the population, and identifying the ills of society with the *sistema dos Santos*. The impact of the youth demonstrations, I argued, is insufficiently captured by the limited number of actual demonstrators; as in the tale of the emperor's clothes, it has more to do with the public questioning of the postwar consensus. More striking perhaps, even the most oppositional positions deployed in these antigovernment protests tapped into existing, culturally significant discursive repertoires to make sense of the situation, manipulating and subverting them to articulate their interests. Identifying the elements of the system that were mobilized then tied back to the various facets analyzed separately in the chapters before, showing again how the dominated and the dominant jointly inhabit and recreate their lifeworlds. Thus, although they ultimately remained ineffective in significantly influencing electoral outcomes, the youth protests shifted the boundary of the acceptable of what can be spoken publicly about politics. This then sketches out the possibility of change within a system that sets strict limits to the open expression of different political opinions.

Making the System Work

Based on my fieldwork and on the stories of my informants, my argument has been shaped by a set of key conceptual assumptions, which I would like to restate here in three points. First, both the dominant and the dominated are constantly jointly remaking the system and both are thus caught up in the same webs of meaning, the discursive framework that delineates what can be said and thought publicly. Thus elements that inform the system, like the often-quoted culture of fear, affect social actors commonly understood to be at opposite ends of the social spectrum. That is, the powerful and the powerless are entangled in the dominant ideology in similar ways. This, I think, helps refine our understanding of hegemony, not as something produced by a dominant group, but as something jointly created, enacted, and lived out by very diverse members of a polity.

Second, the way people position themselves and negotiate these everyday politics is informed fundamentally by the contingencies of living in Luanda. This includes material contingencies like the daily *confusão* of traffic, the high costs of living, and dealing with a cumbersome bureaucracy. But it is also deeply shaped by the historicity and cultural embeddedness of social relations in Angola—between the people and power, between the city and the countryside, between the youth (*jovens*) and the elders (*kotas*). Thus any analysis of a state such as Angola must investigate the connections between the symbolism of the state—cultural forms and processes—and historically constituted systems of inequality and power (Krohn-Hansen and Nustad 2005, 11).

Third, because people are well aware of their complicity in the system, this leads to the formation of often very ambivalent political subjectivities. Unease and dissent, as well as open opposition (though still limited, in most cases, to private spaces), coexist with affirmation, aspiration, and desire, which are all expressed through the system. Here, we should not see people as simply passively bearing the weight of a dominant discourse. Rather, through relational "inventions of the everyday"—that is, through popular practices such as *cunhas*, gossiping, jokes, and spatial mobility—people navigate the complexities of daily life and manage the symbolic and material dimensions of the system.

What this analysis reveals is the agentive, creative, subversive, and aspirational character of these political subjectivities. Contrary to a more Afro-pessimistic take on African political culture, people creatively use the elements of the system to work it: they invoke hierarchy to dodge a police fine, mobilize personal connections for individual advancement, or position themselves vis-à-vis power by relating their individual biographies to an official discourse on national history. By retelling private memories that may fit in or jar with the master narrative of reconstruction, they then express not only alternative versions of history but also alternative political visions of what Angola is, or could be.

Epilogue
Reconfiguring the System

> If the ruling class has lost its consensus, i.e. is no longer "leading" but only "dominant," exercising coercive force alone, this means precisely that the great masses have become detached from their traditional ideologies, and no longer believe what they used to believe previously, etc. The crisis consists precisely in the fact that the old is dying and the new cannot be born; in this interregnum a great variety of morbid symptoms appear.
>
> Antonio Gramsci, *Selection from the Prison Notebooks*

> *A luta continua* (The struggle continues)
>
> Historic MPLA slogan

We can observe in Angola, since the 2012 elections, a great variety of morbid symptoms. Indeed, the MPLA's electoral victory at the polls was interpreted as a plebiscite in favor of President dos Santos's continued hold on to power.[1] Any propensity to engage in meaningful dialogue with the political opposition disappeared, and any manifestation of discontent with the status quo would henceforth be seen as being against the will of "a majority of all Angolans" and as a challenge to the regime's authority, to be met with the full coercive force of state power. It would appear that the cultivation of consent is reaching its limits, with a growing number of citizens questioning the dominant ideology, and that the regime increasingly relies on the armor of coercion to ensure its survival.

Since the end of the main period of fieldwork for this book (October 2011), things have certainly been in flux in Angola. I have followed events from a distance, so this epilogue offers no firsthand account of events. However, having had access to media, social media, mail, and telephone communication with informants, and to screening interviews with Angolan asylum seekers, I give here a very brief summary of subsequent political developments to provide the reader with a further perspective on the ways the system is being remade and reproduced in a moment of crisis. I also sketch out the possibility of change, through the system, from an Angolan perspective.

In November 2013, over a year after António Alves Kamulingue and Isaías Cassule, war veterans and protest organizers, had disappeared, a document was leaked from the Ministry of Interior that detailed in gruesome detail how the two men had been abducted by agents of the state security and information service, tortured to death, and thrown into the crocodile-infested Bengo river.[2]

Following the token dismissal of the Minister of Interior and the opening of an official investigation, seen as insufficient by the family members of the disappeared, UNITA called for a peaceful demonstration on 23 November, demanding the resignation of President dos Santos and stating that the killings were but the last in a long line of crimes perpetrated by the MPLA (including the 27 de Maio). This latter part of the call opened UNITA up to counterattacks, considering the party has never squarely addressed its own violence against civilians during the Angolan conflict. Nonetheless, UNITA's call was endorsed by the other opposition parties—CASA-CE, PRS, and Bloco Democrático—as well as by the "revolutionary youth activists" introduced in chapter 6.

The authorities reacted in predictable fashion, following a well-established script. The police strongly warned against any "illegal" demonstrations, while the political bureau of the MPLA issued a stern statement that, although it condemned the killing of the activists as a "heinous criminal act," strongly discouraged its militants and the population at large from joining the demonstration and asked citizens to let the judicial institutions "calmly do their work." It also denounced UNITA's "irresponsibility" and "lack of respect" for attacking "the country's highest Magistrate, his Excellency the President of the Republic, José Eduardo dos Santos" and causing instability that threatened to "drag the country back to war."[3] A *Jornal de Angola* editorial stated that although freedom of expression was an inalienable value of democracy, no one could ignore the will of the majority, which had voted for the MPLA, or question the independence of the judiciary, demonstrated by the inquiry into the killings. A column published by the Angolan news agency Angop reiterated that Angola's future was rosy and that it was "unanimous" that the enormous progress since the end of the war was the result of hard work that should convince the greatest skeptics. Dissent in dialogue was fine, the piece said, "but no one should . . . obfuscate the glorious moments of the conquest of independence, tarnished by a war that lacerated the country, luckily overcome by the current climate of peace."[4] Finally, the MPLA's youth wing, the JMPLA, "discovered" that its founding anniversary was, in fact, 23 November, not 14 April as previously thought (and celebrated).[5] This gave the police a further excuse to "prevent disruptions" of the JMPLA rally, which had allegedly been announced to authorities much earlier than UNITA's protest march.

On 23 November 2013, Luanda then awoke to a "state of siege."[6] In the early morning, the police surrounded opposition party headquarters and arrested those present, invoking "*orientações superiores*"; in the Coqueiros neighborhood, a leader of CASA-CE's youth department, Manuel Hilberto de Carvalho "Ganga" was shot and killed by the presidential guard (UGP) for allegedly trying to "breach the security perimeter of the presidential palace" while distributing leaflets.[7] Several hundred people who had gathered for the demonstration were dispersed by the police using tear gas, and over three hundred people were arrested.[8] Armed police also surrounded UNITA's headquarters in Bié, Bengo, Benguela, Cabinda, Cunene, Kuando Kubango, and Namibe and prevented any gatherings in the provinces.[9] The next day, a protest by street vendors against police harassment was violently broken up. And on 27 November 2013, a funeral procession for Hilberto Ganga, the murdered party activist, gathered over a thousand people marching toward the Santa Ana cemetery. After a quiet start, the procession increasingly turned into a protest rally, with people chanting "Zédú, assassin!" The funeral march was stopped by armed police with tear gas and water cannons near the Congolenses market, and, after opposition leaders agreed to send people home, only the closest family members were allowed to proceed to the cemetery.

Interviewed on the following day, the Angolan activist and investigative journalist Rafael Marques quoted a street vendor standing by the demonstration, who said "the people of 26 November are no longer the same as the people of 23 November—Angola has changed!"[10] However, the concerted crackdown on this first attempt to organize a peaceful rally, which would have joined (opposition) parties across the board with the more loosely organized "youth revolutionaries," made it clear that the regime would protect its interests with all the means at its disposal.

Since then, the social, economic, and political climate in Angola has only deteriorated further. Following the drop in crude oil prices on the world market in the third quarter of 2014, the Angolan government has had to revisit its budgets, cutting public expenditure by one third for 2015, and taking up new loans and credit lines from various private and state creditors. From January 2015, the economy declined drastically, with tumbling kwanza rates and rising fuel and food prices severely affecting the great majority of the population.[11] Then an internal report revealed that state oil company, Sonangol, was "technically broke" due to its unsustainable operational model. Indeed, Sonangol, long held as the lone "island of competence" in Angola's political-economic landscape (Soares de Oliveira 2007, 595), had been increasingly hollowed out by the systematic outsourcing to subcontractors of core services, most of which followed the immediatist logic of over-invoicing and underperforming.[12] However, rather than admitting any serious economic crisis and facing up to the fact that there had been very little policy learning from the similar but shorter 2008/9 crisis, the government unleashed the most violent persecution of "internal enemies" since the end of the war, indicative of how distrustful the regime had become of anyone who might publicly query and undermine its master narrative.

In mid-April 2015, police and military forces killed an as yet unknown number of adherents of the Adventist offshoot sect A Luz do Mundo (The Light of the World) in Huambo province. The leader of the sect, José Julino Kalupeteca, had been encamped at Monte Sumi with about four thousand followers, singing, praying, and awaiting the end of times. A week after Kalupeteca's followers peacefully turned away the state's census agents, the police returned to arrest Kalupeteca, and a violent confrontation ensued between security forces and Kalupeteca's personal guard, during which, officially, nine police officers and thirteen civilians were killed. Kalupeteca was severely beaten and arrested. Government forces then sealed off the hill as a "military area," as reports of survivors emerged alleging the massacre of over a thousand people, including women and children.[13] The Minister of Justice, Rui Mangueira, furiously rejected calls by the UN High Commissioner for Human Rights to allow for an independent inquiry into the events, saying the country would not accept "that its sovereign institutions be attacked from external institutions," and demanding an apology from the United Nations.[14] In April 2016, Kalupeteca was sentenced by a Huambo court to twenty-eight years in jail for the homicide of nine police officers by a Huambo court.[15]

On 20 June 2015, the police in Luanda arrested thirteen of the youth activists that had been organizing protests since 2011, including Luaty Beirão, Manuel Nito Alves, and Mbanza Hamza. The activists had been meeting in a private house in Vila Alice to discuss two books that outlined strategies for peaceful resistance to oppressive regimes. Their houses were searched and their belongings confiscated. Two days later, the journalist-activist Domingos da Cruz (the author of one of the two books) and an unrelated soldier from the air force were also arrested to give credence to the government's allegations that the group were plotting a coup to overthrow President dos Santos and had received 100 million dollars from "foreign powers" to do so.[16] Two female activists, Rosa Conde and Laurinda Gouveia, were also indicted as co-conspirators but awaiting trial without detention. First the families of the accused, then a larger part of Luandan society, started calling for the release of the "15+2" activists. A protest march by the mothers and wives of the detainees in August was violently repressed by the police with batons and police dogs; further protests were declared "unconstitutional" by Luanda governor Graciano Domingos.[17]

However, when Luaty Beirão's health deteriorated significantly after twenty days of hunger strike, larger parts of Luandan society started identifying with the detainees' cause, including many of the middle class traditionally affiliated with the MPLA, who hitherto had preferred to stay out of politics: *"somos todos revús"* (We are all revolutionaries) signalled a marked change in the popular reception of the revolutionary movement.[18] Prominent personalities, musicians, authors, artists, and politicians—beyond the handful of known "dissidents," and including old, long-time MPLA supporters—came out in defense of the activists. A peaceful vigil in front of the Sagrada Família church in central Luanda congregated a (for Angolan circumstances) impressive number of about two hundred people. The gathering dispersed voluntarily after the police entered the square with dogs and water cannons; a follow-up vigil at the São Domingos church the following week was, however, violently dispersed by the police, who entered the church during service to arrest demonstrators.

When the authorities finally announced a date for the beginning of the trial, an almost fatally weakened Beirão gave up his hunger strike after a symbolic thirty-six days, one day for every year President dos Santos had been in power. The trial of the activists started on 16 November. Much like the Concerned Citizens for Peace and Stability beating up demonstrators in 2011 and 2012 (see chapter 6), a new, "spontaneously formed" civil society movement, the Group Justice without Pressure (Grupo Justiça Sem Pressão) demonstrated in front of the courthouse, intimidating and physically attacking independent journalists trying to cover the trial. Failing to produce any evidence for an actual criminal act, the prosecution leaked crudely manipulated videos of the accused to the press, doctored to show evidence of their intent to violently overthrow the government. Still, facing mounting domestic and international pressure the Constitutional Court on 15 December approved the transfer of the prisoners to home detention, so that they could await the continuation of the trial over the holidays with their families.

The trial resumed in February 2016, taking on increasingly farcical dimensions and including additional, summary sentences against the activists and their lawyers for disrespecting the tribunal. Finally, on 28 March 2016, the trial concluded. Though the charge of attempting to assassinate the president had been quietly dropped, the seventeen activists were found guilty of "prepara-tory acts of rebellion and association of evildoers" (*actos preparatórios de rebelião e associação de malfeitores*) and sentenced to between two and eight years in jail.[19]

Ending the book on a note of civil unrest and antigovernment demonstrations, one has to "fight the impulse to make theory adequate to political desire" (Piot 2010, 169). And yet I felt a summary of events was necessary: things are clearly and visibly in flux, and the idea of "Angolans as a coward people," silenced by a leaden culture of fear that many of my informants still cited in 2010/2011 (and even more so in 2007), must be revisited. Indeed, the increasingly violent repression of antigovernment activism can be read as "the symptom of a hegemonic system losing speed" (Buire 2016, 55); some, for now only loosely organized, social actors are increasingly ready to openly question the postwar consensus of peace and stability in the New Angola.[20] It would appear that the promises of immediatism—the overnight, spectacular wealth made possible by seemingly limitless oil revenues—are dissolving like a mirage in the *cacimbo* (winter) cold, with the end of the oil bonanza clearly showing the limits of this commodified politics.

Angolans are increasingly fed up with the discourse of peace brandished like a weapon by the government to silence its critics: "The Angolans are already tired of this; they just want a normal life. For so many decades we have had an abnormal life. We just want to be able to have a coffee on the corner, buy food in a shop, raise our children."[21] And yet that sort of normality increasingly eludes most Luandans, which makes the disconnect between the MPLA government's populist rhetoric and the people's lived realities ever more glaring. This is compounded by the additional hardships caused by the drying up of oil revenues.

The most visible face of this growing discontent is the youth activists and revolutionary student movement, including the "Angola 15+2." However, at the time of writing, in late 2016, the discontent is spreading both among the "urban youth" as well as among people who are more established and who, until now, had accepted the postwar consensus that places stability and tranquillity over political freedoms.

Even those who have stable jobs and the few who have benefitted from government largesse are increasingly willing to criticize the status quo. As Pitcher (2015) shows, for example, the few who finally got a hold of an apartment in Kilamba thanks to their connections and employment in the civil service might be satisfied with their new standards of living and the services provided by the government, but that does not automatically mean they approve of the government or support the ruling party—quite the contrary, in fact. That such discontent is now spreading even among those people who are materially more secure and among the few who have benefitted from government projects and employment contradicts facile notions of neopatrimonialism or one-dimensional readings of the "politics of the belly."[22] The social groups that have been for years the popular basis of the MPLA's support feel increasingly left out of the regime's project of the New Angola. It is precisely these urban social actors, who historically constituted the natural reservoir of the MPLA's active or tacit support, who have come to feel that their rulers have betrayed their originally proclaimed values of solidarity and social advancement for all to the benefit of a small, predatory elite. And they are no longer willing to turn a blind eye to the violent repression of activists who are, essentially, their social equals. The disconnect between the MPLA's professed political values and lived reality is becoming more visible, and it is precisely because of that that the MPLA's hegemonic project is under increasing pressure. The MPLA's "historical prestige" is being demystified (Gramsci 1971, 145; see also Buire 2016, 69) even among those people who previously have supported and, to an extent, benefitted from the regime.[23]

The material symptoms of a hegemonic system fraying at the seams are plain to see. A garbage crisis (*crise do lixo*) that has plagued Luanda since mid-2015 is but one of the ways the crisis of leadership manifests itself in people's everyday lives. A new waste management model introduced in August 2015 transferred responsibility for rubbish removal from the provincial government to the municipalities. However, because the total budget to do so corresponded to one third of the previous amount—and with the usual, politically connected private companies eating part of the budget along the chain—the city has slowly been transformed into one huge open-air waste dump. The systemic underfunding of the public health system has also resulted in the worst yellow fever outbreak in thirty years, as hospitals have no vaccines, no gloves, no sterile equipment, and even often no running water.[24]

Discontent about the poor handling of the crisis and the monopolization of political and economic power in the hands of President dos Santos and his family is spreading, with even some dyed-in-the-wool MPLA luminaries openly criticizing the current situation as a national disgrace. However, the looting of public assets by politically connected individuals has, if anything, been on the rise. Epitomizing these developments, the president in June 2016 nominated his daughter Isabel dos Santos as the new CEO of Sonangol, a move met with some, albeit ultimately unsuccessful, resistance from MPLA deputies and civil society actors.

The biggest surprise for Angolans and longtime Angola-watchers was the announcement in December 2016 that the MPLA's vice president, Defense

Minister João Lourenço, would run as the party's head of list for the 2017 elections, rather than president dos Santos himself.[25] It would appear that Manuel Vicente—the vice president dos Santos selected and imposed on the party for the 2012 elections and who would have, until now, become his successor if dos Santos had stepped down—was deeply unpopular with the party, and any suspected plans to set up a dynastic succession with one of dos Santos' children as future vice president under Vicente after 2017 were met with resistance from within the party's deciding bodies, the Central Committee and the Political Bureau. However, while Lourenço is younger and more broadly accepted within the party and the army than Vicente was, he is also known as a dos Santos loyalist and hardly appears as a great reformer. Moreover, the accelerated concentration of key assets and posts of economic command in the hands of the dos Santos family ensure that whoever ultimately succeeds dos Santos as president of the republic will be economically beholden to his inner circle. Historically, the system has been extremely resilient to crises, and it remains to be seen whether the regime will not bounce back once again, if and when oil prices recover.

It is moot to speculate how the emerging political subjectivities of increasingly critical "new Angolans" will find their expression in Angola, especially in a political system that is so obviously biased in favor of the ruling party (Roque 2009; 2013; Schubert 2010).[26] We do not know what those who continue to benefit from the system will do when the president leaves, and even those educated young professionals, who are silently critical of the system and the corruption that has gangrened society, are deeply wary of any disorganized regime change, fearing the specter of a violent uprising by the discontented popular masses.[27]

More important, focussing on the person of the president and his likely succession misses out on the more transactional elements of the system. Thus instead of engaging with the question on the minds of many Angola-watchers (what will happen following President dos Santos's death or departure from office), I would like to restate one of the main arguments of this book: we need to pay detailed attention to the more subtle cultural processes and everyday politics of the ordinary in the system of contemporary Angola to find out how a regime such as this one functions. Through this we can then begin to understand how the dominant ideologies that rested on socialist, anticolonial, familial, and revolutionary imaginings of authority and legitimacy are reaching their limits, and how a new kind of political consciousness is emerging, one that is less content with the status quo and formulating a tentative new kind of politics—within and through the repertoires of the system. True, this political awakening has raised hopes among Angolans and Angola observers. However, it will take more than just a change of the figure at the top to fundamentally reorder Angola's social, political, and economic relations, and thus the way the system works. For now, we can simply read the expression of such new political subjectivities—we are all *revús* (revolutionaries)—within the system as the start of a tentative political awakening of a growing minority of Angolans, across ages and social backgrounds, who have, and dare voice, substantive political aspirations for a different kind of social and economic relations.

GLOSSARY AND ABBREVIATIONS

armazém	Warehouse, depot
bairro	Neighborhood, subdivision of a municipality, but also more specifically an informal, unplanned neighborhood
bicha	Queue
B. O.	Bairro Operário, a historic central neighborhood of Luanda, often said to be the birthplace of Angolan nationalism
boleia	A lift, a ride (in a vehicle)
bufo; bufar; bufaria	Snitch, informant; to snitch, to spy, to inform; snitching, informing
candonga	The black/parallel market of the 1980s, eventually used to describe most informal business
candongueiro (táxi)	The blue-and-white, 9–15-passenger minibuses, mostly Toyota HiAce, that ply fixed routes as collective taxis
CASA-CE	Convergência Ampla de Salvação de Angola–Coligação Eleitoral, a new opposition coalition formed in 2012 by UNITA and MPLA dissidents, third force in parliament since the 2012 elections
Casa Militar/Casa Civil	The president's military and civilian cabinet respectively, interposed between the president and the Cabinet of Ministers, with vast financial and executive competences; the former was renamed the Casa de Segurança (Security Cabinet), comprising fifteen units that mirror the public security organs, following the 2012 elections
chefe	Boss, hierarchical superior
cobrador	Fare collector in a collective taxi
DNIC/DPIC	Direcção Nacional/Provincial de Investigação Criminal, National, resp. Provincial Directorate of Criminal Investigation (the criminal department of the police)
FAA	Forças Armadas de Angola (the Angolan Armed Forces, the national army)
FALA	The Armed Forces for the Liberation of Angola (the armed wing of UNITA until partial integration into the FAA in 1991)

FAPLA	The Armed Popular Forces for the Liberation of Angola (the armed wing of the MPLA during the independence struggle and the pre-1991 national army)
FNLA	Frente Nacional de Libertação de Angola (the Angolan National Liberation Front), the oldest of the three historic national liberation movements, formed initially as UPNA/ UPA, today a marginalized opposition party
FSDEA	The Angolan Sovereign Wealth Fund, headed by José Filomeno "Zénú" de Sousa dos Santos (one of President dos Santos's children)
fulano/fulana	A commonly used placeholder name, meaning "this fellow/ person/guy" or "Mister so-and-so"; often used as *fulano de tal*, or expanded into a name, *Fulano Sicrano, Fulano Beltrano*
funge	Staple food, a glutinous, starchy, low-nutrient pap made of manioc or maize meal
gasosa	Fizzy soft drink, by extension a small bribe, a "tip" of a few hundred kwanza
Irmão/Irmã	Brother/Sister, common form of address
JdA	*Jornal de Angola*, the only national daily newspaper (state-controlled)
jovem	Youth (m/f): a wide and flexible social category, often used to address someone you do not know by name, especially in a client/service situation
kamba	Friend (from Kimbundu)
kota	Old one, *mais velho* (from Kimbundu)
kuduro	Angolan dance music genre, "ghetto" music, known for its hard beats, provocative lyrics, and acrobatic dance moves
mais velho/mais velha	Old one (m/f), elder (as a title of respect)
maluco	Crazy, crazy man
Mano/Mana	Colloquial form of *Irmão* (Brother), *Irmã* (Sister), common form of address
Mamã/Papá	Mother/Father (used commonly as forms of address)
matumbo	Dumb, idiot, yokel
MIREX	Ministério das Relações Exteriores (Ministry of Foreign Relations)
moço/moça	Boy/girl, often used in a service context
MPLA	Movimento Popular de Libertação de Angola (Popular Movement for the Liberation of Angola), one of the three national liberation movements and the ruling party of Angola since independence
musseque	"Sandy" neighborhood (from Kimbundu), used during colonial times as a term for the informal, "indigenous" neigh-

	borhoods outside the cement city; also spelled *"musseke,"* *"muceque"* (*"bairro"* more common today)
negócio	Business, enterprise
pastelaria	Bakery-café
PIR	Polícia de Intervenção Rápida (the Rapid Intervention Police or "Ninjas," often deployed as a riot police)
praça	Literally a square, designating in Angola an open-air market
quintal	Courtyard, often also a place where drinks or food, or both, is sold
roboteiro	Porter, young man who, for a small fee, carries heavy loads on a self-made wooden wheelbarrow
rusga	Raid, the capture of boys and young men for forced military service in the 1980s and 1990s
saldo	Cell phone credit, "top-up"; by extension also a small "tip" or bribe
SINSE	Serviço de Inteligência e Segurança do Estado (the State Intelligence and Security Service), commonly known as *segurança* (security service), and previously incarnated as DISA and SINFO
Sonangol	The Angolan state oil company; by law the majority shareholder in all oil exploration joint ventures, and Angola's main revenue earner
UNITA	União Nacional para a Libertação Total de Angola (the National Union for the Total Liberation of Angola), one of the three national liberation movements and the MPLA's opponent in the Angolan conflict (1976–2002), today the major opposition party
zungueira; zunga	Female ambulant seller; ambulant or street commerce

Notes

Introduction

1. Cf. Aretxaga 2003. Thus when I speak of the "relation of people to power," I generally refer to this notion of *o poder* that my informants invoked, not of power as an analytical concept. For ease of reading, however, I have refrained from putting it in quotation marks or writing it as The Power.

2. See Roque 2009; Faria 2013; Roque 2013; and Soares de Oliveira 2015.

3. See UNDP HDI 2012. On urban poverty, see for example Robson and Roque 2001; Cain 2002; Ennes Ferreira 2005; Hodges 2007; Rodrigues 2007; HRW 2010; and Da Rocha 2012.

4. According to the international consultancy firm Mercer, which publishes annual reports on the costs of living for expatriates, Luanda was the most expensive city in 2010, 2011, and 2013, though it was relegated to second spot by Tokyo in 2012 (Mercer 2014). While the usefulness of such rankings may be questioned, costs of living for the most basic goods and services are truly exorbitant, even for normal people not aspiring to an expat lifestyle.

5. This echoes notions in other contexts of a "system" that stands for a specific political regime, as, for example, *nizham* in pre-revolution Egypt (Salvatore 2013, 4), Ledeneva (2013) on the *sistema* in contemporary Russia, or *khozyain* in contemporary Azerbaijan (Tristam Barrett, personal communication, 19.11.2013). See also Rogers 2006 on Russia.

6. Cf. Soares de Oliveira 2015. Also, a quarter of the entire population of the country lives in the capital.

7. Cf. Levitsky and Way 2002; Schedler 2002; and Ottaway 2003.

8. For the sake of simplicity I use the analytical shorthand "neo-authoritarian" to characterize the political set-up of Angola.

9. Often part of the discourse of local NGOs or media reports, this explanation also resonates in other scholarship (e.g., Vallée 2008; Corkin 2013; Ovadia 2013). See also below in greater detail on research on Angola.

10. The question of the lack of contestation of the regime is also a central concern for Tomás (2012).

11. The start of shale gas exploration in the United States and the subsequent changes to the world oil and gas market have somewhat reduced this dependency since 2014, also leading to a slight shift in Western foreign policy attitudes toward Angola (see epilogue).

12. If one thinks of the past presidential election in the United States, the past two general elections and the Brexit referendum in the United Kingdom, for example, or the way the "refugee crisis" is instrumentalized in political discourse.

13. Cf. Piot 2010, 20.

14. For example, Gramsci 1971, 40–42.

15. Cf. Chabal and Daloz 1999.

16. See also Ledeneva 2013, 2: "Kremlinological accounts of '*bulldogs fighting under the carpet*' have certain explanatory power but they excessively personalise the workings of the state."

17. See also Jourde 2009, 203–4.

18. For a good discussion of the problematic nature of the notion of agency, cf. Ahearn 2001; and Kockelmann 2007.

19. E.g., Das and Poole 2004; and Friedman 2011.

20. Cf. Navaro-Yashin 2002, 132.

21. As Messiant (1995b, 4) succinctly put it, "*Ce n'est pas seulement qu'il n'y a pas eu de lieu national permettant une recherche plus ou moins indépendante; il n'y a pas même eu un lieu de recherche dépendante*" (It is not only that there has not been any national space that would allow for any more or less independent research; there has not even been any space for dependent research). In fact, study / research visas as a legal category were only introduced in 2008, two years before I started my field research (see also chapter 4).

22. Although fresh work by a new generation of Angola scholars such as Jess Auerbach, Sylvia Croese, Aharon deGrassi, Claudia Gastrow, Chloé Buire, Paulo Inglês, Gilson Lázaro, and António Tomás is likely to be published over the coming years, which will contribute substantively to the body of existing research.

23. Following Sumich (2008) for Mozambique. See also Krohn-Hansen 2008. A mode of analysis that, perhaps more than just in scholarly research, predominates in policy papers and media accounts of Angola: "Angolan politics is largely a game of second-guessing and conspiracy theories, of strategic, military and family alliances, over which Dos Santos rules absolutely via a carefully crafted web of patronage and influence," *Mail & Guardian*, 14.06.2013, "Dos Santos' Hollow Triumph on TV" (http://mg.co.za/article/2013-06-14-00-dos-santoss-hollow-triumph-on-tv, accessed 14.06.2013).

24. See figure 4, chapter 2 of this volume.

25. The designation "Evangelic" results from the Swiss background and might sound misleading to an Anglophone reader due to its consonance with Evangelical; however, it corresponds to the typology Presbyterian in the Anglo-Saxon context.

26. Though perhaps not the top echelons of Luandan society.

27. On the role of Christianity in Angola, and the importance of protestant missions in the formation of social identities, see for example Pélissier 1978; Heimer 1979; B. Schubert 2000; Péclard 2005, 2012; and Messiant 2006.

28. Cf. Piot 2010, 15, and Friedman 2011, 3.

29. As this was the topic of my father's doctoral thesis in theology after our return to Switzerland. See B. Schubert 1997.

30. This is a bit of a generalization, which I nuance in chapter 6 and the epilogue. For more work on religiosity in Angola, see for example Lübbert Hansen 2006; Sarró and Blanes 2009; and Blanes 2011, 2012.

31. As well as in other contexts, of course (e.g., Barber 1997; Fernandes 2003; Shipley 2009; Eisenberg 2012).

1. 2002, Year Zero

1. Rádio Mais, a private radio station, is owned by Media Nova SA, a holding allegedly controlled by General "Kopelipa," General "Dino," and Vice-President Manuel Vicente.

2. On the Architect of Peace trope, see also Lázaro 2012.

3. Scholars tend to distinguish two (1975–91 and 1993–2002) or even three (1975–91, 1992–94, and 1998–2002) phases of the civil war. I use the more general terms "Angolan conflict" and "civil war" to denote the entire period of 1975–2002, unless otherwise specified.

4. "Continuing struggle," based on the MPLA's socialist slogan *"a luta continua!"* (The struggle continues).

5. According to the notion of the New Angola circulated across social strata, its rightful place is a dominant one, ideally "above" South Africa in terms of socioeconomic development and influence within SADC, and surpassing Nigeria as Africa's largest oil exporter.

6. This echoes a widespread fatalism about any form of *"situação,"* a sort of agentless, generalized situation in which individual actors are helpless. See Pearce 2005.

7. See Foucault 1995. See also Crehan 1997, 31–33 on the power of naming.

8. Cf. Humphrey 2005, for the links between architecture and ideology.

9. Research on urban planning and development in Luanda includes Jenkins, Robson, and Cain 2002; Cain 2002; Croese 2012; Buire 2014; and Gastrow 2014a.

10. See also Ranger 2004; Kössler 2010; and Becker 2011.

11. See also Buur 2010; Machava 2011; and Sumich 2012.

12. Based on research in Maputo, Mozambique (March–May 2016) and personal communication with Justin Pearce (April 2016).

13. See Marcum 1969; Marcum 1978; Pélissier 1978; Heimer 1979; Messiant 2006; Pearce 2015a; and Péclard 2015.

14. Factors that influenced the division between three liberation movements include social conflicts between urban and rural population, historic regional and denominational divides, the politicization of ethnicity, and Cold War dynamics. See, for example, Heywood 2000; Péclard 2005; Messiant 2006; and Birmingham 2006, chap. 7.

15. For accounts of the tumultuous 1974–75 period, see Kapuścinski 1987 and especially Pearce 2015a, chapter 1.

16. FNLA started out in 1954 as the Union of Peoples of Northern Angola (UPNA). It changed its name to Union of Peoples of Angola (UPA) in 1959; and in 1961, to FNLA. See Marcum 1969.

17. An attack perpetrated by Luandan nationalists not affiliated with the MPLA. See Messiant 1998, 160–61. Attempts to also claim ownership of the Baixa de Cassange revolt were less successful.

18. Interviews Martins, Baixa, 17.02.2011; Fragoso, Vila Alice, 09.06.2011, Fundação 27 de Maio, 23.09.2011, 19.10.2011; L. P., B. O., 01.06.2011.

19. Interview with Moisés Sotto Mayor, son of Virgílio Sotto Mayor, Fundação 27 de Maio, 19.10.2011

20. According to Moisés Sotto Mayor, his father Virgílio had nursed a feverish Manuel Pedro Pacavira back to health when they were both detained in Missombo prison,

and Pacavira had confessed during his fever to having collaborated with PIDE. After his release from prison in 1971, Sotto Mayor senior integrated the MPLA and was made a military commander, but he defended the by then unpopular opinion that all nationalist forces of Angola should unite. His execution, after a military trial, for excessive use of force against civilians in August 1975, in this reading, was then instigated by Pacavira to erase this inconvenient knowledge and silence Sotto Mayor's advocating for greater recognition of the independent nature of the attack on the São Paulo prison. Interview with Moisés Sotto Mayor, 19.10.2011.

21. See, for example, *Angop*, 15.12.2010, "Lei dos feriados nacionais dignifica datas significativas da nação" (http://www.portalangop.co.ao/motix/pt_pt/noticias/politica/2010/11/50/Lei-dos-Feriados-Nacionais-dignifica-datas-significativas-Nacao,7a36d8a0-8f6a-4137-97bc-dc0604cebf00.html, accessed 02.11.2012).

22. Iko Carreira, one of the MPLA's leading figures and Angola's first defense minister, is rumored to have been a fighter pilot for the Portuguese army and to have participated in the bombing, a further reason not to commemorate the event.

23. Cf. Duncan 2013, 11, 14.

24. See, for example, Pawson 2014, 51.

25. As quoted in Portuguese newspaper *Económico*, 03.07.2015, "Angola: Eduardo dos Santos diz que 'não é sensato' deixar o poder antes de 2017": *"Não se deve permitir que o povo angolano seja submetido a mais uma situação dramática como a que viveu em 27 de maio de 1977, por causa de um golpe de Estado. (. . .) Quem escolhe a via da força para tomar o poder ou usar para tal meios anticonstitucionais, não é democrata"* (http://economico.sapo.pt/noticias/angola-eduardo-dos-santos-diz-que-nao-e-sensato-deixar-o-poder-antes-de-2017_222719.html, accessed 24.08.2015).

26. E.g., Stockwell 1978.

27. E.g., Sitte 1981; Bridgland 1988.

28. It also dropped the "PT" (Workers' Party) from its name at its March 1990 Central Committee Meeting. See Pazzanita 1991 and Hodges 2001, 11.

29. *JdA*, 01.07.1992, "UNITA acusada de montar operação militar no Bié."

30. *JdA*, 16.09.1992, "UNITA fere e mata agente da Polícia no Kwanza-Sul."

31. *JdA*, 20.09.1992, "UNITA espanca crianças por trajarem camisolas do MPLA."

32. *JdA*, 13.10.1992, "UNITA mantém a nação sob ameaça de Guerra." All *JdA* titles referenced above accessed at the Municipal Library of Luanda (Biblioteca Municipal de Luanda).

33. Leandro, B. O., 16.06.2011.

34. A tried and tested tactic of the MPLA as it appears. See the rumors spread on FNLA's cannibalism on the eve of independence, above.

35. *JdA*, 13.10.1992, "UNITA fere e mata agente da Polícia no Kwanza-Sul."

36. P. Inglês, personal communication, 9.1.2015; B. Schubert, personal communication, 11.1.2015.

37. Candidate's biography for José Eduardo dos Santos from the MPLA 2012 electoral campaign homepage (http://www.mpla2012.ao/candidatos, accessed 31.10.2014).

38. Popular comments usually subvert this as "architect of hunger," or "architect of corruption," thus calling into question the official representation of the Architect of Peace as a "spontaneous," popular title of honor for the president (see chapter 6).

39. On high modernism see Scott 1998. On the MPLA's postwar high modernist development vision see Soares de Oliveira 2015. On the New Man in Angola see Collier. 2013.

40. CEAST Conference on National Reconciliation, Catholic University of Angola, Luanda, 24.03.2011.

41. Defining "social justice" as a merely economic question is in line also with the depoliticization of the conflict.

42. *VOA Português*, 20.11.2012, "Vitorino Nhany: 'Na independência passamos de regime colonial para neo-colonial'" (http://www.voaportugues.com/content/article/1547502.html, accessed 20.11.2012).

43. *DW*, 11.11.2014, "Angola precisa de uma segunda independência": *"Falta a independência total, que é baseada na liberdade—que não existe—na justiça social, no respeito dos direitos humanos, na igualdade de oportunidades"* (http://www.dw.de/angola-precisa-de-uma-segunda-independ%C3%AAncia/a-18055564, accessed 12.11.2014).

44. Some of these "provisional" tent settlements in Zango have been there for several years now, despite government promises to resettle inhabitants to more appropriate houses. See Buire 2014, Croese 2010, 2017, and Gastrow 2014a on "urban requalification."

45. Much like other "Dubais" as, for example, Astana (Kazakhstan; see Laszczkowski 2011), Baku (see Grant 2014), or, ironically, Cabinda, the oil-rich northern Angolan province, where claims for independence against the MPLA government of Angola are sometimes also framed in similar ideas.

46. See also chapter 3. On the roots of urban modernity, see Messiant 2006 and Moorman 2008.

47. Pawson expresses a similar sentiment in her account of walking through Luanda's *baixa* (2014, 131).

48. Cf. Azaryahu 1996, 316, and Kössler 2007, 365.

49. There is a "Peace Arch" in Luena, the capital of the remote province of Mexico, to commemorate the signing of the memorandum.

50. On the functioning of *candonga*, see B. Schubert 1997, chap. 5, and Kasack 1992, 54–62.

51. *Angop*, 29.07.2011, "Início de obras no antigo Roque Santeiro é um marco histórico, segundo PR" (http://www.angop.ao/angola/pt_pt/noticias/politica/2011/6/30/Inicio-obras-antigo-Roque-Santeiro-marco-historico-segundo,f54cbf49-2a2d-4135-ae86-d2bffea17040.html, accessed 04.02.2017).

52. See, for example, in the comments section of *Club-K*, 29.07.2011, reproducing the *Angop* piece of the previous note (http://www.club-k.net/, accessed 08.01.2015).

53. See Gastrow (2014b) and Soares de Oliveira (2015) for more information on how money is made in the property market.

54. For studies of the Roque, see Ducados and Ennes Ferreira 1998; Lopes 2004; and Tomás 2012.

55. Though the MPLA's appropriation of history is perhaps less straightforward than in neighboring countries, all nationalist narratives do this, a point made by Zinn (2005). See also, for example, Hobsbawm and Ranger 1983; McClintock 1995; and Chatterjee 2007.

56. The Luena Memorandum of 2002 amounted to little more than a technical agreement that formalized the government of Angola's military victory over UNITA (Pearce 2005).

2. Sambizanga

1. Historically, Luanda was divided between the *cidade* (the colonial cement city) and the *musseques* (the surrounding indigenous, informal quarters, built on sandy ground). Due to the gradual upgrading of certain old-standing slums and the pejorative associations with *musseque* the more neutral *bairro* (neighborhood) has come to largely replace *musseque* in popular usage, thereby eventually engendering a slippage of meaning through which *bairro* nowadays usually connotes the unplanned, peripheral neighborhoods—though some of these areas have now permanent, "good" homes (Gastrow 2017, 2–3). The status of Sambizanga was changed from municipality to district in the administrative reorganization of the Province of Luanda in 2011; see chapter one and below for details.

2. See also chapters 1 and 3, on the controversy around the birthplace of President dos Santos.

3. See, for example, Labanyi 2010; Navaro-Yashin 2009; Wise 2010; and Fontein 2011.

4. See, for example, Azaryahu 1996; Hall 2006; Field 2007; Kaplan 2011; and Schramm 2011.

5. I am very grateful to James Ferguson for his stimulating comments on my argument here.

6. Cf. Piot 2010.

7. Although the observations and descriptions are a montage, for verifiability I have referenced the quotes of my informants with date and place.

8. See also Duncan (2013, 14) on popular memories of religious violence in Indonesia, and on how people base their assumptions about the future on their present understanding of past experiences.

9. See figure 2 at the beginning of the book. After the reform, the five central municipalities were transformed into districts within the new municipality of Luanda. The seven new municipalities, Luanda, Cazenga, Cacuaco, Ícolo e Bengo, Viana, Belas, and Quissama, now extend over the entire province.

10. The constituent *bairros* of the commune of Sambizanga are Santo Rosa, Mota, Sambizanga-Lixeira, and Bairro Madeira, while those of the commune of N'Gola Kiluanji are N'Gola Kiluanji, Os Kwanzas, Bairro Campismo, Bairro Uíge, Bairro dos Ossos, Petrangol, São Pedro da Barra, Bairro da EMCIB, and Porto Pesqueiro da Boavista.

11. Isilda Hurst, Alvalade, 05.01.2011. She also said that the fairly new model neighborhood of Nova Vida also brought mid- to upper-level functionaries in contact in unexpected ways that were likely to stimulate political consciousness and create an unpleasant surprise for the government.

12. This reflects the government's practice of nurturing and actively "organizing" civil society associations, and its suspicion (and repression) of any "disorganized" civic activism. See Schubert 2010.

13. Adriano, B. O., 24.06.2011.

14. Adriano, Maculusso, 12.08.2011.

15. Though his material leads him to somewhat different conclusions, Holbraad similarly reports from Cuba how people might criticize the general situation but still defend *la revolución* as their own (2014, 367).

16. *Langas* is a derogatory term for northern Angolans, or "Congolese," as they are seen.

17. This included the use of shibboleths, like *arroz* (ɐroʃ, rice) and *hoje* (oʒə, today), which Bakongo tend to pronounce as *aroz* (ɐrˈɔʃ, with a very liquid "r" approximating an "l") and *hoze* (ozə) (cf. Cole 2006, 225, on Madagascar).

18. A variation on Neto's *"a luta continua, a vitória é certa"* (The struggle continues; victory is certain). Chinguito, B. O., 07.09.2011.

19. See chapter 3.

20. On the Halloween Massacres and Bloody Friday, see HRW 1994 and Mabeko-Tali 1995.

21. See chapter 3. See also Inglês 2016. On the people of the MPLA/UNITA, see Pearce 2015. On dehumanizing devices, see the vast literature on the Rwandan genocide.

22. Alberto, B. O., 19.02.2011.

23. Cf. Cole 2006, 231–38.

24. Incidentally, this CHD complex is now managed by a company owned by First Lady Ana Paula dos Santos. No tenders were published for the contract.

25. Indeed, parts of Boa Vista were the first scene of the forced clearances for urban requalification. See, for example, HRW 2007 and 2011.

26. See chapter 3, on "foreignness" and Angolanness.

27. Leandro, São Paulo, 16.06.2011.

28. In the original: *"Dai o celebre provérbio, que outros depois copiaram, se não tem no Roque e porque ainda não foi inventado. Aqui se encontrava a verdadeira bolsa de valores de Angola, onde se estabelecia o curso real das moedas e o preço dos produtos. E de onde partiram as mercadorias para os outros mercados e para os vendedores de rua da cidade."* Pepetela (2001, 84).

29. For a more comprehensive explanation of the earlier system of *candonga*, see Kasack 1992, 54–62 and B. Schubert 1997, chap. 5; for moneymaking practices today, see chapter 5.

30. On the development of road transport in Angola, see Lopes 2009.

31. Mob lynching remains a popular form of extrajudicial justice both in the *bairros* and in the countryside. See also Calvão 2013, 129.

32. For more detailed ethnographic and sociological analyses of the former Roque, see Ducados and Ennes Ferreira 1998; Lopes 2004; and Tomás 2012.

33. I organized several group meetings, mainly in the Roque and Bairro Operário parishes.

34. Hence the name of this *bairro*, Madeira (wood).

35. Mamã Adelina, Roque parish, 22.12.2010.

36. Mamã Luisa, Bairro Operário parish, 17.11.2010.

37. In fact, only a few weeks after this meeting, a teenage gang assaulted and severely beat up Irmão Batista, taking his cell phone and a USB stick.

38. Mamã Laurinda, Roque parish, 22.12.2010.

39. This is something Moorman also notes (2008, 17).

40. See also Mendes, Silva, and Cabecinhas (2011) on the mythical status 27 May has acquired among secondary school students despite its absence from history curricula.

41. Cf. Wedeen 1999, 32, 45.

42. Cf. Kesselring 2016.

43. Nguyen 2015, chap. 9.

44. Piot (2010, 37) reports very similar processes for Togo under Eyadéma. See also Fontein 2009b.

45. Waldemar Bastos, "A Velha Chica," on *Estamos Juntos* (1982), EMI Brazil.

46. See also havemos de voltar, 18.03.2011, "Xé Menino, fala política" (http://havemosdevoltar.wordpress.com/2011/03/18/xe-menino-fala-politica/, accessed 13.08.2012).

47. Lucas Pedro, B. O., 01.06.2011.

48. Chinguito and Gégé, B. O., 11.03.2011.

49. One of them even showed me photos of himself, wearing white underwear marked with the red P for political and tied with ropes to a tree trunk in his back yard, a most astonishing (I thought) reenactment or staging of his experiences to demonstrate and validate his identity as a survivor.

50. As well as, one should add, serving the political ambitions of the Foundation's leader, General (Retd.) Silva Mateus, the leader of the so-called União de Tendências within the MPLA.

51. The delicious Angolan staple dishes prepared by Mãe Tété and her staff were my sustenance on many a workday in the Bairro Operário.

52. Due to this, the frequent power and water failures, and my quintal neighbors' liberal use of my water tank, the pump needed constant venting, and running water was more the exception than the rule.

53. Cf. Ferguson 1999.

3. Angolanidade

1. Many comments, however, were also very mocking in tone, rightly predicting the MPLA would claim the triumph for its own benefit. See Club-K, 13.09.2011, "Angolana Leila Lopes eleita Miss Universo" (www.club-k.net/bastidores/8786-angolana-leila-lopes-eleita-miss-universo2011-.html, accessed 18.03.2013).

2. Cf. Hangen 2005, 51. See also Kaarsholm 2012.

3. See, for example, Sökefeld 2001 for a review of identity and its analytical value.

4. Cf. Rubbers 2009, 286. As these terms are problematic, one would conventionally put them in inverted commas at every mention to denote that they should not be taken at face value, and constantly scrutinized. For ease of reading, however, I will refrain from doing so.

5. See, for example, Pélissier 1978; Messiant 2006; and Mabeko-Tali 2001b.

6. See also Ferreira 2012 and Candido 2013, as well as Melnysyn 2017.

7. That is, aspiring to more autonomy from the metropolis without relinquishing their social and political status. See also Corrado 2008.

8. I return to the question of family links in greater detail in chapter 4.

9. Turning Brazil's "inferiority complex about its multiracial past" on its head (Bender 1978, 5), Freyre theorized that the sexual procreation of the white man with the "Negro or mulatto girl who is easily to be had" on the old sugar plantations resulted in an advanced, meta-racial Brazilian identity (1986, 279) that became the "dominant theme in twentieth century [Brazilian] politics and culture" (Edmonds 2010, 127).

10. Under the Salazar regime, the racialized hierarchy in the Overseas Province of Angola was, starting from the top: Portuguese first class (Metropolis-born), Portuguese

second class, or Euro-African (born in Angola to two white Portuguese parents), *mestiço* (mixed race), *assimilado* (assimilated black African), and finally *indígena*, the "uncivilized" majority of black Africans who, until the abolition of the Estatuto do Indigenato in 1961, had no citizenship rights and could be drafted into forced labor, which was a key factor for the economic profitability of the colony. See, for example, Messiant 2006 and Tavares Pimenta 2012.

11. See also Duffy 1962, chap. 6; and Clarence-Smith 1985, 179.

12. There were stirrings of Angolan nationalism among *mestiço* and *assimilado* elites as early as the mid-nineteenth century, as Wheeler (1969) shows.

13. In the works of writers such as Uanhenga Xitu, Luandino Vieira, Agostinho Neto, and Fernando Costa Andrade, for example.

14. Several MPLA leaders, including Neto, also had white wives, which further undermined their position with those advocating a more African nationalism.

15. On the role of missionary ethnographers and "conservation anthropology," see, for example, Harries 2007.

16. See also Péclard 2012, 152.

17. Quite similarly to the other settler colonies in the subregion.

18. Referring to the Revolta do Leste, Daniel Chipenda's 1974 revolt on the eastern front. See Mabeko-Tali 2001a, 137.

19. For a useful critique of that explanation, see Péclard 2012, 153–55.

20. See, for example, *O País*, 06.11.2012, "Por uma Angola mais 'in África'" (http://www.opais.net/pt/revista/?det=29798&id=1640&mid=, accessed 14.10.2013).

21. See also the *topos* of the culture of fear in chapter 2.

22. *O País*, 16.10.2010, "Irene Alexandra Neto: Não estamos presos ao passado." In author's possession.

23. That is probably a rather understated way of putting it.

24. Or maybe rather a "Unitel-version" considering the very similar aesthetics of the advertisements of Angola's largest mobile network provider, incidentally owned by Isabel dos Santos (see later in this chapter).

25. Cf. Moorman 2014, 35. Rap has taken over as underground, subversive music, propagated on the soundsystems of the taxis (with artists like MCK, Brigadeiro 10 pacotes, Ikonoklasta).

26. Dog Murras is a great example of some of the creative reappropriations of contradictory registers within the system (see chapter 6). He has deployed nationalist imagery (the Angolan flag) to represent Angola internationally but used socialist iconography (Che Guevara, the Youth Pioneers) to elliptically criticize the government. Despite the ghetto aesthetics of kuduro, he is easily middle class: his parents were nationalists, as his given name, Murtala, indicates. Many thanks to Marissa Moorman for pointing this out to me.

27. See, for example, MPLA, 16.09.13, "Dia do Herói Nacional: MPLA recorda Agostinho Neto como patriota convicto" (http://www.mpla.ao/imprensa.52/noticias.55/dia-do-heroi-nacional-mpla-recorda-agostinho-neto-como-patriota-convicto.a1114.html, accessed 23.10.2013).

28. *VOA Português*, 07.08.2012, "MPLA instaura processo contra deputado que questionou a origem de José Eduardo dos Santos" (http://www.voaportugues.com/content/mpla-ataca-deputado-unita/1474575.html, accessed 16.04.2013).

29. See, for example, Banégas 2006; Jackson 2006; Marshall-Fratani 2006; and Alexander and McGregor 2007.

30. Roque Santeiro, 12.02.2011.

31. B. O. parish, 20.03.2011.

32. A few informants conceded that having foreign-born parents was, as such, nothing unusual in Africa, but that they were making a point: "That's normal in Africa. So many people had to emigrate because of the wars. Even Kabila (Jr.) was not born in Congo but in Tanzania. The grandfather of Agostinho Neto was Senegalese. This is normal. But we're saying this [the president's alleged birth in São Tomé] *because we are mistreated.* There was a time when there was a huge lack of cement in Angola. And there were ships full of Angolan cement going to São Tomé. Back then the market was really closed. So we are really demonizing him, like he did it with Holden and Savimbi— we're just paying him back in his own money." (Lucas Pedro, B. O., 01.06.2011).

33. Incidentally, when people in the street did not assume I was a Russian or a Czech, they often called out *"latón!"* or *"pula!"* to me to make sense of my presence.

34. See, for example, Stoler 2002 and Edmonds 2010.

35. It is also commonly said that the flight crews at the national carrier TAAG are almost exclusively lighter-skinned and white.

36. This is a practice we know from other settings. In Nepal, for example, Susan Hangen (2005, 51) analyzes how subaltern groups deploy racial discourses as a fundamentally "oppositional identity." Similarly, for Angola, Krug interprets constructions of alternative ideas of *angolanidade* "as an ongoing struggle by nonelite actors" (2011, 110).

37. As Kyle (2005), for example, suggests.

38. People used to say, very derogatively, *"é proveniente"* (he is originating) of someone of UNITA, meaning that he *"provém das matas"* (comes from the bush).

39. Conversation with Gilson Lázaro, UAN Campus, 29.10.2010.

40. This echoes Ferguson's anecdote about the values attached to different types of housing in his experience in Lesotho (2006, 18). See also chapter 1 in this volume and Soares de Oliveira 2015. Admittedly, the MPLA's 2012 electoral manifesto included a provision on the promotion of "national languages" at secondary school, but it remains to be seen whether and how this will be implemented.

41. Cf. Birmingham 2012, 218.

42. In Portuguese these *populações* are construed as being different from the people; see chapter 2.

43. This often includes virulent anti-Muslim statements that equate Guineans and Malians with terrorists. It also includes growing hostility against low-skilled Chinese economic migrants. See Quintão and Santos 2012 on perceptions of Chinese wage dumping in the construction sector.

44. As a personal aside: when I first travelled to Ghana in 2008, I was completely flabbergasted to see men of wealth and important social standing wearing the traditional *kente* cloth at official functions—but my bewilderment is clearly linked to my Angolan socialization where European suits are de rigueur for office-holders.

45. For a more detailed discussion of what this might entail for the study of the "African middle class" viewed through the prism of Luanda, see Schubert 2016b.

46. With the rare exception of people like the MP Makuta Nkonda, who presents himself as a "son of farmers" of the North and speaks a rough, heavily accented Portuguese—also a political tactic to denote authenticity and being down-to-earth.

47. Cf. Roth-Gordon 2009, 59.

48. For the linguistically inclined reader, the comparison was between the [diʃer] of Lisbon Portuguese with the [deʃser] of Luandan Portuguese.

49. See also chapter 4 on the use of kinship terms in everyday interactions.

50. *Angop*, 14.09.2011, "OMA prepara recepção para Miss Universo 2011" (http://www.portalangop.co.ao/motix/pt_pt/noticias/lazer-e-cultura/2011/8/37/OMA -prepara-recepcao-para-Miss-Universo-2011,ff26a24d-58eb-4859-97cf-7fb1dcfd4179 .html, accessed 18.03.2013).

51. *Angop*, 13.09.2011, "MPLA felicita eleição da angolana Leila Lopes ao título de Miss Universo" (http://www.portalangop.co.ao/motix/pt_pt/noticias/lazer-e-cultura/2011 /8/37/MPLA-felicita-eleicao-angolana-Leila-Lopes-titulo-Miss-Universo,4c5e5243-4043 -4129-9788-8b7cc84ce3b4.html, accessed 18.03.2013).

52. The new, third party, CASA-CE, deploys "pan-Angolan themes" in its discourse, precisely to appeal to more educated audiences, as well as to avoid the perceived dead-end of UNITA's ethno-regional mobilization (thanks to Ricardo Soares de Oliveira for highlighting that point to me). I have heard informally, however, that CASA-CE also tried to mobilize in some more remote provincial localities deploying a racial (or tribalist, in old parlance) discourse during its 2012 electoral campaign.

53. As has happened in Côte d'Ivoire (Marshall-Fratani 2006), South Africa and Zimbabwe (Ndlovu-Gatsheni 2009), and Gabon (Rich 2009), for example.

4. Cunhas

1. *Club-K*, 21.01.2014, "Falso filho de JES na cadeia" (http://club-k.net/index. php?option=com_content&view=article&id=17235:falso-filho-de-jes-na-cadeia&catid=8:bastidores&Itemid=125, accessed 22.01.2014).

2. According to the Portuguese etymological dictionary *Houaiss*, a *cunha* historically also designated a military strategy of inserting elements of one's own troops into enemy territory or of breaking up especially vulnerable enemy units.

3. As well as status markers and consumption (see chapter 5).

4. Because he was born in Angola, he was eligible for citizenship.

5. See introduction, on research methodology. In fact, given that I did not have a car, I applied for a driver's license mainly to experience the process firsthand.

6. For a similar argument about encountering bureaucracy as a foreign/native anthropologist in China, see Yang 1994, 10.

7. Cf. Mbembe 1999, 112.

8. A phenomenon aptly termed *excesso de doutorismo* (excess of doctor-ism).

9. Equivalent to something like "Petro rules!" referring to the Atlético Petróleos de Luanda soccer club.

10. Although today widespread beyond circles of churchgoing Angolans, it was, during the time of the civil war, also a form of distancing oneself from the official "comrade" (*camarada*) of socialist parlance. The FNLA is today still often called the "party of brothers" (*partido dos irmãos*).

11. It is unsurprising, considering the ambiguous status of whiteness in Angola, that João would term this a *falta de respeito* (see chapter 3).

12. The choice of the correct form of address in Angolan Portuguese depends on a number of factors, the most decisive being age and the degree of intimacy (Silva-Brummel 1984, 277).

13. Field notes, UNITEL, São Paulo, 18.04.2011.

14. See, for example, chapter 3 on returned young Angolans.

15. In fact, his given name, José, and his (given) father's name, Eduardo. See the note on language, names, and money in the preface.

16. This could be seen as in opposition to the state's Althusserian interpellation of "citizens" (cf. Holston 2008; Roth-Gordon 2009).

17. E.g., Comaroff and Comaroff 1991, 227.

18. I am grateful to Sylvia Croese for reminding me of this point.

19. At the time of research, many services were shifting from paper-based to IT-based processing, often causing further delays.

20. Concerning the ethical challenges of doing fieldwork in Angola, see the introduction. Note also again the idioms of mobility—*dar entrada* (give entrance) to a process, *levantar* (raise) the documents, the *saída* (coming out) of an approval, and so on.

21. Given the high formal hurdles for the attribution of even a simple ordinary visa, government plans to make Angola a premier destination for international tourism have been, until now, empty talk.

22. Indicative again of the spatially differentiated nature of class in Luanda (see chapter 3).

23. Cf. Rodrigues 2007a and Tomás 2012.

24. Most famously in the *blat* exchange of favors in Russia (Ledeneva 1998) and *guanxi* in China (Yang 1994), but also in Romania (Stan 2012) and the former soviet Central Asian republics (e.g., Werner 1998).

25. See chapter 5. See also, for example, Birmingham 2012; Heywood 2002; and Messiant 2006.

26. She was thus part of what could be termed upper middle class (see chapter 3).

27. Fulano is the generic placeholder name in Portuguese, hence the repetition (see also glossary).

28. After whom one of Luanda's central maternity hospitals is named.

29. To paraphrase the title of Pepetela's historical novel *A Gloriosa Família* (1997) on the fictional Van Dum family.

30. José Filomeno de Sousa dos Santos, one of the president's sons and then vice president of the board of the first Angolan investment bank, Quantum Capital, rebranded Banco Kwanza Invest after money-laundering allegations. See, for example, http://www.exameangola.com/pt/?det=24024&id=1999&mid= (accessed 22.03.2012). In the meantime, he was made one of the three directors of the board of the Angolan Sovereign Wealth Fund.

31. Being so vague and ill-defined, it is of course a highly evocative term that works well, especially when applied to "dysfunctional" African politics, hence the idea's popularity, also in media accounts of Africa. However, I think its evocative power works just as well when applied to the context of German academia.

32. See Pitcher, Moran, and Johnston 2009.

33. Cf. Childs (1949, 58) on Ovimbundu and Miller (1976, 45) on Mbundu social organization.

34. This imagery was also used by civil society activist José "Zé Tó" Patrocínio in an interview on the government's financial support to associations: "The government is treating some associations like stepchildren and others like children," *VOA Português*, 20.01.2016, "Omunga diz que Fundo Soberano não pode financiar organizações não governamentais" (http://www.voaportugues.com/a/omunga-diz-que-fundo-soberano-nao-pode-financiar-organizacoes-nao-governantais/3154647.html, accessed 17.06.2016). See also chapter 5 and Schubert (2010) on the two civil societies.

35. Cf. Schatzberg 1993, 452.

36. Filipe, B. O., 19.04.2011.

37. See, for example, Childs (1949, 36, 41–42, 51–52) on familiarity and forms of address, and Miller (1976, 45, 78, 82) on "perpetual kinship."

38. The *alambamento* is often more important than the wedding and is performed later at the civil registry (and often also at a church).

39. E.g., Cohen 1969, Fortes 1970.

40. E.g., Ogola 2006.

41. Chama cha Mapinduzi, or CCM, the successor party to Nyerere's TANU and the ruling party of Tanzania since independence.

42. *Mail & Guardian*, 19.10.2012, "Angolan Wealth Fund Gets President's Son on Board" (http://mg.co.za/article/2012-10-19-00-angolan-wealth-fund-gets-presidents-son-on-board, accessed 30.04.2013). Shortly afterward, the other two administrators were sidelined, leaving Zénú in sole control of the FSDEA.

43. *Forbes*, 23.01.2013, "Isabel dos Santos, Daughter of Angola's President, Is Africa's First Woman Billionaire" (http://www.forbes.com/sites/kerryadolan/2013/01/23/isabel-dos-santos-daughter-of-angolas-president-is-africas-first-woman-billionaire/, accessed 30.04.2013). In all fairness, a few months later, after an outcry from national and international Angola observers, Forbes published a much more critical article in collaboration with Rafael Marques, on the sources of Isabel's wealth: *Forbes*, 14.08.2013, "Daddy's Girl: How An African 'Princess' Banked $3 Billion in a Country Living on $2 a Day" (http://www.forbes.com/sites/kerryadolan/2013/08/14/how-isabel-dos-santos-took-the-short-route-to-become-africas-richest-woman/, accessed 20.11.2013).

44. *FT*, 29.04.2013, "Lunch with the FT: Isabel dos Santos" (http://www.ft.com/intl/cms/s/2/6ffd2edc-955e-11e2-a4fa-00144feabdc0.html, accessed 30.04.2013).

45. *Maka Angola*, 18.03.2013, "Os ovos podres do Presidente e a culpa do MPLA" (http://makaangola.org/2013/04/18/os-ovos-podres-do-presidente-e-a-culpa-do-mpla-2/, accessed 02.05.2013).

46. *Club-K*, 9 June 2016, " 'Fui escolhida por causa da minha experiência no sector privado'—diz PCA da Sonangol" (http://www.club-k.net/index.php?option=com_content&view=article&id=24611%3Afui-escolhida-por-causa-da-minha-experiencia-no-sector-privado-diz-pca-da-sonangol&catid=23%3Apolitica&Itemid=1123&lang=pt, accessed 10.06.2016).

47. Though Neto is sometimes referred to as the "Father of the Nation." On the modernizing paradigm, see chapter 1. On African tradition and creole modern, see chapter 3.

48. Cf. Schatzberg 1993, 455.

49. Repeated in the formulaic *"O resgate dos valores morais e cívicos"* (The rescue of moral and civil values).

50. Cf. Moorman 2014, 26, 33–34.

51. Cf. Wedeen 1999, 67.

52. This is because we're amongst Catholics here; Protestants don't (overtly) drink. Obs: Semana Social da CEAST, Largo das Escolas, 12.01.2011.

53. See also Inglês 2016, 155.

54. FT, 29.04.2013, "Lunch with the FT: Isabel dos Santos," as quoted in note 45.

55. Cf. Aretxaga 2003, 402–3.

56. At the time of print, Lourenço was the MPLA's top nominee for the August 2017 elections, making him the likely successor of President dos Santos.

57. Cf. Wedeen 1999, 4.

5. A Culture of Immediatism

1. Although Angola has known double-digit yearly GDP growth rates since 2002, the dramatic drop in world oil prices in late 2014 severely affected the Angolan economy. The dynamics described here thus refer to the situation before the latest economic crisis.

2. See, for example, *The Economist*, 03.12.2011, "Africa Rising"; *Time*, 03.12.2012, "Africa Rising"; and the conclusion of this volume. For further discussion specifically about the Luandan middle class, see Schubert 2016b.

3. Most notably, in the Baixa (downtown central Luanda) the new headquarters of De Beers Angola/Endiama, the state diamond company, and Sonangol, the state oil company, as well as commercial banks. See also Soares de Oliveira 2007, 613.

4. As well as luxury boutiques and hotels in Lisbon, I should add. See Filipe 2013.

5. See Thornton 1980; Heywood 2002; Birmingham 2006; and Corrado 2008.

6. Pepetela's *Predadores* (2005) draws a satirical portrait of a thinly fictionalized *Empresário de confiança* (trusted/privileged entrepreneurs) and his ideological elasticity, from the heady days of independence to the crass capitalism of the 2000s.

7. On music and national identity, see again Moorman 2008, especially the last chapter on kuduro and new Angolan nationalism, as represented by the sponsorship of Dog Murras's CD production by influential generals. See also Alisch and Siegert 2011; Tomás 2014; and Moorman 2014.

8. *Sábado*, 18.08.2012, "A vida de luxo na cidade mais cara do mundo."

9. Cf. Soares de Oliveira 2015, 148–50. After two years at the top of the list (2010, 2011), Luanda briefly lost the top spot to Tokyo in the 2012 report, reclaimed it in 2013–15 (Mercer 2014), and dropping again to nr. 2 in 2016. Regime-affiliated commenters stated that this was great free publicity for Luanda; more independent voices said the only thing cheap in Luanda were people's salaries.

10. An image that is actively cultivated by the government with the help of Brazilian and European PR agencies, and depicted on embassy websites, as well as by the National Investment Promotion Agency, ANIP; see chapter 1.

11. Government 2014 population census; World Bank estimates for 2014.

12. Sample prices at the time of research were about 2.50 dollars for a liter of milk and 5 dollars for 12 eggs, though the oil price crisis from late 2014 on drove prices further up: in March 2015, the *cesta básica*, a basket of 9 essential foodstuffs used as reference, was priced at 50 dollars. Rising demand in housing by international oil companies

for their staff, combined with supply constraints after the end of the war, also sent rental prices up to about 15,000 dollars per month for a basic 2-bedroom flat in downtown Luanda, though prices have dropped a little from about 2014 due to increased supply and easing demand.

13. See Gastrow 2017, 1–2. On urban poverty, see Cain 2002; Pacheco et al. 2006; Power 2011; and Croese 2012.

14. Interview PQ, Baixa, 1.11.2010.

15. Cf. Moorman 2014, 30: "In Luanda, then, the body is ground zero of economic and physical survival and the locus of material and psychic investments."

16. In Portuguese, a popular neighborhood; not yet a fully informal *musseque* (shantytown/slum), but at the periphery of the cement city and inhabited by the popular classes.

17. As well as to the researcher on a European grant.

18. E.g., Bayart 1989 and Schatzberg 2001.

19. Cf. Bourdieu 1979.

20. Cf. Fehérváry 2002; Vigh 2008; and Jansen 2014.

21. The figure Leandro quotes seems low but is indicative of persistent salary inequalities between local and expatriate workers in many African oil industries. In Equatorial Guinea, for example, Appel quotes her informants with the memorable "We are working like Americans but being paid like Africans" (Appel 2012, 706).

22. This echoes Filip de Boeck's observation from Kinshasa, where he notes that Slum dwellers who suffer from forced evictions still endorse and voice desires for the new, modern settlement they have to make way for (2011, 278).

23. Cf. Ferguson 1999.

24. Irene Neto, Fundação Agostinho Neto, 29.08.2011.

25. As on rapper MCK's track, "O País do Pai Banana," on *Proibido Ouvir Isto* (Luanda: 2011): *Polícia já não quer gasosa, agora é saldo* (The police don't want *gasosa* anymore; now it's saldo).

26. Quite typically for the nature of Angola's politically connected oligopolies, Isabel dos Santos, after taking the helm of Sonangol in 2016, decreed that the company would source all its cabazes for the Christmas season from the Candando supermarket chain, which is owned by none other than Isabel dos Santos.

27. Never mind that there are, in fact, simply not enough jobs for the existing skill base.

28. See Archambault (2015, 257) on the intimate economy and commodification of love relationships in Mozambique. See also Archambault (2012, 406–7), on the practice of soliciting phone credit through "*bips.*"

29. Unease about the commodification of social relationships is, however, not limited to people left outside. The author João Melo, an old-time MPLA member and MP noted for his sometimes virulent attacks of the opposition, writes in his collection of short stories *O homem que não tira o palito da boca* (2009) of shady deals, base desires, and couples breaking up because of a general's offering a car and an apartment to the girl.

30. Cf. Wedeen 1999, 25.

31. Echoing the other, often-mentioned "weapons of the regime," the media and the police (Schubert 2010, 665).

32. Though the government has been adept at renegotiating new credit lines following the 2014 oil-price crash, the oil-driven growth miracle looks increasingly hollow; see Epilogue.

33. Cf. Sumich 2015, on Mozambique.

34. I found my *quarto-sala* in São Paulo (chapter 2) through such an *intermediária*, Tia Maria.

35. See note 12, above.

36. Cf. Gastrow 2014b, 232–33; Pitcher and Moorman 2015.

37. In that case not referring to the abovementioned, better-known Isabel dos Santos, but to her half-sister Welwitschea José "Tchizé" dos Santos Pego; Simão, Baixa, 24.06.2011.

38. Cf. Barreau-Tran 2015; Schubert 2016b.

39. A well-known and often satirized equation, as stories and jokes about the president, ministers, or generals and their *catorzinhas* (little fourteens) and mistresses abound. See also Melo 2009; Schubert 2010, 668.

40. The saying goes that all academics were *comPrados*—a pun on *comprar* (to buy) and the popular Toyota Prado luxury SUV.

41. A strategy that is increasingly backfiring, though: at a rally in support of the president's candidacy as the MPLA's head of list for the 31 August 2012 elections, held at the national stadium on 23 June 2012, the audience were more interested in singers Yuri da Cunha and Yola Araújo than in the president's planned appearance. Despite First Provincial Secretary Bento Bento's exhortations, applause for dos Santos remained lukewarm, and dos Santos ended up not appearing. See *Maka Angola*, 23.06.2012, "Yola Araújo mais popular que Dos Santos" (http://makaangola.org/2012/06/23/yola-araujo-mais-popular-que-dos-santos/>, accessed 07.2012).

42. Cf. Smith 2008.

43. Cf. Pearce 2012a, 208.

44. Or, again, as MCK put it, *"eles fizeram da miséria um negócio"* (They made a business of misery); song quoted above.

45. It has been claimed that the appointment of Isabel dos Santos as CEO of Sonangol and of Zénú dos Santos as the head of the FSDEA (see chapter 4) is precisely to ensure that whoever becomes President dos Santos' political successor will be economically dependent on the goodwill of the dos Santos family.

46. See also Vallée 2008, 38.

47. Manuel Ennes Ferreira, personal communication, 12.02.2016.

48. Cf. Jansen 2014.

6. Against the System, within the System

1. Cf. Piot 2010, 20.

2. Arguably, there had not been any openly antigovernment demonstrations since the 27 de Maio 1977. See Pawson 2007; 2014.

3. Respectively Agostinho Neto, of the MPLA; Jonas Savimbi, of the UNITA; and Holden Roberto, of the FNLA.

4. Many Angolan public figures, politicians, and generals are widely known by their noms de guerre and referred to by these nicknames (for example, Gen. Manuel Hélder Vieira Dias "Kopelipa," or Julião Mateus Paulo "Dino Matross"). See also later in

this chapter ("The Fighting People of Angola") on war names. For an analysis of naming practices during the independence struggle, see Brinkman 2004.

5. The 2010 constitution formalized Angola's "hyper-presidentialism," indicating how the law is used as a tool to legalize the president's control over the country (Lima, 2015, 185–86). The formal civil liberties enshrined in this "model constitution" then open up the law as a new arena of contestation, too, a theme I do not develop here but which certainly warrants further investigation.

6. For Dino Matross's statements, see, for example: *VOA News*, 18.02.2011, "Angola: MPLA diz que Luanda não será o Cairo" (http://www.voanews.com/portuguese /news/revolucao-angola-receios-116480948.html, accessed 15.12.2011); *Radio Nacional de Angola*, 20.02.2011, "Dino Matross: Nação angolana não deve confundir realidade do país com a dos países árabes de África" (http://www.angonoticias.com/Artigos /item/29081, accessed 15.12.2011).

7. *O País*, 07.03.2011, "MPLA denuncia cabala contra Angola" (http://www.opais .net/pt/opais/?id=1929&det=19449&mid=, accessed 15.12.2011).

8. B. O., 03.03.2011.

9. See http://www.youtube.com/watch?v=_mhF7tDoekg (accessed 10.12.2011).

10. This song itself also echoed an earlier song "Milhorró" by the Kiezos, in which the refrain was *"vão, vão-se embora! Isto assim não pode ser!"* (Go, go away! It cannot be that way!), written at a period during the colonial time where PIDE regularly found *"Fora! Voltam para vossa terra!"* (Out! Go back to your country!) written on the walls of the *musseques* (Moorman 2008, 3, 128–30). Flores himself has also become more outspoken on the issue of political repression since 2015.

11. As I discuss in the introduction, I followed the advice of the people around me (cf. Kovats-Bernat 2002, 3): although I did not hole up for three days, I carefully avoided the Independence Square and surroundings.

12. UNITEL is largely owned by Isabel dos Santos, one of the president's daughters; MOVICEL is owned by a consortium of high-ranking FAA generals. For more details on the business dealings of Angola's elite, see Marques de Morais 2010 and Filipe 2013.

13. I discuss the idea of the "two civil societies" in greater detail in J. Schubert (2010).

14. *JdA*, 06.03.2011, "Quatro milhões de pessoas nas ruas de todo o país" (http:// jornaldeangola.sapo.ao/20/0/quatro_milhoes_de_pessoas_nas_ruas_de_todo_o _pais, accessed 20.12.2011).

15. *Angonoticias*, 05.03.2011, "Marcha do MPLA juntou três milhões contra os 'aventureiros'" (http://www.angonoticias.com/Artigos/item/29271, accessed 20.12.2011).

16. *AP*, 05.03.2011, "More than 20,000 Demonstrate Peacefully in Angola" (http:// news.yahoo.com/more-20-000-peacefully-demonstrate-angola-20110305-075536-717 .html, accessed 20.12.2011).

17. Interview with Isabel, Piscina do Alvalade, 08.03.2011.

18. According to Roque (2013, 3), quoting Angolan observers, the pro-peace rally cost the MPLA around twenty million US dollars.

19. See, for example, *IPS*, 10.03.2011, "Mass Protests Fail but Angolan Activists Remain Defiant" (http://www.ips.org/africa/2011/03/mass-protests-fail-but-angolan -activists-remain-defiant/, accessed 20.12.2011).

20. *VOA Português*, 07.03.2011, "Polícia angolana prende manifestantes e trava protesto anti-governamental" (http://www.voanews.com/portuguese/news/Policia

-angolana-prende-manifestantes-e-trava-protesto-anti-governamental-117533114
.html, accessed 19.01.2012).

21. I am specifically thinking about the outrage seen in the Western media when the Islamic State uses social media for its propaganda goals.

22. The diversity and heterogeneity is also reflected in the loose, informal character of those various groupings and in the shifting group names they employ (see later in the chapter, section "The Fighting People of Angola").

23. Cf. Eckert 2011, 312.

24. Cf. Archambault 2012, 396, for Mozambique.

25. The interview, a previously scripted and rather uncritical conversation for the Portuguese news channel *SIC Notícias*, was in fact dos Santos's first public interview in twenty-two years (see *SIC Notícias*, 06.06.2013, "Primeira grande entrevista concedida pelo Presidente de Angola em 22 anos" (http://sicnoticias.sapo.pt/mundo/2013/06/06/primeira-grande-entrevista-concedida-pelo-presidente-de-angola-em-22-anos, accessed 19.06.2013).

26. Similar to Equatorial Guinea; cf. Campos-Serrano 2013, 318.

27. Cf. Fontein 2012 for the case of Zimbabwe.

28. Cf. Brinkman 2004.

29. Nito Alves's case is slightly more complex: his full name is Manuel Chivonda Baptista Nito Alves, as his father was a supporter of the 1977 Nito Alves. The contemporary Nito Alves, conscious of the historic name he bears, was politicized in the 2011 demonstrations and became Angola's youngest prisoner of conscience in September 2013, having been imprisoned without trial for printing shirts with the president's effigy marked "Horrible Dictator Out!" See Amnesty International's call for his release (http://www.amnesty.org/en/library/asset/AFR12/005/2013/en/61e7519c-c31e-489b-86f3-c58f799afbac/afr120052013en.html, accessed 26.11.2013); *Guardian*, 03.10.2013, "Nito Alves: The Teenage Reincarnation of Resistance in Angola" (http://www.theguardian.com/commentisfree/2013/oct/03/nito-alves-teenage-resistance-angola, accessed 03.12.2013).

30. Mbanza Hamza, personal communication, 13.06.2013, caps his.

31. *Club-K*, 18.09.2011, "Angola suspeita que França esteja por detrás das manifestações em Luanda" (http://www.club-k.net/index.php?option=com_content&view=article&id=8857:angola-suspeita-que-franca-esteja-por-detras-da-manifestacao-de-3-de-setembro-&catid=23:politica&Itemid=123, accessed 19.06.2013).

32. See, for example, *Angop*, 02.03.2011, "Detectadas munições anti-aérea em navio norte-americano baseado no Lobito" (http://www.portalangop.co.ao/motix/pt_pt/noticias/politica/2011/2/9/Detectadas-municoes-anti-aerea-navio-norte-americano-baseado-Lobito,fe0b4573-e117-4455-8550-4654d34da3b9.html, accessed 19.12.2011).

33. Group interview, Roque parish, 22.12.2010.

34. *Angola24horas.com*, 04.03.2011, "Perdemos o medo, mãe!" (www.angola24horas.com/index.php?/item/4236-perdemos-o-medo-mae, accessed 03.11.2013). See also Roque 2013, 2.

35. *VOA Português*, 03.09.2011, "Brutalidade policial trava manifestação em Luanda" (http://www.voaportugues.com/content/luanda-09-03-2011-voanews-129184138/1261043.html, accessed 19.06.2013).

36. *Club-K*, 12.09.2011, "Juiz do caso manifestantes recusa vídeo da violência policial" (http://club-k.net/index.php?option=com_content&view=article&id=8773:juiz -do-caso-manifestantes-recusa-video-da-violencia-policial&catid=2&Itemid=88, accessed 19.06.2013).

37. A patently absurd argument because Islam is extremely marginal in Angola (and de facto is not recognized as a religion) and because there is no precedent of militant religious activism.

38. *Angop*, 13.09.2011, "'Os jovens estão a ser manipulados por adultos inconsequentes'—diz Líder da JMPLA" (http://club-k.net/index.php?option=com _content&view=article&id=8777:qos-jovens-estao-a-ser-manipulados-por -adultos -inconsequentesq-diz-lider-da-jmpla&catid=23:politica&Itemid=2, accessed 04.01.2012).

39. *JdA*, 09.09.2011, "Portugueses perdem o juizo" (http://jornaldeangola.sapo.ao /19/46/portugueses_perdem_juizo, accessed 04.01.2012).

40. The election date, originally scheduled for the first weekend of September, was changed to the week before, three days after the president's seventieth birthday celebrations.

41. Two veteran activists who were organizing the 7 June protest, António Alves Kamulingue and Isaías Cassule, disappeared without a trace on 22 May 2012, ahead of this first demonstration; their whereabouts remained unknown until November 2013.

42. *VOA Português*, 03.06.2012, "Angola: Polícia dispersa manifestantes com armas de fogo" (http://www.voaportugues.com/content/article-06-20-2012-luandademonstratio ns-159745535/1450724.html, accessed 03.06.2013).

43. Youth protesters were by then commonly known as Movimento Revolucionário (MR, Revolutionary Movement), which makes it sound like a more unitary, organized movement than it actually is.

44. *News24*, 18.05.2012, "Angolan Election Commission Head Removed" (http:// www.news24.com/Africa/News/Angolan-election-commission-head-removed -20120518, accessed 03.06.2013).

45. Though to give credit where it's due, as Sylvia Croese argues, the government has delivered about 100,000 public housing units in Luanda alone over the past few years. While national reconstruction has served to enrich the elite, "under certain conditions patrimonial rule may even be central to producing developmental outcomes" (2017, 82).

46. Lauding, for example, the "perfect miracle of national reconstruction" (*JdA*, 12.08.2012, "O milagre perfeito," http://jornaldeangola.sapo.ao/opiniao/a_palavra _do_director/o_milagre_perfeito, accessed 09.02.2017) and underlining that "democracy has to follow the rules" (*JdA*, 22.07.2012, "A democracia tem regras," http:// jornaldeangola.sapo.ao/opiniao/a_palavra_do_director/a_democracia_tem_regras, accessed 09.02.2017) to discredit any opposition demonstrations.

Conclusion

1. The author lists "North Korea (DPRK), Azerbaijan, Turkmenistan, Kazakhstan, Uzbekistan, Belorussia (Belarus), and Cuba," together with Russia, China, and Iran

(Monday 2011, 812). In Africa, one could add Gabon, Mozambique, and the Republic of Congo, to name but the three most obvious examples.

2. Cf. Quayson (2014, 240–41), on Accra.

3. Cf. Gastrow 2017, 2.

4. Cf. Wedeen (1999) on Syria.

Epilogue

1. As this was the first time he had been formally elected, the two-term limit would theoretically only apply to him in 2022, allowing him to stand again as his party's presidential candidate in 2017, which he initially appeared to intend to do.

2. HRW, 22.11.2013, "Angola: Officials Implicated in Killing Protest Organizers" (http://www.hrw.org/news/2013/11/22/angola-officials-implicated-killing-protest-organizers, accessed 28.11.2013).

3. *Angonotícias*, 20.11.2013, "MPLA acusa UNITA de tentar criar caos, anarquia e violência" (http://www.angonoticias.com/Artigos/item/40639/mpla-acusa-unita-de-tentar-criar-caos-anarquia-e-violencia, accessed 28.11.2013).

4. *Angop*, 22.11.2013, "Todos pela defesa da paz!" (http://www.portalangop.co.ao/angola/pt_pt/noticias/politica/2013/10/47/Todos-pela-defesa-paz,b37c2d34-e722-4d2e-9399-6c671970c678.html, accessed 28.11.2013).

5. *Club-K*, 20.11.2013, "JMPLA descobre que foi fundada a '23 de novembro'" (http://www.club-k.net/index.php?option=com_content&view=article&id=16794:jmpla-descobre-que-foi-fundada-a-23-de-novembro&catid=23:politica&Itemid=123, accessed 28.11.2013).

6. *Club-K*, 23.11.2013, "Angola em estado de sítio: Polícia invade sede da UNITA à tiros" (http://www.club-k.net/index.php?option=com_content&view=article&id=16836:angola-em-estado-de-sitio-policia-invade-sede-da-unita-a-tiros&catid=23:politica&Itemid=123, accessed 28.11.2013).

7. *Maka Angola*, 23.11.2013, "Guarda Presidencial mata activista político" (http://www.makaangola.org/2013/11/guarda-presidencial-mata-activista-politico/, accessed 10.02.2017).

8. *Al Jazeera*, 23.11.2013, "Angolan Police Teargas Opposition Protesters" (http://www.aljazeera.com/news/africa/2013/11/angolan-police-teargas-opposition-protesters-2013112315371418886.html, accessed 28.11.2013).

9. *DW*, 25.11.2013, "Angola regressa à calma após um morto e 292 detenções em manifestação" (http://www.dw.de/angola-regressa à-calma-após-um-morto-e-292-detenções-em-manifestação/a-17253675, accessed 28.11.2013).

10. *DW*, 27.11.2013, "Marchantes gritavam 'Zedú assassino,' diz Rafael Marques ao descrever cortejo de Manuel Ganga" (http://www.dw.de/marchantes-gritavam-zedú-assassino-diz-rafael-marques-ao-descrever-cortejo-de-manuel-ganga/a-17258512, accessed 28.11.2013).

11. It is one of the ironies of Angola's ambivalent relation with the Bretton Woods institutions that the IMF had for years called for the phasing out of fuel subsidies claiming that subsidies distorted the market and created false incentives and that the government only cut the subsidies when faced with another crisis. This led to the almost doubling of petrol and diesel prices at the pumps and eventually resulted in a violent

taxi driver strike in Luanda in October 2015, after which the government agreed to a 50 percent rise in transport fares, again chiefly affecting the poorest segment of the population, who spend a large part of their disposable income on transport.

12. *VOA Português*, 22.06.2015, "Modelo operacional da Sonangol está falido, diz relatório" (http://www.voaportugues.com/content/modelo-operacional-da-sonangol-esta-falido/2832514.html, accessed 16.06.2016).

13. Aslak Orre, *CMI News*, 19.05.2015, "Covering Up a Massacre in Angola?" (http://www.cmi.no/news/?1549-massacre, accessed 16.06.2016).

14. *VOA Português*, 23.05.2015, "Angola volta a rejeitar pedido da ONU para investigação a confrontos no Huambo" (http://www.voaportugues.com/a/angola-volta-a-rejeitar-pedido-da-onu-para-investigacao-a-confrontos-no-huambo/2786904.html, accessed 16.06.2016).

15. *Rede Angola*, 05.04.2016, "Kalupeteka condenado a 28 anos de prisão" (http://www.redeangola.info/kalupeteka-condenado-a-28-anos-de-prisao/, accessed 16.06.2016).

16. *Maka Angola*, 25.06.2016, "Angolan Authorities Detain Youth Protesters as 'Coup Plotters'" (https://www.makaangola.org/2015/06/angolan-authorities-detain-youth-protesters-as-%c2%93coup-plotters%c2%94/, accessed 16.06.2016).

17. *Maka Angola*, 16.09.2015, "Solidarity Meeting with Political Prisoners Gathers a Thousand People" (https://www.makaangola.org/2015/09/solidarity-meeting-with-political-prisoners-gathers-a-thousand-people/, accessed 16.06.2016).

18. It also changed the popular perception of Luaty Beirão. After his first appearance around the 2011 protests, many people saw him as a wastrel and a spoiled child of the regime (his father was a close ally of dos Santos and had run the president's foundation for several years), with his *mestiço* background and foreign education discrediting him in their view. Following the hunger strike, he has become the face of the Angolan protesters, even though he has repeatedly denied seeking any leadership role. This has afforded the movement more visibility abroad but has also led to levels of hero worship around the iconic figure of Luaty that are problematic for the movement itself.

19. *Rede Angola*, 28.03.2016, "Activistas condenados de dois a oito anos de prisão" (http://www.redeangola.info/activistas-condenados/, accessed 16.06.2016). After the activists had spent a year in detention, on 29 June 2016 the Supreme Court upheld the defense's habeas corpus petition and ordered the release of the accused "under terms of identity and residence" pending the decision of their appeal (http://www.redeangola.info/defesa-confirma-libertacao-de-activistas-hoje/, accessed 29.06.2016). It remains, however, unclear whether and how this signals a newly independent judiciary, or rather a relaxation based on *orientações superiores*. At the time of writing, I suspect the latter because we are entering the run-up to the 2017 elections.

20. In addition to the cases of Monte Sumi and the trial of the "15+2," one could also mention the sham trial of Rafael Marques and his conviction for "slander" in April 2015, as well as the sentencing of Cabindan civil society activist Marcos Mavungo in September 2015 for having unsuccessfully tried to organize a demonstration. Mavungo's prison sentence was overturned by the Supreme Court in May 2016, and he was freed after more than a year in detention.

21. Irene Neto, FAAN, Baixa, 29.08.2011.

22. Bayart 1989.

23. See Sumich 2015 for similar dynamics in Mozambique.

24. WHO, March 2016, "Angola Grapples with Worst Yellow Fever Outbreak in 30 Years" (http://www.who.int/features/2016/angola-worst-yellow-fever/en/, accessed 16.06.2016). See also Rafael Marques's grim report on *Maka Angola*, 07.03.2016, "The Children's Corridor of Death in Angola's Second Hospital" (https://www.makaangola.org/2016/03/the-childrens-corridor-of-death-in -angolas-second-hospital/, accessed 16.06.2016).

25. *Rede Angola*, 14.12.2016, "MPLA assume reforma de José Eduardo dos Santos" (http://www.redeangola.info/mpla-assume-reforma-de-jose-eduardo-dos-santos/, accessed 10.02.2017).

26. That is especially true given UNITA's failure to renew its leadership for the 2017 elections; under such circumstances, can opposition politics really present a credible political alternative?

27. Personal communication with informants, July 2016.

References

Ahearn, Laura M. 2001. "Language and Agency." *Annual Review of Anthropology* 30: 109–37. doi:10.2307/3069211.

Alexander, Jocelyn, and JoAnn McGregor. 2007. "Veterans, Violence, and Nationalism in Zimbabwe." In *States of Violence: Politics, Youth, and Memory in Contemporary Africa*, edited by Edna G. Bay and Donald L. Donham, 215–35. Charlottesville: University of Virginia Press.

Alisch, Stefanie, and Nadine Siegert. 2011. "Angolanidade Revisited: Kuduro." *NoRient: Network for Local and Global Sounds and Media Culture*, June. http://norient.com/academic/kuduro/.

Amundsen, Inge, and Cristiana Abreu. 2006. "Civil Society in Angola: Inroads, Space and Accountability." CMI Report 2006: 14. Bergen: Christian Michelsen Institute.

Anderson, Benedict. 1983. *Imagined Communities*. London: Verso.

Appel, Hannah. 2012. "Offshore Work: Oil, Modularity, and the How of Capitalism in Equatorial Guinea." *American Ethnologist* 39 (4): 692–709. doi:10.1111/j.1548-1425.2012.01389.x.

Archambault, Julie Soleil. 2012. "'Travelling While Sitting Down': Mobile Phones, Mobility and the Communication Landscape in Inhambane, Mozambique." *Africa* 82 (3): 393–412.

——. 2015. "Taking Love Seriously in Human-Plant Relations in Mozambique: Towards an Anthropology of Affective Encounters." *Cultural Anthropology* 31 (2): 244–71.

Aretxaga, Begoña. 2000. "A Fictional Reality. Paramilitary Death Squads and the Construction of State Terror in Spain." In *Death Squad: The Anthropology of State Terror*, edited by Jeffrey A. Sluka, 46–69. Philadelphia: University of Pennsylvania Press.

——. 2003. "Maddening States." *Annual Review of Anthropology* 32: 393–410.

Autesserre, Séverine. 2012. "Dangerous Tales: Dominant Narratives on the Congo and their Unintended Consequences." *African Affairs* 111 (443): 202–22. doi:10.1093/afraf/adr080.

Azaryahu, Maoz. 1996. "The Power of Commemorative Street Names." *Environment and Planning D: Society and Space* 14 (3): 311–30. doi:10.1068/d140311.

Banégas, Richard. 2006. "Côte d'Ivoire: Patriotism, Ethnonationalism and Other African Modes of Self-Writing." *African Affairs* 105 (421): 535–52. doi:10.1093/afraf/adl035.

Barbeitos, Arlindo. 1997. "Une perspective angolaise sur le lusotropicalisme." *Lusotopie* 1997: 309–25.

Barber, Karin. 1997. *Readings in African Popular Culture*. Bloomington: Indiana University Press.

Barreau-Tran, Léa. 2015. "Itinéraires d'une commerçante angolaise dans la mondialisation." *Lesedi : Lettre D'information de l'Institut Français d'Afrique Du Sud-Recherche* 18: 5–12.

Bayart, Jean-François. 1989. *L'État en Afrique: La politique du ventre*. Paris: Fayard.

———. 2000. "Africa in the World: A History of Extraversion." *African Affairs* 99 (395): 217–67.

Bayart, Jean-François, Stephen Ellis, and Béatrice Hibou. 1999. *The Criminalization of the State in Africa*. Bloomington: Indiana University Press.

Beck, Teresa Koloma. 2009. "Staging Society: Sources of Loyalty in the Angolan UNITA." *Contemporary Security Policy* 30 (2): 343–55. doi:10.1080/13523260903060235.

———. 2013. *The Normality of Civil War*. Frankfurt: Campus Verlag.

Becker, Gay, Yewoubdar Beyene, and Pauline Ken. 2000. "Memory, Trauma, and Embodied Distress: The Management of Disruption in the Stories of Cambodians in Exile." *Ethos* 28 (3): 320–45. doi:10.1525/eth.2000.28.3.320.

Becker, Heike. 2011. "Commemorating Heroes in Windhoek and Eenhana: Memory, Culture and Nationalism in Namibia, 1990–2010." *Africa* 81 (4): 519–43.

Bender, Gerald J. 1978. *Angola under the Portuguese: The Myth and the Reality*. Berkeley: University of California Press.

Biehl, João, and Ramah McKay. 2012. "Ethnography as Political Critique." *Anthropological Quarterly* 85 (4): 1209–27. doi:10.1353/anq.2012.0057.

Bierschenk, Thomas, and Jean-Pierre Olivier de Sardan, eds. 2014. *States at Work: Dynamics of African Bureaucracies*. Leiden: Brill.

Birmingham, David. 1978. "The Twenty-Seventh of May: An Historical Note on the Abortive 1977 'Coup' in Angola." *African Affairs* 77 (309): 554–64.

———. 1988. "Carnival at Luanda." *Journal of African History* 29 (Special Issue 01): 93–103. doi:10.1017/S002185370003601X.

———. 1993. *Frontline Nationalism in Angola and Mozambique*. Trenton, NJ: Africa World Press.

———. 2002. "Angola." In *A History of Postcolonial Lusophone Africa*, edited by Patrick Chabal, 137–84. London: C. Hurst.

———. 2006. *Empire in Africa: Angola and Its Neighbours*. Athens: Ohio University Press.

———. 2012. "Is 'Nationalism' a Feature of Angola's Cultural Identity?" In *Sure Road? Nationalisms in Angola, Guinea-Bissau and Mozambique*, edited by Eric Morier-Genoud, 217–30. Leiden: Brill.

Birth, Kevin. 2006. "Past Times: Temporal Structuring of History and Memory." *Ethos* 34 (2): 192–210. doi:10.1525/eth.2006.34.2.192.

Bissell, William Cunningham. 2005. "Engaging Colonial Nostalgia." *Cultural Anthropology* 20 (2): 215–48. doi:10.1525/can.2005.20.2.215.

Blanes, Ruy Llera. 2011. "Unstable Biographies. The Ethnography of Memory and Historicity in an Angolan Prophetic Movement." *History and Anthropology* 22 (1): 93–119. doi:10.1080/02757206.2011.546854.

———. 2012. "Moral Circumscriptions: Involuntary Mobility, Diaspora and Ideological Configurations in the Angolan Tokoist Church." *Canadian Journal of African*

Studies / La Revue Canadienne Des Études Africaines 46 (3): 367–80. doi:10.1080 /00083968.2012.737525.

Blundo, Giorgio. 2006. "Dealing with the Local State: The Informal Privatization of Street-Level Bureaucracies in Senegal." *Development and Change* 37 (4): 799–819. doi:10.1111/j.1467-7660.2006.00502.x.

Blundo, Giorgio, and Jean-Pierre Olivier de Sardan. 2006. *Everyday Corruption and the State: Citizens and Public Officials in Africa.* Cape Town: David Philip.

Bourdieu, Pierre. 1979. *La distinction: Critique sociale du jugement.* Paris: Minuit.

Bourgois, Philippe. 1990. "Confronting Anthropological Ethics: Ethnographic Lessons from Central America." *Journal of Peace Research* 27 (1): 43–54.

Bratton, Michael, and Nicolas van de Walle. 1994. "Neopatrimonial Regimes and Political Transitions in Africa." *World Politics* 46 (4): 453–89. doi:10.2307/2950715.

Bridgland, Fred. 1988. *Jonas Savimbi: A Key to Africa.* Sevenoaks: Coronet.

Brinkman, Inge. 2004. "Language, Names, and War: The Case of Angola." *African Studies Review* 47 (3): 143–63.

Brittain, Victoria. 2002. "Jonas Savimbi, 1934–2002." *Review of African Political Economy* 29 (91): 128–30. doi:10.1080/03056240208704591.

Bryant, Rebecca. 2013. "History's Remainders: Belonging, Temporality, and Unfinished Pasts." Paper presented at the Social Anthropology Seminar Series 2013/2014, University of Edinburgh, 25 October 2013.

Bryceson, Deborah Fahy. 2000. "Of Criminals and Clients: African Culture and Afro-Pessimism in a Globalized World." *Canadian Journal of African Studies / Revue Canadienne Des Études Africaines* 34 (2): 417–42. doi:10.2307/486424.

Buire, Chloé. 2012. "Exploring Urban Identities in Luanda." Fieldwork Report, CUBES, University of the Witwatersrand.

——. 2014. "The Dream and the Ordinary: An Ethnographic Investigation of Suburbanisation in Luanda." *African Studies* 73 (2): 290–312. doi:10.1080/0002 0184.2014.925229.

——. 2016. "L'hégémonie politique à l'épreuve des musiques urbaines à Luanda, Angola." *Politique africaine,* 141 (April): 53–76.

Buur, Lars. 2010. "Xiconhoca: Mozambique's Post-Independence Traitor." In *Traitors: Suspicion, Intimacy, and the Ethics of State-Building,* edited by Sharika Thiranagama and Tobias Kelly, 24–47. Philadelphia: University of Pennsylvania Press.

Cabrita Mateus, Dalila, and Álvaro Mateus. 2011. *Angola 61 Guerra Colonial: Causas e consequências. O 4 de Fevereiro e o 15 de Março.* Alfragide: Texto editores.

Cain, Allan. 2002. "Urban Poverty and Civic Development in Post-War Angola." CMI Report 2002: 8. Bergen: Christian Michelsen Institute.

Calvão, Filipe. 2013. "The Transporter, the Agitator, and the Kamanguista: Qualia and the In/visible Materiality of Diamonds." *Anthropological Theory* 13 (1–2): 119–36. doi:10.1177/1463499613483404.

Campos-Serrano, Alicia. 2013. "Extraction Offshore, Politics Inshore, and the Role of the State in Equatorial Guinea." *Africa: The Journal of the International African Institute* 83 (2): 314–39.

Candido, Mariana P. 2013. *An African Slaving Port and the Atlantic World: Benguela and Its Hinterland.* Cambridge: Cambridge University Press.

Ceuppens, Bambi, and Peter Geschiere. 2005. "Autochthony: Local or Global? New Modes in the Struggle over Citizenship and Belonging in Africa and Europe." *Annual Review of Anthropology* 34 (January): 385–407. doi:10.2307/25064891.

Chabal, Patrick. 2009. *Africa: The Politics of Suffering and Smiling.* London: Zed Books.

Chabal, Patrick, and Jean-Pascal Daloz. 1999. *Africa Works: Disorder as Political Instrument.* Bloomington: Indiana University Press.

——. 2006. *Culture Troubles: Politics and the Interpretation of Meaning.* Chicago, IL: University of Chicago Press.

Chalfin, Brenda. 2006. "Global Customs Regimes and the Traffic in Sovereignty: Enlarging the Anthropology of the State." *Current Anthropology* 47 (2): 243–76. doi:10.1086/499548.

Chatterjee, Partha. 2007. *The Nation and Its Fragments: Colonial and Postcolonial Histories.* Princeton, NJ: Princeton University Press.

Childs, Gladwyn Murray. 1949. *Umbundu Kinship and Character: Being a Description of the Social Structure and Individual Development of the Ovimbundu of Angola, with Observations Concerning the Bearing on the Enterprise of Christian Missions of Certain Phases of the Life and Culture Described.* London: Oxford University Press.

Cilliers, Jakkie, and Christian Dietrich. 2000. *Angola's War Economy: The Role of Oil and Diamonds.* Pretoria: Institute for Security Studies.

Clarence-Smith, Gervase. 1980. "Review Article: Class Structure and Class Struggles in Angola in the 1970s." *Journal of Southern African Studies* 7 (1): 109–26.

——. 1985. *The Third Portuguese Empire, 1825–1975: A Study in Economic Imperialism.* Manchester: Manchester University Press.

Cohen, Abner. 1969. "Political Anthropology: The Analysis of the Symbolism of Power Relations." *Man* 4 (2): 215–35. doi:10.2307/2799569.

Cole, Jennifer. 2001. *Forget Colonialism? Sacrifice and the Art of Memory in Madagascar.* Berkeley: University of California Press.

——. 2006. "Malagasy and Western Conceptions of Memory: Implications for Postcolonial Politics and the Study of Memory." *Ethos* 34 (2): 211–43. doi:10.1525/eth.2006.34.2.211.

Collier, Delinda. 2013. "A 'New Man' for Africa: Some Particularities of the Marxist Homem Novo within Angolan Cultural Policy." In *De-Centering the Cold War*, edited by Fabio Lanza and Jadwiga Pieper Mooney, 187–206. London: Routledge.

Collier, Paul, and Anke Hoeffler. 2000. "Greed and Grievance in Civil War." Working Paper Series 2000-18, Centre for the Study of African Economies, Institute of Economics and Statistics, University of Oxford.

Comaroff, Jean, and John L. Comaroff. 1991. *Of Revelation and Revolution.* Vol. 1, *Christianity, Colonialism and Consciousness in South Africa.* Chicago, IL: University of Chicago Press.

——. 1999. "Occult Economies and the Violence of Abstraction: Notes from the South African Postcolony." *American Ethnologist* 26 (2): 279–303.

——. 2012. "Theory from the South: Or, How Euro-America Is Evolving toward Africa." *Anthropological Forum* 22 (2): 113–31.

Comaroff, Jean, and John L. Comaroff, eds. 2001. *Millennial Capitalism and the Culture of Neoliberalism.* Durham, NC: Duke University Press.

Comerford, Michael J. 2005. *The Peaceful Face of Angola: Biography of a Peace Process (1991–2002)*. Luanda: M. Comerford.

Corkin, Lucy. 2013. *Uncovering African Agency: Angola's Management of China's Credit Lines*. Farnham: Ashgate.

Corrado, Jacopo. 2008. *The Creole Elite and the Rise of Angolan Protonationalism: 1870–1920*. Amherst, NY: Cambria Press.

Cramer, Christopher. 2006. *Civil War Is Not a Stupid Thing: Accounting for Violence in Developing Countries*. London: Hurst.

Crehan, Kate. 1997. *The Fractured Community: Landscapes of Power and Gender in Rural Zambia*. Berkeley: University of California Press.

——. 2002. *Gramsci, Culture and Anthropology*. Berkeley: University of California Press.

Croese, Sylvia. 2010. "Angola: Rebuilding by Demolishing—the Politics of National Reconstruction." *Pambazuka* 475. http://pambazuka.org/en/category/features/63298.

——. 2012. "One Million Houses? Chinese Engagement in Angola's National Reconstruction." In *China and Angola: A Marriage of Convenience?*, edited by Marcus Power and Ana Cristina Alves, 124–44. Cape Town: Pambazuka.

——. 2017. "State-Led Housing Delivery as an Instrument of Developmental Patrimonialism: The Case of Post-War Angola." *African Affairs* 116 (462): 80–100. doi:10.1093/afraf/adw070.

Da Rocha, Alves. 2012. *Economic Growth in Angola to 2017: The Main Challenges*. Angola Brief. Bergen: Christian Michelsen Institute.

Das, Veena, and Deborah Poole. 2004. *Anthropology in the Margins of the State*. Santa Fe, CA: School for Advanced Research Press.

Dean, M. 1999. *Governmentality: Power and Rule in Modern Society*. London: Sage

de Boeck, Filip. 2011. "Inhabiting Ocular Ground: Kinshasa's Future in the Light of Congo's Spectral Urban Politics." *Cultural Anthropology* 26 (2): 263–86. doi:10.1111/j.1548-1360.2011.01099.x.

de Certeau, Michel. 1988. *The Practice of Everyday Life*. Translated by Steven F. Rendall. Berkeley: University of California Press.

deGrassi, Aaron. 2008. "'Neopatrimonialism' and Agricultural Development in Africa: Contributions and Limitations of a Contested Concept." *African Studies Review* 51 (3): 107–33. doi:10.1353/arw.0.0087.

Derluguian, Georgi M. 2005. *Bourdieu's Secret Admirer in the Caucasus*. Chicago, IL: University of Chicago Press.

Diani, Mario. 2011. "Networks and Internet into Perspective." *Swiss Political Science Review* 17 (4): 469–74. doi:10.1111/j.1662-6370.2011.02040.x.

Dorman, Sara Rich. 2009. "Patrick Chabal: An Appreciation?" *Critical African Studies* 1 (2): 10–18. doi:10.1080/20407211.2009.10530746.

Dorman, Sara Rich, Daniel Patrick Hammett, and Paul Nugent, eds. 2007. *Making Nations, Creating Strangers: States and Citizenship in Africa*. Leiden: Brill.

Ducados, Henda Lucia, and Manuel Ennes Ferreira. 1998. *O financiamento informal e as estratégias de sobrevivência económica das mulheres em Angola: A kixikila no município do Sambizanga (Luanda)*. Documentos de trabalho n° 53-1998. CEsA - ISEG, Lisboa.

Duffy, James. 1962. *Portugal in Africa*. Harmondsworth: Penguin.

Duncan, Christopher R. 2013. *Violence and Vengeance: Religious Conflict and Its Aftermath in Eastern Indonesia*. Ithaca, NY: Cornell University Press.

Eckert, Julia. 2011. "Introduction: Subjects of Citizenship." *Citizenship Studies* 15 (3–4): 309–17. doi:10.1080/13621025.2011.565153.

Edmonds, Alexander. 2010. *Pretty Modern: Beauty, Sex, and Plastic Surgery in Brazil*. Durham, NC: Duke University Press.

Eisenberg, Andrew J. 2012. "Hip-Hop and Cultural Citizenship on Kenya's 'Swahili Coast.'" *Africa: The Journal of the International African Institute* 82 (4): 556–78.

Englund, Harri. 2006. *Prisoners of Freedom: Human Rights and the African Poor*. Berkeley, CA: University of California Press.

Ennes Ferreira, Manuel. 2005. "Development and the Peace Dividend Insecurity Paradox in Angola." *European Journal of Development Research* 17 (3): 509–24. doi:10.1080/09578810500209650.

Erdmann, Gero, and Ulf Engel. 2007. "Neopatrimonialism Reconsidered: Critical Review and Elaboration of an Elusive Concept." *Commonwealth & Comparative Politics* 45 (1): 95–119. doi:10.1080/14662040601135813.

Escobar, Arturo. 1996. "Constructing Nature: Elements for a Poststructural Political Ecology." In *Liberation Ecologies: Environment, Development, Social Movements*, edited by Richard Peets and Michael John Watts, 46–68. London: Routledge.

Fanon, Frantz. 2004. *The Wretched of the Earth*. New York: Grove Press.

Faria, Paulo C. J. 2013. "The Dawning of Angola's Citizenship Revolution: A Quest for Inclusionary Politics." *Journal of Southern African Studies* 39 (2): 293–311. doi:10.1080/03057070.2013.798541.

Fauvet, Paul. 1977. "The Rise and Fall of Nito Alves." *Review of African Political Economy* 9: 88–104.

Fehérváry, Krisztina. 2002. "American Kitchens, Luxury Bathrooms, and the Search for a 'Normal' Life in Postsocialist Hungary." *Ethnos* 67 (3): 369–400. doi:10.1080/0014184022000031211.

Feldman, Allen. 1991. *Formations of Violence: The Narrative of the Body and Political Terror in Northern Ireland*. Chicago, IL: University of Chicago Press.

——. 1994. "On Cultural Anesthesia: From Desert Storm to Rodney King." *American Ethnologist* 21 (2): 404–18.

Ferguson, James. 1994. *The Anti-Politics Machine: "Development," Depoliticization, and Bureaucratic Power in Lesotho*. Minneapolis: University of Minnesota Press.

——. 1999. *Expectations of Modernity: Myths and Meanings of Urban Life on the Zambian Copperbelt*. Berkeley: University of California Press.

——. 2006. *Global Shadows: Africa in the Neoliberal World Order*. Durham, NC: Duke University Press.

Fernandes, Sujatha. 2003. "Fear of a Black Nation: Local Rappers, Transnational Crossings, and State Power in Contemporary Cuba." *Anthropological Quarterly* 76 (4): 575–608. doi:10.2307/3318281.

Ferrão, Raquel. 2012. "A Insurgência da UNITA e comunidades de sofrimento em Angola." Paper presented at Constructions of the Nation after Large-Scale Violence, River Crossing Lodge, Windhoek, 14–19 October 2012.

Ferreira, Roquinaldo. 2012. *Cross-Cultural Exchange in the Atlantic World: Angola and Brazil during the Era of the Slave Trade*. Cambridge: Cambridge University Press.

Field, Sean. 2007. "Sites of Memory in Langa." In *Imagining the City: Memories and Cultures in Cape Town*, edited by Sean Field, Renate Meyer, and Felicity Swanson, 21–36. Cape Town: HSRC Press.

Filipe, Celso. 2013. *O poder angolano em Portugal: Presença e influência do capital de um país emergente*. Lisbon: Planeta Manuscrito.

Fitzpatrick, Sheila. 1999. *Everyday Stalinism: Ordinary Life in Extraordinary Times: Soviet Russia in the 1930s*. Oxford: Oxford University Press.

Fontein, Joost. 2009a. "The Politics of the Dead: Living Heritage, Bones and Commemoration in Zimbabwe." *ASA Online* 1 (2): 1–27.

——. 2009b. "Anticipating the Tsunami: Rumours, Planning and the Arbitrary State in Zimbabwe." *Africa: Journal of the International African Institute* 79 (3): 369–98. doi:10.3366/E0001972009000862.

——. 2010. "Between Tortured Bodies and Resurfacing Bones: The Politics of the Dead in Zimbabwe." *Journal of Material Culture* 15 (4): 423–48. doi:10.1177/1359183510383105.

——. 2011. "Graves, Ruins, and Belonging: Towards an Anthropology of Proximity." *Journal of the Royal Anthropological Institute* 17 (4): 706–27. doi:10.1111/j.1467-9655.2011.01715.x.

——. 2012. "Re-Making the Dead, Uncertainty and the Torque of Human Materials in Northern Zimbabwe." Paper presented at CAS@50, University of Edinburgh, 6–8 June 2012.

Fortes, Meyer. 1970. *Kinship and the Social Order: The Legacy of Lewis Henry Morgan*. London: Routledge & Kegan Paul.

Foucault, Michel. 1978. *The History of Sexuality*. Vol. I, *The Will to Knowledge*. Translated by Alan Sheridan. London: Penguin.

——. 1995. *Discipline and Punish: The Birth of the Prison*. Translated by Alan Sheridan. New York: Vintage Books.

Freyre, Gilberto. 1986. *The Masters and the Slaves*. Translated by Samuel Putnam. 2nd English ed. Berkeley: University of California Press.

Friedman, John T. 2011. *Imagining the Post-Apartheid State: An Ethnographic Account of Namibia*. New York: Berghahn.

Friedman, Jonathan. 1994. "The Political Economy of Elegance: An African Cult of Beauty." In *Consumption and Identity*, edited by Jonathan Friedman, 120–34. Chur, Switzerland: Harwood Academic.

Gal, Susan. 1987. "Codeswitching and Consciousness in the European Periphery." *American Ethnologist* 14 (4): 637–53. doi:10.2307/645318.

Gastrow, Claudia. 2014a. "'Vamos construir!': Revendications foncières et géographie du pouvoir à Luanda, Angola." *Politique Africaine* 132: 49–72.

——. 2014b. "Negotiated Settlements: Housing and the Aesthetics of Citizenship in Luanda, Angola." PhD diss., University of Chicago.

——. 2016. "Aesthetic Dissent: Urban Redevelopment and Political Belonging in Luanda, Angola." *Antipode* 49 (2): 1–20. doi:10.1111/anti.12276.

——. 2017. "Cement Citizens: Housing, Demolition and Political Belonging in Luanda, Angola." *Citizenship Studies* 9: 1–16. doi:10.1080/13621025.2017.1279795.

Gell, Alfred. 1986. "Newcomers to the World of Goods: Consumption among the Muria Gonds." In *The Social Life of Things: Commodities in Cultural Perspective*, edited by Arjun Appadurai, 110–38. Cambridge: Cambridge University Press.

Geschiere, Peter. 1997. *The Modernity of Witchcraft: Politics and the Occult in Postcolonial Africa*. Charlottesville: University of Virginia Press.

Geschiere, Peter, and Stephen Jackson. 2006. "Autochthony and the Crisis of Citizenship: Democratization, Decentralization, and the Politics of Belonging." *African Studies Review* 49 (2): 1–7. doi:10.2307/20065238.

Gonçalves, Euclides. 2013. "Orientações Superiores: Time and Bureaucratic Authority in Mozambique." *African Affairs* 112 (449): 602–22.

Gramsci, Antonio. 1971. *Selections from the Prison Notebooks of Antonio Gramsci*. London: Lawrence and Wishart.

Grant, Bruce. 2014. "The Edifice Complex: Architecture and the Political Life of Surplus in the New Baku." *Public Culture* 26 (3): 501–28. doi:10.1215/08992363-2683648.

Green, Linda. 1994. "Fear as a Way of Life." *Cultural Anthropology* 9 (2): 227–56. doi:10.1525/can.1994.9.2.02a00040.

Greenhill, Kelly M., and Solomon Major. 2007. "The Perils of Profiling: Civil War Spoilers and the Collapse of Intrastate Peace Accords." *International Security* 31 (3): 7–40.

Gropas, Maria. 2007. "The Repatriotization of Revolutionary Ideology and Mnemonic Landscape in Present-Day Havana." *Current Anthropology* 48 (4): 531–49. doi:10.1086/518299.

Hagmann, Tobias. 2006. "Ethiopian Political Culture Strikes Back: A Rejoinder to J. Abbink." *African Affairs* 105 (421): 605–12. doi:10.1093/afraf/adl020.

——. 2009. "Africa: The Politics of Suffering and Smiling. By Patrick Chabal." *International Affairs* 85 (6): 1283–84.

Hall, Martin. 2006. "Identity, Memory and Countermemory." *Journal of Material Culture* 11 (1–2): 189.

Hall, Stuart. 1996. "Introduction: Who Needs Identity?" In *Questions of Cultural Identity*, 1–17. London: Sage.

Hamilton, Russell G. 1982. "A Country Also Built of Poems: Nationalism and Angolan Literature." *Research in African Literatures* 13 (3): 315–26.

Hangen, Susan. 2005. "Race and the Politics of Identity in Nepal." *Ethnology* 44 (1): 49–64. doi:10.2307/3773959.

Hanks, William F. 2005. "Pierre Bourdieu and the Practices of Language." *Annual Review of Anthropology* 34: 67–83.

Harries, Patrick. 2007. *Butterflies and Barbarians: Swiss Missionaries and Systems of Knowledge in South-East Africa*. Athens: Ohio University Press.

Hastrup, Kirsten, and Peter Elsass. 1990. "Anthropological Advocacy: A Contradiction in Terms?" *Current Anthropology* 3: 301–10.

Hasty, Jennifer. 2005. "The Pleasures of Corruption: Desire and Discipline in Ghanaian Political Culture." *Cultural Anthropology* 20 (2): 271–301. doi:10.2307/3651536.

Heiman, Rachel, Carla Freeman, and Mark Liechty. 2012. "Introduction: Charting an Anthropology of the Middle Classes." In *The Global Middle Classes: Theorizing through Ethnography*, edited by Rachel Heiman, Carla Freeman, and Mark Liechty, 3–29. Santa Fe, NM: School for Advanced Research Press.

Heimer, Franz-Wilhelm. 1979. *Der Entkolonisierungskonflikt in Angola*. Munich: Weltforum-Verlag.

Henighan, Stephen. 2006. "'Um James Bond subdesenvolvido': The Ideological Work of the Angolan Detective in Pepetela's Jaime Bunda Novels." *Portuguese Studies* 22 (1): 135–52. doi:10.2307/41105257.

Herzfeld, Michael. 2005. *Cultural Intimacy: Social Poetics in the Nation-State*. New York: Routledge.

——. 2006. "Spatial Cleansing, Monumental Vacuity, and the Idea of the West." *Journal of Material Culture* 11 (1–2): 127–49. doi:10.1177/1359183506063016.

Heywood, Linda M. 2000. *Contested Power in Angola, 1840s to the Present*. Rochester, NY: University of Rochester Press.

——. 2002. "Portuguese into African: The Eighteenth-Century Central African Background to Atlantic Creole Cultures." In *Central Africans and Cultural Transformations in the American Diaspora*, edited by Linda Marinda Heywood, 91–114. Cambridge: Cambridge University Press.

Heywood, Linda M., and John K. Thornton. 2007. *Central Africans, Atlantic Creoles, and the Foundation of the Americas, 1585–1660*. Cambridge: Cambridge University Press.

Hibou, Béatrice. 2004. "From Privatising the Economy to Privatising the State: An Analysis of the Continual Formation of the State." In *Privatising the State*, 1–46. London: Hurst.

Hobsbawm, Eric, and Terence Ranger. 1983. *The Invention of Tradition*. Cambridge: Cambridge University Press.

Hodges, Tony. 2001. *Angola: From Afro-Stalinism to Petro-Diamond Capitalism*. Bloomington: Indiana University Press.

——. 2004. *Angola: Anatomy of an Oil State*. Bloomington: Indiana University Press.

——. 2007. "The Economic Foundations of the Patrimonial State." In *Angola: The Weight of History*, edited by Patrick Chabal and Nuno Vidal, 175–99. London: Hurst.

Holbraad, Martin. 2014. "Revolución o muerte: Self-Sacrifice and the Ontology of Cuban Revolution." *Ethnos* 79 (3): 365–87. doi:10.1080/00141844.2013.794149.

Holston, James. 2008. *Insurgent Citizenship: Disjunctions of Democracy and Modernity in Brazil*. Princeton, NJ: Princeton University Press.

HRW (Human Rights Watch). 1994. *Angola: Arms Trade and Violations of the Laws of War Since the 1992 Elections*. New York: Human Rights Watch.

——. 2007. "They Pushed Down the Houses." Forced Evictions and Insecure Land Tenure for Luanda's Urban Poor. New York: Human Rights Watch. https://www.hrw.org/sites/default/files/reports/angola0507web.pdf.

——. 2010. "Angola: Oil Wealth Eludes Nation's Poor." *Human Rights Watch*, 13 April 2010 (http://www.hrw.org/news/2010/04/12/angola-oil-wealth-eludes-nation-s-poor).

——. 2011. "Angola: Stop Forced Evictions." *Human Rights Watch*, 25 August 2011 (http://www.hrw.org/news/2011/08/25/angola-stop-forced-evictions).

——. 2012a. "Angola: Violent Crackdown on Critics." *Human Rights Watch*, 2 April 2012 (http://www.hrw.org/news/2012/04/02/angola-violent-crackdown-critics).

——. 2012b. "Angola: Protesters Detained, Disappeared." Human Rights Watch, 5 July 2012 (http://www.hrw.org/news/2012/07/05/angola-protesters-detained-disappeared).

———. 2012c. "Angola: Stop Stifling Free Speech." *Human Rights Watch*, 1 August 2012 (http://www.hrw.org/news/2012/08/01/angola-stop-stifling-free-speech).

Humphrey, Caroline. 2005. "Ideology in Infrastructure: Architecture and Soviet Imagination." *Journal of the Royal Anthropological Institute* 11 (1): 39–58. doi:10.1111/j.1467-9655.2005.00225.x.

Igreja, Victor. 2008. "Memories as Weapons: The Politics of Peace and Silence in Post-Civil War Mozambique." *Journal of Southern African Studies* 34 (3): 539–56.

Inglês, Paulo. 2016. "Reconfiguração social em Angola: Ordem local e quotidiano pós-conflito." PhD thesis, ISCTE-IUL (University Institute of Lisbon).

Jackson, Stephen. 2006. "Sons of Which Soil? The Language and Politics of Autochthony in Eastern D.R. Congo." *African Studies Review* 49 (2): 95–123. doi:10.1353/arw.2006.0107.

———. 2010. " 'It Seems to Be Going': The Genius of Survival in Wartime DR Congo." In *Hard Work, Hard Times: Global Volatility and African Subjectivities*, edited by Anne-Maria Makhulu, Beth A Buggenhagen, and Stephen Jackson, 48–68. Berkeley: University of California Press.

Jansen, Stef. 2014. "Hope For/Against the State: Gridding in a Besieged Sarajevo Suburb." *Ethnos* 79 (2): 238–260. doi:10.1080/00141844.2012.743469.

Jenkins, Paul, Paul Robson, and Allan Cain. 2002. "Local Responses to Globalization and Peripheralization in Luanda, Angola." *Environment and Urbanization* 14 (1): 115–27. doi:10.1177/095624780201400110.

Jourde, Cédric. 2009. "The Ethnographic Sensibility: Overlooked Authoritarian Dynamics and Islamic Ambivalences in West Africa." In *Political Ethnography: What Immersion Contributes to the Study of Power*, edited by Edward Schatz, 201–16. Chicago, IL: University of Chicago Press.

Kaarsholm, Preben. 2012. "Africa: The Politics of Suffering and Smiling by Patrick Chabal." *Journal of Modern African Studies* 50 (2): 357–59. doi:10.1017/S0022278X12000080.

Kaplan, Brett Ashley. 2011. *Landscapes of Holocaust Postmemory*. New York: Routledge.

Kapuściński, Ryszard. 1987. *Another Day of Life*. London: Picador.

Karlström, Mikael. 2003. "On the Aesthetics and Dialogics of Power in the Postcolony." *Africa* 73 (1): 57–67.

Kasack, Sebastian. 1992. "Perspektiven für partizipatives Squatterupgrading in Luanda/Angola. Eine Feasibility-Studie im Quartier Lixeira, Bairro Sambizanga." Bonn: Rheinische Friedrich-Wilhelms-Universität.

Kassembe, Dia. 1995. *Angola: 20 Ans de Guerre Civile—Une Femme Accuse*. Paris: L'Harmattan.

Kesselring, Rita. 2016. *Bodies of Truth Law, Memory, and Emancipation in Post-Apartheid South Africa*. Stanford, CA: Stanford University Press.

Kibble, Steve. 2006. "Angola: Can the Politics of Disorder Become the Politics of Democratisation and Development?" *Review of African Political Economy* 33 (109): 525–42.

Kockelman, Paul. 2007. "Agency: The Relation between Meaning, Power, and Knowledge." *Current Anthropology* 48 (3): 375–401. doi:10.1086/512998.

Koechlin, Lucy. 2013. *Corruption as an Empty Signifier: Politics and Political Order in Africa*. AEGIS. Leiden: Brill.

Kössler, R. 2007. "Facing a Fragmented Past: Memory, Culture and Politics in Namibia." *Journal of Southern African Studies* 33 (2): 361–82.

——. 2010. "Images of History and the Nation: Namibia and Zimbabwe Compared." *South African Historical Journal* 62 (1): 29–53. doi:10.1080/02582471003778318.

Kovats-Bernat, J. Christopher. 2002. "Negotiating Dangerous Fields: Pragmatic Strategies for Fieldwork amid Violence and Terror." *American Anthropologist* 104 (1): 1–15.

Krohn-Hansen, Christian. 2005. "Negotiated Dictatorship: The Building of the Trujillo State in the South-Western Dominican Republic." In *State Formation: Anthropological Perspectives*, edited by Christian Krohn-Hansen and Knut G. Nustad, 96–122. London: Pluto Press.

——. 2008. *Political Authoritarianism in the Dominican Republic*. New York: Palgrave Macmillan.

Krohn-Hansen, Christian, and Knut G. Nustad, eds. 2005. *State Formation: Anthropological Perspectives*. London: Pluto Press.

Krug, Jessica. 2011. "The Strange Life of Lusotropicalism in Luanda: On Race, Nationality, Gender, and Sexuality in Angola." In *Black Subjects in Africa and Its Diasporas: Race and Gender in Research and Writing*, edited by Benjamin Talton and Quincy T. Mills, 109–27. New York: Palgrave Macmillan.

Kyle, Steven. 2005. "The Political Economy of Angolan Growth: Social and Regional Structure." *Review of African Political Economy* 32 (104/5): 269–93.

Labanyi, Jo. 2010. "Doing Things: Emotion, Affect, and Materiality." *Journal of Spanish Cultural Studies* 11 (3–4): 223–33. doi:10.1080/14636204.2010.538244.

Laszczkowski, Mateusz. 2011. "Building the Future: Construction, Temporality, and Politics in Astana." *Focaal* 2011 (60): 77–92. doi:10.3167/fcl.2011.600107.

Lázaro, Gilson. 2012. "Violência, trauma e reconciliação em Angola." Paper presented at Constructions of the Nation after Large-Scale Violence, River Crossing Lodge, Windhoek, 14–19 October 2012.

Ledeneva, Alena V. 1998. *Russia's Economy of Favours: Blat, Networking and Informal Exchange*. Cambridge: Cambridge University Press.

——. 2013. *Can Russia Modernise?: Sistema, Power Networks and Informal Governance*. Cambridge: Cambridge University Press.

Legg, Stephen. 2007. "Reviewing Geographies of Memory/Forgetting." *Environment and Planning A* 39 (2): 456–66. doi:10.1068/a38170.

Lentz, Carola. 1998. "The Chief, the Mine Captain and the Politician: Legitimating Power in Northern Ghana." *Africa: Journal of the International African Institute* 68 (1): 46–67. doi:10.2307/1161147.

Levitsky, Steven, and Lucan Way. 2002. "The Rise of Competitive Authoritarianism." *Journal of Democracy* 13 (2): 51–65.

Liechty, Mark. 2005. "Carnal Economies: The Commodification of Food and Sex in Kathmandu." *Cultural Anthropology* 20 (1): 1–38. doi:10.2307/3651575.

Lima, Juliana. 2015. "Le point de vue de Juliana Lima." In "Autour d'un livre," coordinated by Didier Péclard. *Politique africaine*, no. 139 (December): 171–94.

Lopes, Carlos M. 2004. "Candongeiros, kinguilas, roboteiros e zungueiras: Uma digressão pela economia informal de Luanda." Paper presented at VIII Congresso Luso-Afro-Brasileiro de Ciências Sociais, CES, Coimbra, 16–18 September 2004.

———. 2009. "Hug Me, Hold Me Tight! The Evolution of Passenger Transport in Luanda and Huambo (Angola), 1975–2000." In *The Speed of Change: Motor Vehicles and People in Africa, 1890–2000*, edited by Jan-Bart Gewald, Sabine Luning, and Klaas Van Walraven, 107–26. Leiden: Brill.

Lübbert Hansen, Mille. 2006. "'God for Everyone: Everyone for Himself'? An Angolan Example of Civil Society beyond the Blueprints." Roskilde: Roskilde University.

Mabeko-Tali, Jean-Michel. 1995. "La chasse aux zaïrois à Luanda." *Politique Africaine* 57: 71–84.

———. 2001a. *Dissidências e poder de estado: O MPLA perante si próprio (1962–1977); Ensaio de história política.* Vol. 1, *1962–1974.* Luanda: Nzila.

———. 2001b. *Dissidências e poder de estado: O MPLA perante si próprio (1962–1977); Ensaio de história política.* Vol. 2, *1974–1977.* Luanda: Nzila.

Machava, Benedito Luís. 2011. "State Discourse on Internal Security and the Politics of Punishment in Post-Independence Mozambique (1975–1983)." *Journal of Southern African Studies* 37 (3): 593–609.

Mahmood, Saba. 2005. *Politics of Piety: The Islamic Revival and the Subject of Feminism.* Princeton, NJ: Princeton University Press.

Maier, Karl. 1996. *Angola: Promises and Lies.* London: Serif.

Malaquias, Assis. 2007. "Angola: How to Lose a Guerrilla War." In *African Guerillas: Raging against the Machine*, edited by Morten Bøås and Kevin C. Dunn. Boulder, CO: Lynne Rienner.

Malinowski, Bronisław. 1922. *Argonauts of the Western Pacific: An Account of Native Enterprise and Adventure in the Archipelagoes of Melanesian New Guinea.* London: Routledge.

Malkki, Liisa. 1995. *Purity and Exile: Violence, Memory, and National Cosmology among Hutu Refugees in Tanzania.* Chicago, IL: University of Chicago Press.

Mamdani, Mahmood. 2001. *When Victims Become Killers : Colonialism, Nativism, and the Genocide in Rwanda.* Princeton, NJ: Princeton University Press.

Marcum, John. 1969. *The Angolan Revolution.* Vol. 1, *The Anatomy of an Explosion (1950–1962).* Cambridge, MA: MIT Press.

———. 1978. *The Angolan Revolution.* Vol. 2, *Exile Politics and Guerrilla Warfare (1962–1976).* Cambridge, MA: MIT Press.

———. 1987. "The People's Republic of Angola: A Radical Vision Frustrated." In *Afro-Marxist Regimes: Ideology and Public Policy*, edited by Edmond J. Keller and Donald Rothchild, 67–83. Boulder, CO: Lynne Rienner.

Marques de Morais, Rafael. 2010. "The Angolan Presidency: The Epicentre of Corruption." *Pambazuka.* http://www.pambazuka.org/en/category/features/66476.

Marshall-Fratani, Ruth. 2006. "The War of 'Who Is Who': Autochthony, Nationalism, and Citizenship in the Ivoirian Crisis." *African Studies Review* 49 (2): 9–43. doi:10.1353/arw.2006.0098.

Mbembe, Achille. 1999. "Du gouvernement privé indirect." *Politique Africaine* 73: 103–21.

——. 2001. *On the Postcolony*. Berkeley: University of California Press.

——. 2002. "African Modes of Self-Writing." Translated by Steven Rendall. *Public Culture* 14 (1): 239–73.

McClintock, Anne. 1995. *Imperial Leather: Race, Gender and Sexuality in the Colonial Contest*. New York: Routledge.

Meagher, Kate. 2006. "Cultural Primordialism and the Post-Structuralist Imaginaire: Plus Ça Change . . ." *Africa: Journal of the International African Institute* 76 (4): 590–97. doi:10.2307/40027300.

Médard, Jean-François. 1982. "The Underdeveloped State in Tropical Africa: Political Clientelism or Neo-Patrimonialism?" In *Private Patronage and Public Power: Political Clientelism in the Modern State*, edited by Cristopher Clapham, 162–92. London: Frances Pinter.

Melnysyn, Shana. 2017. "Vagabond States: Trade, Boundaries, and Belonging in Early 20th Century Portuguese Angola." PhD diss., University of Michigan.

Melo, João. 2009. *O homem que não tira o palito da boca*. Lisbon: Caminho.

Mendes, Júlio, Eugénio Silva, and Rosa Cabecinhas. 2011. "Memória colectiva e identidade nacional: Jovens angolanos face à História de Angola." *Anuário Internacional de Comunicação Lusófona*, 2011: 205–21.

Mercer. 2014. *2014 Cost-of-Living Survey*. London: Mercer.

Messiant, Christine. 1994. "Angola, les voies de l'ethnisation et de la décomposition. I—de la guerre à la paix (1974–1991): Le conflit armé, les interventions internationales et le peuple angolais." *Lusotopie* 1/2: 155–210.

——. 1995a. "Avant-propos. L'Angola dans la guerre." *Politique Africaine* 57: 3–9.

——. 1995b. "Angola, les voies de l'ethnisation et de la décomposition. II—Transition à la démocratie ou retour à la guerre? L'épanouissement des deux 'partis armés' (Mai 1991–Septembre 1994)." *Lusotopie* 3: 181–212.

——. 1998. "'Chez nous, même le passé est imprévisible': L'expérience d'une recherche sur le nationalisme angolais, et particulièrement le MPLA: sources, critique, besoins actuels de la recherche." *Lusotopie* 5: 157–97.

——. 1999. "La Fondation Eduardo Dos Santos (FESA): À propos de 'l'investissement' de la société civile par le pouvoir angolais." *Politique Africaine* 73: 81–101.

——. 2002. "Fin de la guerre, enfin, en Angola. Vers quelle paix?" *Politique Africaine* 86: 183–95.

——. 2004. "Why Did Bicesse and Lusaka Fail? A Critical Analysis." In *"From Military Peace to Social Justice? The Angolan Peace Process,"* edited by Guus Meijer. Special issue, *Accord*, no. 15 (2004): 16–23.

——. 2006. *1961. L'Angola colonial, histoire et société. Les prémisses du mouvement nationaliste*. Basel: P. Schlettwein.

——. 2007. "The Mutation of Hegemonic Domination." In *Angola: The Weight of History*, edited by Patrick Chabal and Nuno Vidal, 93–123. London: Hurst.

——. 2008. *L'Angola postcolonial: 2. Sociologie politique d'une oléocratie*. Paris: Karthala.

Miller, Joseph C. 1976. *Kings and Kinsmen: Early Mbundu States in Angola*. Oxford: Clarendon Press.

Miranda, Armindo. 2004. "Angola 2003/2004: Waiting for Elections." CMI Report 2004: 11. Bergen: Christian Michelsen Institute.

Monday, Chris. 2011. "Family Rule as the Highest Stage of Communism." *Asian Survey* 51 (5): 812–43. doi:10.1525/as.2011.51.5.812.

Moorhouse, Karin, and Wei Cheng. 2005. *No One Can Stop the Rain: A Chronicle of Two Foreign Aid Workers during the Angolan Civil War*. London, ON: Insomniac Press.

Moorman, Marissa J. 2008. *Intonations: A Social History of Music and Nation in Luanda, Angola, from 1945 to Recent Times*. Athens: Ohio University Press.

——. 2014. "Anatomy of Kuduro: Articulating the Angolan Body Politic after the War." *African Studies Review* 57 (3): 21–40. doi:10.1017/asr.2014.90.

Mosse, David, and David Lewis, eds. 2005. *The Aid Effect: Giving and Governing in International Development*. Ann Arbor, MI: Pluto Press.

Murray Li, Tania. 2007. *The Will to Improve: Governmentality, Development, and the Practice of Politics*. Durham, NC: Duke University Press.

Musaraj, Smoki. 2011. "Tales from Albarado: The Materiality of Pyramid Schemes in Postsocialist Albania." *Cultural Anthropology* 26 (1): 83–110.

Myers, Garth. 2011. *African Cities: Alternative Visions of Urban Theory and Practice*. London: Zed Books.

Navaro-Yashin, Yael. 2002. *Faces of the State: Secularism and Public Life in Turkey*. Princeton, NJ: Princeton University Press.

——. 2009. "Affective Spaces, Melancholic Objects: Ruination and the Production of Anthropological Knowledge." *Journal of the Royal Anthropological Institute* 15 (1): 1–18. doi:10.1111/j.1467-9655.2008.01527.x.

——. 2012. *The Make-Believe Space: Affective Geography in a Postwar Polity*. Durham, NC: Duke University Press.

Ndjio, B. 2008. "Millennial Democracy and Spectral Reality in Post-Colonial Africa." *African Journal of International Affairs* 11 (2): 115–56. doi:10.4314/ajia.v11i2.57267.

Ndlovu-Gatsheni, Sabelo J. 2009. "Africa for Africans or Africa for 'Natives' Only? 'New Nationalism' and Nativism in Zimbabwe and South Africa." *Africa Spectrum* 44 (1): 61–78.

Nguyen, Viet Thanh. 2015. *The Sympathizer*. New York: Grove/Atlantic.

Nuijten, Monique, and Gerhard Anders, eds. 2007. *Corruption and the Secret of Law: A Legal Anthropological Perspective*. Aldershot: Ashgate.

Ogola, George. 2006. "The Idiom of Age in a Popular Kenyan Newspaper Serial." *Africa: Journal of the International African Institute* 76 (4): 569–89. doi:10.2307/40027299.

Ortner, Sherry B. 1990. "Patterns of History: Cultural Schemas in the Foundings of Sherpa Religious Institutions." In *Culture through Time: Anthropological Approaches*, edited by Emiko Ohnuki-Tierney, 57–93. Stanford, CA: Stanford University Press.

——. 1998. "Identities: The Hidden Life of Class." *Journal of Anthropological Research* 54 (1): 1–17. doi:10.2307/3631674.

Ottaway, Marina. 2003. *Democracy Challenged: The Rise of Semi-Authoritarianism*. Washington, DC: Carnegie Endowment for International Peace.

Oushakine, Serguei Alex. 2006. "The Politics of Pity: Domesticating Loss in a Russian Province." *American Anthropologist* 108 (2): 297–311. doi:10.2307/3804792.

Ovadia, Jesse Salah. 2013. "The Reinvention of Elite Accumulation in the Angolan Oil Sector: Emergent Capitalism in a Rentier Economy." *Cadernos de Estudos Africano* 25: 33–63.

Pacheco, Fernando, Mamadú Jao, Teresa Cravo, and Ulrich Schiefer. 2006. "The Role of External Development Actors in Post-Conflict Scenarios." Working Paper 258, Oficina do CES, Centro de Estudos Sociais, Coimbra, September 2006.

Pawson, Lara. 2007. "The 27 May in Angola: A View from below." *Relações Internacionais* 14: 1–18.

——. 2014. *In the Name of the People: Angola's Forgotten Massacre*. London: I.B. Tauris.

Pazzanita, Anthony G. 1991. "The Conflict Resolution Process in Angola." *The Journal of Modern African Studies* 29 (1): 83–114.

Pearce, Justin. 2005. *An Outbreak of Peace: Angola's Situation of Confusion*. Claremont: David Philip.

——. 2012a. "Changing Nationalisms: From War to Peace in Angola." In *Sure Road? Nationalisms in Angola, Guinea-Bissau and Mozambique*, edited by Eric Morier-Genoud, 199–216. Leiden: Brill.

——. 2012b. "Control, Politics and Identity in the Angolan Civil War." *African Affairs* 111 (444): 442–65. doi:10.1093/afraf/ads028.

——. 2015a. *Political Identity and Conflict in Central Angola, 1975–2002*. Cambridge: Cambridge University Press.

——. 2015b. "Contesting the Past in Angolan Politics." *Journal of Southern African Studies* 41 (1): 103–19. doi:10.1080/03057070.2015.991189.

Péclard, Didier. 2005. "Etat Colonial, Missions Chrétiennes et Nationalisme En Angola, 1920–1975. Aux Racines Sociales de l'UNITA." PhD thesis, Université de Paris, Paris.

——. 2012. "UNITA and the Moral Economy of Exclusion in Angola, 1966–1977." In *Sure Road? Nationalisms in Angola, Guinea-Bissau and Mozambique*, edited by Eric Morier-Genoud, 149–76. Leiden: Brill.

——. 2015. *Les incertitudes de la nation en Angola: Aux racines sociales de l'Unita*. Paris: Karthala.

Pedersen, Morten Axel, and Morten Nielsen. 2013. "Trans-Temporal Hinges: Reflections on an Ethnographic Study of Chinese Infrastructural Projects in Mozambique and Mongolia." *Social Analysis* 57 (1): 122–42. doi:10.3167/sa.2013.570109.

Pélissier, René. 1978. *La Colonie du Minotaure: Nationalismes et révoltes en Angola (1926–1961)*. Orgeval: Montamets.

Pepetela. 1997. *A gloriosa família*. Lisbon: Dom Quixote.

——. 2001. *Jaime Bunda, agente secreto: Estória de alguns mistérios*. Lisbon: Dom Quixote.

——. 2005. *Predadores*. Lisbon: Dom Quixote.

Phillips, Kristin D. 2010. "Pater Rules Best: Political Kinship and Party Politics in Tanzania's Presidential Elections." *PoLAR: Political and Legal Anthropology Review* 33 (1): 109–32. doi:10.1111/j.1555-2934.2010.01095.x.

Piot, Charles. 2010. *Nostalgia for the Future: West Africa after the Cold War*. Chicago, IL: University of Chicago Press.

Pitcher, Anne. 2015. "Kilamba, Angola: Dystopian Ghost City or Middle Class Dreamscape?" Paper presented at the 6th European Conference on African Studies, Sorbonne, Paris, 8–10 July 2015.

Pitcher, Anne, and Kelly M. Askew. 2006. "African Socialisms and Postsocialisms." *Africa* 76 (1): 1–14. doi:10.2307/40026154.

Pitcher, Anne, and Marissa J. Moorman. 2015. "City Building in Post-Conflict, Post-Socialist Luanda. Burying the Past with Phantasmagorias of the Future." In *African Cities Reader III: Land, Property and Value*, edited by Ntone Edjabe and Edgar Pieterse, 123–35. Vlaeberg: African Centre for Cities & Chimurenga Magazine.

Pitcher, Anne, Mary H. Moran, and Michael Johnston. 2009. "Rethinking Patrimonialism and Neopatrimonialism in Africa." *African Studies Review* 52 (1): 125–56. doi:10.1353/arw.0.0163.

Power, Marcus. 2011. "Angola 2025: The Future of the 'World's Richest Poor Country' as Seen through a Chinese Rear-View Mirror." *Antipode* 0: 1–26.

Power, Marcus, and Ana Cristina Alves, eds. 2012. *China and Angola: A Marriage of Convenience?* Cape Town: Pambazuka Press.

Pratt, Jeff C. 2003. *Class, Nation, and Identity: The Anthropology of Political Movements*. London: Pluto Press.

Primorac, Ranka. 2007. "The Poetics of State Terror in Twenty-First Century Zimbabwe." *Interventions* 9 (3): 434–50. doi:10.1080/13698010701618687.

Quayson, Ato. 2014. *Oxford Street, Accra: City Life and the Itineraries of Transnationalism*. Durham, NC: Duke University Press Books.

Quintão, Amália, and Regina Santos. 2012. "Chinese Corporate Practices in Angola: Myths and Facts." In *China and Angola: A Marriage of Convenience?*, edited by Marcus Power and Ana Cristina Alves, 145–61. Cape Town: Pambazuka Press.

Ranger, Terence. 2004. "Nationalist Historiography, Patriotic History and the History of the Nation: The Struggle over the Past in Zimbabwe." *Journal of Southern African Studies* 30 (2): 215–34.

Rich, Jeremy. 2009. "Nous, les Équatos: Equatorial Guinean Immigrants in Contemporary Gabon." *Afro-Hispanic Review* 28 (2): 113–30.

Richardson, Tanya. 2008. *Kaleidoscopic Odessa: History and Place in Contemporary Ukraine*. Toronto: University of Toronto Press.

Robson, Paul, and Sandra Roque. 2001. *Here in the City There Is Nothing Left over for Lending a Hand*. Luanda: DW & ADRA.

Rodrigues, Cristina Udelsmann. 2007a. "Survival and Social Reproduction Strategies in Angolan Cities." *Africa Today* 54 (1): 91–105.

——. 2007b. "From Family Solidarity to Social Classes: Urban Stratification in Angola (Luanda and Ondjiva)." *Journal of Southern African Studies* 33 (2): 235–50. doi:10.1080/03057070701292566.

Rogers, Douglas. 2006. "How to Be a Khoziain in a Transforming State: State Formation and the Ethics of Governance in Post-Soviet Russia." *Comparative Studies in Society and History* 48 (4): 915–45.

Roitman, Janet L. 2005. *Fiscal Disobedience: An Anthropology of Economic Regulation in Central Africa*. Princeton, NJ: Princeton University Press.

Roque, Paula Cristina. 2009. "Angola's Façade Democracy." *Journal of Democracy* 20 (4): 137–50.

——. 2011. "Angola: Parallel Governments, Oil and Neopatrimonial System Reproduction." Situation report prepared for the Institute for Security Studies, Johannesburg, 6 June 2011.

———. 2013. "Angola's Second Post-War Elections: The Alchemy of Change." May 2013. Situation report prepared for the Institute for Security Studies, Johannesburg, May 2013.

Roque, Sandra. 2011. "Cidade and Bairro: Classification, Constitution and Experience of Urban Space in Angola." *Social Dynamics* 37 (3): 332–48. doi:10.1080/0 2533952.2011.658282.

Roseberry, William. 1994. "Hegemony and the Language of Contention." In *Everyday Forms of State Formation: Revolution and the Negotiation of Rule in Modern Mexico*, edited by Gilbert M. Joseph and Daniel Nugent, 355–66. Durham, NC: Duke University Press.

Rose-Redwood, Reuben S. 2008. "'Sixth Avenue Is Now a Memory': Regimes of Spatial Inscription and the Performative Limits of the Official City-Text." *Political Geography* 27 (8): 875–94. doi:10.1016/j.polgeo.2008.11.002.

Roth-Gordon, Jennifer. 2009. "The Language That Came down the Hill: Slang, Crime, and Citizenship in Rio de Janeiro." *American Anthropologist* 111 (1): 57–68. doi:10.2307/40300786.

Rubbers, Benjamin. 2009. "The Story of a Tragedy: How People in Haut-Katanga Interpret the Post-Colonial History of Congo." *Journal of Modern African Studies* 47 (2): 267–89. doi:10.1017/S0022278X09003838.

Salvatore, Armando. 2013. "New Media, the 'Arab Spring,' and the Metamorphosis of the Public Sphere: Beyond Western Assumptions on Collective Agency and Democratic Politics." *Constellations* 20 (2): 1–12. doi:10.1111/cons.12033.

Sarró, Ramon, and Ruy Llera Blanes. 2009. "Prophetic Diasporas: Moving Religion Across the Lusophone Atlantic." *African Diaspora* 2 (1): 52–72. doi:10.1163/187254609X430786.

Sarró, Ramon, Ruy Llera Blanes, and Fátima Viegas. 2008. "La guerre dans la paix. Ethnicité et angolanité dans l'Église Kimbanguiste de Luanda." *Politique Africaine* 110: 84–101. doi:10.1163/187254609X430786.

Schatzberg, Michael G. 1993. "Power, Legitimacy and 'Democratisation' in Africa." *Africa* 63 (4): 445–61.

———. 2001. *Political Legitimacy in Middle Africa: Father, Family, Food*. Bloomington: Indiana University Press.

Schedler, A. 2002. "The Menu of Manipulation." *Journal of Democracy* 13 (2): 36–50.

Scheper-Hughes, Nancy. 1995. "The Primacy of the Ethical: Propositions for a Militant Anthropology." *Current Anthropology* 36 (3): 409–40.

Schramm, Katharina. 2011. "Introduction: Landscapes of Violence—Memory and Sacred Space." *History & Memory* 23 (1): 5–22.

Schubert, Benedict. 1997. *Der Krieg und die Kirchen: Angola 1961–1991*. Lucerne: Exodus.

———. 2000. *A guerra e as igrejas: Angola, 1961–1991*. Basel: P. Schlettwein.

Schubert, Jon. 2010. "'Democratisation' and the Consolidation of Political Authority in Post-War Angola." *Journal of Southern African Studies* 36 (3): 657–72.

———. 2015. "2002, Year Zero: History as Anti-Politics in the New Angola." *Journal of Southern African Studies* 41 (4): 835–52.

———. 2016a. "'A Culture of Immediatism': Co-Optation and Complicity in Post-War Angola." *Ethnos* 82 (2): 1–19. doi:http://dx.doi.org/10.1080/00141844.2015 .1133687.

———. 2016b. "Emerging Middle-Class Political Subjectivities in Post-War Angola." In *The Rise of Africa's Middle Class*, edited by Henning Melber, 147–58. London: Zed Books.

Scott, James C. 1990. *Domination and the Arts of Resistance: Hidden Transcripts*. New Haven, CT: Yale University Press.

———. 1998. *Seeing Like a State*. New Haven, CT: Yale University Press.

Shipley, Jesse Weaver. 2009. "Aesthetic of the Entrepreneur: Afro-Cosmopolitan Rap and Moral Circulation in Accra, Ghana." *Anthropological Quarterly* 82 (3): 631–68. doi:10.2307/20638655.

Silva-Brummel, Maria Fernanda. 1984. "As formas de tratamento no português angolano." In *Umgangssprache in der Iberoromania*, edited by Heinz Kröll, Günter Holtus, and Edgar Radtke, 271–88. Tübingen: Gunter Narr Verlag.

Silverstein, Paul A. 2002. "An Excess of Truth: Violence, Conspiracy Theorizing and the Algerian Civil War." *Anthropological Quarterly* 75 (4): 643–74. doi:10.2307/3318165.

Simone, AbdouMaliq. 2004. *For the City Yet to Come: Changing African Life in Four Cities*. Durham, NC: Duke University Press.

Sitte, Fritz. 1981. *Flug in die Angola-Hölle: Der vergessene Krieg*. Vienna: Verlag Styria.

Smith, Daniel Jordan. 2008. *A Culture of Corruption: Everyday Deception and Popular Discontent in Nigeria*. Princeton, NJ: Princeton University Press.

Soares de Oliveira, Ricardo. 2007. "Business Success, Angola-Style: Postcolonial Politics and the Rise and Rise of Sonangol." *Journal of Modern African Studies* 45 (4): 595–619. doi:10.1017/S0022278X07002893.

———. 2011. "Illiberal Peacebuilding in Angola." *Journal of Modern African Studies* 49 (2): 287–314. doi:10.2307/23018923.

———. 2015. *Magnificent and Beggar Land: Angola Since the Civil War*. London: Hurst.

Sogge, David. 2011. "Angola: Reinventing Pasts and Futures." *Review of African Political Economy* 38 (127): 85–92. doi:10.1080/03056244.2011.552678.

Sökefeld, Martin. 2001. "Reconsidering Identity." *Anthropos* 96 (2): 527–44.

Stan, Sabina. 2012. "Neither Commodities nor Gifts: Post-Socialist Informal Exchanges in the Romanian Healthcare System." *Journal of the Royal Anthropological Institute* 18 (1): 65–82.

Stern, Steve J. 2004. *Remembering Pinochet's Chile: On the Eve of London 1998*. Durham, NC: Duke University Press.

Stockwell, John. 1978. *In Search of Enemies: A CIA Story*. London: Deutsch.

Stoler, Ann L. 2002. *Carnal Knowledge and Imperial Power: Race and the Intimate in Colonial Rule*. Berkeley: University of California Press.

Sturken, Marita. 1997. *Tangled Memories: The Vietnam War, the AIDS Epidemic, and the Politics of Remembering*. Berkeley: University of California Press.

Sumich, Jason. 2008. "Politics after the Time of Hunger in Mozambique: A Critique of Neo-Patrimonial Interpretation of African Elites." *Journal of Southern African Studies* 34 (1): 111–25. doi:10.1080/03057070701832916.

———. 2012. "'An Imaginary Nation': Nationalism, Ideology and the Mozambican National Elite." In *Sure Road? Nationalisms in Angola, Guinea-Bissau and Mozambique*, edited by Eric Morier-Genoud, 127–47. Leiden: Brill.

——. 2015. "The Uncertainty of Prosperity: Dependence and the Politics of Middle-Class Privilege in Maputo." *Ethnos* 81 (5): 1–21. doi:10.1080/00141844.2014.1002860.

Tavares Pimenta, Fernando. 2012. "Angola's Euro-African Nationalism: The United Angolan Front." In *Sure Road? Nationalisms in Angola, Guinea-Bissau and Mozambique*, edited by Eric Morier-Genoud, 177–97. Leiden: Brill.

Thiranagama, Sharika, and Tobias Kelly, eds. 2010. *Traitors: Suspicion, Intimacy, and the Ethics of State-Building*. Philadelphia: University of Pennsylvania Press.

Thornton, John. 1980. "The Slave Trade in Eighteenth Century Angola: Effects on Demographic Structures." *Canadian Journal of African Studies / Revue Canadienne Des Études Africaines* 14 (3): 417–27.

Thornton, John K. 2002. "Religious and Ceremonial Life in the Kongo and Mbundu Areas, 1500–1700." In *Central Africans and Cultural Transformations in the American Diaspora*, edited by Linda M. Heywood, 71–90. Cambridge: Cambridge University Press.

Thrift, Nigel. 2004. "Intensities of Feeling: Towards a Spatial Politics of Affect." *Geografiska Annaler: Series B, Human Geography* 86 (1): 57–78. doi:10.1111/j.0435-3684.2004.00154.x.

Tomás, António. 2012. "Refracted Governmentality: Space, Politics and Social Structure in Contemporary Luanda." PhD diss., Columbia University, New York.

——. 2014. "Becoming Famous: Kuduro, Politics and the Performance of Social Visibility." *Critical Interventions* 8 (2): 261–75. doi:10.1080/19301944.2014.938987.

Tréfon, Théodore. 2004. "Introduction. La réinvention de l'ordre à Kinshasa." In *Ordre et désordre à Kinshasa: Réponses populaires à la faillite de l'Etat*, edited by Théodore Tréfon, 13–32. Paris: L'Harmattan.

Trouillot, Michel-Rolph. 2001. "The Anthropology of the State in the Age of Globalization: Close Encounters of the Deceptive Kind." *Current Anthropology* 42 (1): 125–38.

Tsing, Anna Lowenhaupt. 2005. *Friction: An Ethnography of Global Connection*. Princeton, NJ: Princeton University Press.

Vallée, Olivier. 2008. "Du palais aux banques: la reproduction élargie du capital indigène en Angola." *Politique Africaine* 110: 21–46.

Venâncio, José Carlos. 1998. "Etnicidade e nacionalidade na África de lingua portuguesa: Algumas referências sobre a situação pós-colonial." In *Pós-colonialismo e identidade*, edited by Victor M. P. Da Rosa and Susan P. Castillo, 79–86. Porto: Universidade Fernando Pessoa.

Verdery, Katherine. 1996. *What Was Socialism, and What Comes Next?* Princeton, NJ: Princeton University Press.

Vigh, Henrik. 2008. "Crisis and Chronicity: Anthropological Perspectives on Continuous Conflict and Decline." *Ethnos* 73 (1): 5–24. doi:10.1080/00141840801927509.

Vines, Alex, Nick Shaxson, and Lisa Rimli. 2005. "Drivers of Change: Angola—An Overview." Report prepared for Chatham House, London, April 2005.

Vom Bruck, Gabriele. 2005. "The Imagined 'Consumer Democracy' and Elite (Re)Production in Yemen." *Journal of the Royal Anthropological Institute* 11 (2): 255–75. doi:10.1111/j.1467-9655.2005.00235.x.

Wagner, Günter. 1940. "The Political Organization of the Bantu of Kavirondo." In *African Political Systems*, edited by Meyer Fortes and Edward Evan Evans-Pritchard, 197–238. London: KPI.

Wai, Zubairu. 2012. "Neo-Patrimonialism and the Discourse of State Failure in Africa." *Review of African Political Economy* 39 (131): 27–43. doi:10.1080/03056244.2012.658719.

Weate, Jeremy. 2003. "Achille Mbembe and the Postcolony: Going beyond the Text." *Research in African Literatures* 34 (4): 27–41. doi:10.1353/ral.2003.0116.

Wedeen, Lisa. 1999. *Ambiguities of Domination: Politics, Rhetoric, and Symbols in Contemporary Syria*. Chicago, IL: University of Chicago Press.

——. 2008. *Peripheral Visions: Publics, Power, and Performance in Yemen*. Chicago, IL: University of Chicago Press.

Werbner, Richard P. 1998. "Smoke from the Barrel of a Gun: Postwars of the Dead, Memory and Reinscription in Zimbabwe." In *Memory and the Postcolony: African Anthropology and the Critique of Power*, edited by Richard P Werbner, 71–102. London: Zed Books.

Werner, Cynthia. 1998. "Household Networks and the Security of Mutual Indebtedness in Rural Kazakstan." *Central Asian Survey* 17 (4): 597–612. doi:10.1080/02634939808401058.

West, Harry G. 2003. "Voices Twice Silenced: Betrayal and Mourning at Colonialism's End in Mozambique." *Anthropological Theory* 3 (3): 343–65.

Wheeler, Douglas L. 1969. "'Angola Is Whose House?' Early Stirrings of Angolan Nationalism and Protest, 1822–1910." *African Historical Studies* 2 (1): 1–22. doi:10.2307/216324.

White, Geoffrey M. 1999. "Emotional Remembering: The Pragmatics of National Memory." *Ethos* 27 (4): 505–29. doi:10.1525/eth.1999.27.4.505.

Wise, Amanda. 2010. "Sensuous Multiculturalism: Emotional Landscapes of Inter-Ethnic Living in Australian Suburbia." *Journal of Ethnic and Migration Studies* 36 (6): 917–37. doi:10.1080/13691831003643355.

Yang, Mayfair M. 1994. *Gifts, Favors, and Banquets: The Art of Social Relationships in China*. Ithaca, NY: Cornell University Press.

Young, Crawford. 2007. "The Illusion of Cultural Identity, by Jean-François Bayart." *African Affairs* 106 (422). 155–57. doi:10.1093/afraf/adl045.

Zinn, Howard. 2005. *A People's History of the United States*. New York: HarperCollins.

INDEX

CPSIA information can be obtained
at www.ICGtesting.com
Printed in the USA
FFOW03n1803071017
40684FF